Systemic Black American Poverty in Northwest Louisiana

Systemic Black American Poverty in Northwest Louisiana

The Two Parishes of Caddo and Bossier

STEPHEN PINKNEY

WIPF & STOCK · Eugene, Oregon

SYSTEMIC BLACK AMERICAN POVERTY IN NORTHWEST LOUISIANA
The Two Parishes of Caddo and Bossier

Wipf & Stock
An Imprint of Wipf and Stock Publishers
199 W. 8th Ave., Suite 3
Eugene, OR 97401

www.wipfandstock.com

PAPERBACK ISBN: 979-8-3852-4695-3
HARDCOVER ISBN: 979-8-3852-4696-0
EBOOK ISBN: 979-8-3852-4697-7

DEDICATION

The ultimate dedication of my dissertation and this book goes to my mother and stepfather, Angela and Hiram Clay, and Robert Thomas Jr., my father. It also goes to my daughter Ty Pinkney who is an inspiration to me. In addition, the dedication of this book goes to the Pinkney, Thomas, and Clay families. I also want to give special thanks to Theresa Thomas Moore for her encouragement, support, and prayers.

My special appreciation goes to scholars Dr. Frances Cress Welsing (deceased), Neeley Fuller Jr. (deceased), Dr. Anthony Browder, Dr. Booker T. Coleman, and Dr. Huey P. Newton (deceased). Their work, knowledge, activism, courage, and success motivated and inspired me to pursue a PhD and become a scholar.

Finally, I express my sincere and profound appreciation to my professional planning colleagues for listening to my ideas, collaborating, and being a positive influence, and to Sasidhar Parasa for assisting me in learning models and mapping. Also, I extend my gratitude to Hiram Clay, my stepfather, for always being available for me in my time of need and assisting with solutions. I want to thank everyone mentioned for their contributions and support.

Contents

List of Tables

List of Figures

Acronyms

ACS	American Community Survey
ALICE	Asset Limited, Income Constrained, and Employed
AMI	Area Median Income
CBD	Central Business District
DDD	Downtown Development District
FBA	Foundational Black American
GE	General Electric
GIS	Geographic Information System
GM	General Motors
HBCU	Historically Black Colleges and Universities
IRC	Internal Revenue Code
IRS	Internal Revenue Service
LSU	Louisiana State University
NCLB	No Child Left Behind
SNDi	Street-Network Disconnectedness Index
UAW	United Automobile, Aerospace and Agricultural Implement Workers of U.S.
US	United States
USDA	US Department of Agriculture

Acknowledgments

I WANT TO EXPRESS my sincere and special appreciation to the chairperson of my dissertation committee, Dr. Glenn Johnson. I am grateful for his dedication, constructive guidance, and motivation during my dissertation. I also want to thank him for the wealth of knowledge and skills he imparted to me throughout my doctoral journey. His advice and mentoring contributed immensely to the successful completion of my dissertation. I thank him for the opportunity to work and learn from him.

My special gratitude also goes to Dr. Lalita Sen and Dr. David Baker. Their great professional advice and guidance were of tremendous assistance throughout my dissertation. Certainly, I appreciate their constructive instructions, vigilance, and wisdom. These professors' mentorship, dedication, and expertise motivated me to complete this dissertation and my academic program.

My special thanks goes to Dr. Robert Bullard. I appreciate his high-level global expertise and the valuable professional skills he imparted to me in my doctoral program. I appreciate the opportunity he granted me to present my research works at the HBCU Climate Change Conference. I also want to express my profound and sincere gratitude to Dr. Robert Bullard as my committee member, for his professional skills, support, and contributions towards the completion of my dissertation. Finally, I am thankful for the funding I received as a research assistant at the Bullard Center for Environmental and Climate Justice at Texas Southern University.

Finally, my special appreciation goes to Drs. Beverly Wright, Earthea Nance, and Bumseok Chun for their valuable roles and encouragement in my study and throughout the dissertation. I would also like to express my special thanks to all UPEP faculty, staff, friends, colleagues, and the ACTS Houston Community Organization in Pleasantville, Texas, for their supportive thoughts and encouragement.

Abstract

THERE ARE MANY STATES, counties, and cities in the United States of America where people do not have access to basic necessities such as food, housing, proper medical facilities, access to schools, and any transportation, etc. The reason for this situation is due to the issue of poverty. Poverty is an unacceptably low-standard way of life that is a complex human phenomenon. It has multiple causes, manifestations, and dimensions.[1] Caddo Parish, Louisiana, is such a place that has high poverty among Black people. The population of African American people in Caddo Parish is larger than the Whites who live there, and African American poverty has more than doubled that of the White residents. African American poverty in Caddo Parish is higher than the poverty average in the state of Louisiana and is higher than the United States average. The neighboring parish of Bossier is experiencing the same issue as the African Americans in Caddo Parish. Caddo and Bossier Parishes connect by their two largest cities in the parishes, named the Shreveport–Bossier City metropolitan area. Both cities' poverty level among Black people is higher than the United States national average.

This case study explores and argues how systemic racism has blended into urbanization, sprawl, and politics. The research explores how these factors cause poverty in the Black community and have plagued their progress from the colonization of Louisiana through the American Civil War to the present time in Caddo Parish, Louisiana. Dr. Robert Bullard mentions that

> racism is and continues to be a conspicuous part of the American sociopolitical system. As a result, Black people in particular, and ethnic and racial minority groups of color, find themselves at a disadvantage in contemporary society.[2]

---

1. Odhiambo et al., *Quantitative and Qualitative Methods*, 14–37.
2. Bullard, "Legacy of American Apartheid," 445.

The factor of poverty has caused population change in Shreveport and Bossier City. Shreveport has seen a population decline, whereas Bossier has seen an increase in population. However, Caddo Parish still has a larger population.[3] African American homeownership is low considering the heavy populations of these people in the Shreveport–Bossier City area, and is disproportionate to the White residents. This study will examine housing discrimination in these areas because housing discrimination denies a substantial segment of the African American community a basic form of wealth accumulation and investment through homeownership.[4]

There are development plans to make the area a more attractive and dynamic location for corporate investments, expansions, and expansion for the future Shreveport-Bossier area. This development attempts to modernize the metropolitan areas' environmental sustainability, neighborhoods, housing stock, infrastructure, and transportation. Further considerations include aiding with workforce training and business attraction through local organizations and the city's programs. Eliminating cost-burdened and extremely cost-burdened residences and improving housing conditions for residents with housing maintenance issues are major concerns.

The purpose of this case study is to shed light on the history of racism, bad politics, sprawl, spatial mismatch, lack of homeownership, population trends, transportation issues, lack of employment opportunities, high crime, bank deserts, health care, present Jim Crow laws, and the miseducation of African Americans in Louisiana as these factors play on their social and economic place in northwest Louisiana. The researcher will use qualitative research to answer questions with spatial and statistical analysis to provide visuals of the data collected on the census tracts. There will be some quantitative information within the qualitative findings. There will be some quantitative information within the qualitative findings. Researchers use qualitative research with some quantitative results because they consider both methods extremely effective for poverty analysis and give a more holistic view to a given study.[5]

The purpose of this book is to research and understand African American poverty in Caddo Parish, how they ended up in this predicament, and present solutions to rectify the situation. The adverse effects of urbanization and sprawl result in poverty. These harmful effects,

3. Bayliss, "Census 2020."

4. Bullard et al., "Suburban Sprawl," 936–39.

5. Odhiambo et al., *Quantitative and Qualitative Methods*, 14–37.

including the study area, are frequently seen in the African American / Black community. Negative effects of urbanization can be a lack of resources, poverty, unemployment, and overcrowding. Furthermore, the migration from rural areas to metropolitan areas causes congestion that impedes growth and bolsters the negative issues from geographically concentrated poverty, such as crime and violence in Shreveport.

This study highlights poverty, education, unemployment, homeownership, and renters, and it contrasts and compares variables in Caddo Parish to Bossier Parish with Black versus White residents with GIS mapping. The GIS mapping shows the disproportionate percentages in each factor for the Black population versus the White population for both Caddo Parish and Bossier Parish.

The project distinctively shows (1) inequity and inequality in homeownership, (2) the poor education and miseducation in the Louisiana school system, (3) how incarceration ratios are disproportionate, (4) the lack of employment opportunities in the area, and (5) inequity in public and personal transportation. Furthermore, the results show the negative effects of Black versus White birth rates, IRS inequalities, health care inequalities, and how the factors mentioned in this study are blended in racism, which has kept Blacks in poverty in Caddo Parish and Bossier Parish from the colonization of Louisiana to the last thirty years. Lastly, this study presents mapping, snapshots, and negative effects of food deserts, banking deserts, payday loan companies, eyesore neighborhoods, nonwalkable and nonbikeable communities, and lack of sufficient medical facilities in predominately Black neighborhoods in the study area.

Despite the Civil Rights Movement and other justice movements, there are still disparities in wealth, employment, health care, education, laws, housing, transportation, poverty, and other factors. To bring change, urban planners and/or environmental justice activists must work diligently to overcome and subdue obstacles to create smart growth, cleaner, greener communities, and sustainable communities while simultaneously promoting equality and eliminating inequities.

CHAPTER 1

Introduction

THE RESEARCH WILL EXAMINE factors contributing to systemic African American poverty in Caddo Parish and Bossier Parish, Louisiana. The significant factors are educational attainment (i.e., bachelor's, master's, doctorate, and professional degrees), unemployment/underemployment (hourly jobs versus salary jobs), income, homeownership, renter status, cost of living, transportation, and incarceration. The researcher will provide both parishes' thirty-year (1990–2020) historical context. The researcher will focus on employment trends and opportunities which would include job losses / job gains. It will be essential to examine the percentage of African Americans compared to Whites who had government jobs over the last three decades. Government jobs provide more stability for individuals, and individuals have a great chance of being promoted with these jobs. Oil and gas jobs are high paying, and it will be essential to see how many African Americans have them. The researcher will also examine how college degrees provide upward opportunities for African Americans. The researcher will explain the barriers and restrictions in these parishes that resulted in sustaining systemic racism.

The research will examine the homeownership of African Americans in both parishes while looking for trends and patterns that will explain low rates of homeownership and high rates of renters. As we know, owning homes is a sign of stability and contributes to a more vital community/parish versus a community/parish with exceptionally high rates of renters. The researcher will examine the cost of living (COL) rates in both parishes and explain their relationship to poverty. The researcher will also see if the average wages in the parishes are lower than the cost of living and provide an explanation accordingly. The researcher will examine the number of African Americans who work in a retail, entry-level casino, and fast-food jobs (usually part time), resulting in many impoverished individuals. It is important to note that many individuals who are employed (e.g., work two part-time jobs) are still poor or living in poverty.

The researcher will examine the increase and decrease of major industries in the two parishes. It is also important to examine and document the population growth and decline over the last thirty years. Finally, the researcher will examine four types of poverty (i.e., housing, transportation, energy, and food insecurity) and their impact on African Americans in Caddo Parish and Bossier Parish.

The researcher is from Caddo Parish, Louisiana, and believes in grassroots activism. The researcher strongly believes in the statement that

> it is hoped that an examination of African American activism in Louisiana will result in greater awareness and mutual respect amongst environmental, civil rights, and social justice groups as well as among political leaders, corporate elites, and governmental officials. As environmental grassroots activists address individual community concerns, they are also promoting human rights, efficacy, and greater stakeholder participation and public involvement in environmental decision-making.[1]

The researcher does believe in environmental justice. Environmental justice is the meaningful involvement and fair treatment of all people regardless of national origin, color, race, and income with respect to the implementation, development, and enforcement of environmental laws, policies, and regulations. No group of people, including ethnic, socioeconomic, or racial groups, should endure or tolerate a disproportionate share of pessimistic environmental consequences resulting from municipal, industrial, and commercial operations or execution of tribal, local, state, and federal programs and policies.[2]

1.1 STUDY RATIONALE

In Caddo Parish, Louisiana, African Americans have seen more than their fair share of oppression. Systemic racism has affected Black lives

1. Johnson, "Grassroots Activism," 285.
2. Johnson, "Grassroots Activism," 285.

in America since the fall of 1492.[3] The gruesome life of slavery from the northern states of the US made its way to Louisiana officially in 1708 with the help of Pierre Le Moyne D'Iberville. D'Iberville was the person to help build the French colony of Louisiana. The colonization effects still show their residual effects and systemic orchestrations in 2022.[4] Today African Americans in Caddo Parish are faced with the effects of racism, poverty, urbanization, politics, miseducation, sprawl, unemployment, unlawful incarceration, low unemployment rates, population trends, unfair housing practices, low wages, a small amount of business ownership representation, food deserts, banking deserts, and high-interest payday loans companies.

Currently, African American poverty in Caddo Parish is higher than the national average.[5] Knowing these statistics, being born and raised in Caddo Parish, the researcher wanted to know why such a situation existed. According to a 2017 article that presented data from a survey from WalletHub, Louisiana was labeled to have the "worst public education system in the United States"[6] and is ranked fifty-first in state rankings for school safety. Shreveport City is the largest city in Caddo Parish, the third-largest city in Louisiana, and the land mass has more than quadrupled while its population grew one and a half times from 1950 to 2009. Since 1980, the city's land area has grown 26% while the population remained stable, with more than 74% of Caddo Parish's population living in Shreveport. The city of Shreveport's story of physical development has been one of sprawl without growth.[7]

The Louisiana Housing Census of 1990 to 2020 shows Caddo Parish African American / Black homeownership versus White homeownership disparities. Chapter 2 will provide homeownership data. Many African American renters are in Caddo Parish, especially in Shreveport City. Some African Americans pay larger amounts to rent than they would be paying for homeownership if given similar circumstances. Understanding why there is such a vast gap between African Americans and Whites in homeownership should provide answers to how this can cause persistent poverty for African Americans in Caddo Parish.

3. Sertima, *They Came Before Columbus*, 43–270.
4. Rodrigue, "French Colonial Louisiana."
5. World Population Review, "Caddo Parish," 1.
6. McElfresh, "Louisiana's Education."
7. Shreveport Metropolitan Planning Commission, "Population," 3–26.

Travel time and distance of travel can be a factor that affects the poverty of individuals. Transportation is vital to our everyday lives. There are costs associated with transportation, public transportation, and buying a vehicle. Transportation also profoundly affects residential and industrial growth and physical and social mobility. Transportation decision-making—whether at the federal, regional, state, or local level—often mirrors the power arrangements of the dominant society and its institutions.[8] Lack of power causes transportation issues for minorities since they are not the dominant society. This paper will also research the commute times to work and/or to the central business district of the people from Caddo Parish. The goal is to show the disparity in commute times between minorities versus Whites. Employment trends will be a factor that could affect African American poverty because it will indeed affect the income of this group of people. Businesses owned by minorities will be data the researcher will need to provide to show the lack of Black business ownership that could provide jobs for African Americans, act as the primary source of income for African Americans, and provide generational wealth for African American families. Understanding current and future business patterns are key to implementing planning strategies. This information may give some idea of how to educate people in this study area to increase the employment rate for local people and pursue a better quality of life.[9] Population trends can be affected by employment opportunities, job types, and pay wages.

There have been a couple of action plans for the Caddo Parish Shreveport–Bossier City metropolitan area for improvement. The first plan is the *Consolidated Plan 2019–2023 and 2019 Annual Action Plan* for the city of Shreveport. The second plan is the *Great Expectations: Shreveport-Caddo 2030 Master Plan*. The *Consolidated Plan 2019–2023 and 2019 Annual Action Plan* is to create more opportunities for business owners in Shreveport's central business district, reduce homelessness, increase the potential for more homeownership, and expand job creation. The *Shreveport-Caddo 2030 Master Plan* is a plan centers around population and land use trends. The plan aims is to find ways to better utilize land with less sprawl.[10] The *Shreveport-Caddo Master Plan* area shares land use and population characteristics with shrinking cities, which include

---

8. Bullard et al., "Suburban Sprawl," 936–39.

9. McCargo et al., *Building Black Homeownership*, 5–11.

10. Shreveport Metropolitan Planning Commission, "Population," 3–26.

high levels of vacancy and blight. The researcher presents the history and development of Caddo Parish, and that Shreveport-Caddo can no longer sustain the sprawl without growth development model that has characterized its last thirty years.[11]

None of the current or past plans include specific plans for African Americans, which will help bring equality and equity to the African American community in Caddo Parish. The plans also do not include what the researcher is proposing, which is to shed light on the inequities and inequalities. The researcher is looking for action regarding such disadvantages. This book is for research and a plan to help Caddo Parish and assist other communities. This research will help attract native Caddo Parish workers who migrated to other cities because they could not find employment in Caddo Parish or obtain the income they needed to live the lifestyle they wanted.

1.2 RESEARCH AIM AND OBJECTIVES

The purpose of this book is to research and understand African American poverty in Caddo Parish, how they ended up in this predicament, and present solutions to rectify the situation. The researcher wants to present why African Americans ended up in this situation because if the research can show why this situation has occurred, then it is less likely these people will fall into the same pitfalls if the problems are solved. The researcher will examine African American poverty by looking at the long history of poor education, politics, planning, housing, and racism, along with statistical data and GIS mapping from analyzing census tract data from Caddo Parish. The research will examine the last thirty years (1990–2020) of African American poverty in Caddo Parish

- to show how racism has affected African American poverty in Caddo Parish,
- to provide details of urbanization effects on African American poverty in Caddo Parish,
- to show how lack of planning has caused issues with sprawl without growth,
- to provide detail on housing discrimination and lack of African American homeownership in Caddo Parish,

11. Shreveport Metropolitan Planning Commission, "Population," 3–26.

- to provide detail on the lack of Black business ownership,
- to investigate the miseducation of African Americans in Louisiana,
- to find where the disconnect is between African Americans and job opportunities,
- to provide links between transportation and poverty,
- to investigate how employment trends affect population growth and population decline,
- to show links between poverty and health,
- to give details on how payday loans affect low-income people.

The researcher will use qualitative research to answer these questions with the inclusion of spatial and statistical analysis to provide visuals of the data collected on the census tracts. There will be some quantitative information within the qualitative findings.

1.3 RESEARCH QUESTIONS

Research Question #1:   Is there a relationship between poverty due to the negative effects of urbanization and politics?

Research Question #2:   Is there a relationship between systemic racism, poverty, urbanization, and politics, and do these relationships affect lack of African American wealth in the Caddo Parish?

Research Question #3:   Is there a comparison between African American versus White poverty in Caddo Parish and African American versus White poverty in neighboring Bossier Parish?

Research Question #4:   Is there a relationship between population trends and job opportunities in Caddo Parish?

1.4 STUDY STRUCTURE

This research entails historical research, modern research, and statistical data-based information along with GIS mapping to give a visual view of

Caddo Parish's demographical position of the factors involved. The researcher plans to show the inequalities and inequities in Caddo Parish towards African Americans and to present policy recommendations for the issues rather than letting them mount and fester. The book will consist of an abstract and five chapters. The first chapter will provide the introduction, demographics, and background of the research provided. Chapter 1 has presented research questions. Chapter 2 will review the literature and discuss poverty and the history of racism in Caddo Parish. Chapter 3 will discuss the focus areas of urbanization and politics and how it relates to poverty. Chapter 4 presents the data found, analysis of data, and GIS mapping. Chapter 5 will consist of policy recommendations and proposals for the issues, a summary, a discussion, and a conclusion.

CHAPTER 2

Review of Literature

INTRODUCTION

WHEN TRIBAL SOCIETY BEGAN to transform into civil society, poverty began to appear worldwide. At one point in time, wealth was given to us by nature due to the fact nature provided everything for us. Individuals and communities shared goods they had among each other that they needed or lacked. There was no cost associated with the majority of goods. Then the population of the world grew. Along with the population increase, we witnessed the growth of supply and demand, farming and agriculture, the need for fertile land, and animal domestication. Furthermore, there were social distinctions between class, race, and prestige, while seeing old traditions vanishing contributed to significant changes in society across the globe. The fight for wealth, luxury, prestige, and necessities brought on wealth for a few individuals and certain families, but not compared to the masses that experienced individual and generational poverty.[1] One major event for the pursuit of wealth and power which triggered African American poverty in the US was the transatlantic slave trade. The first section of chapter 2 will discuss poverty, African American / Black poverty in Caddo Parish, Caddo Parish African American / Black poverty links between institutional racism, and the other discussed areas of human activity including the focus areas for this research.

---

1. Rajkumar, "Poverty," 1–49.

2.1 POVERTY

What is poverty? One could say that, in the developed world, our under-standing of poverty is often based on what we see in our own country.[2] Having traveled to places inside of the United States and having seen large populations of people of direct African descent experiencing poverty in every city raised many questions for the researcher. There are many cities in the United States where people do not have access to basic necessities such as food, homes, any transportation, proper medical facilities, and access to schools. The researcher has had many discussions where folks living in the United States understood they were poor but felt better off than some people outside of the US in other poverty-stricken countries. Poverty can be economical, marginalized, and/or feeling dependent on someone or some entity. The basic definition of poverty is living without the basic necessities of life: water, housing, and/or food.[3] In the United States, poverty is calculated by the US Census Bureau set on a threshold. The United States' numerical definition of poverty is a family of four with an income of less than $69 per day or an individual with an income of less than $34 per day.[4] Nevertheless, the researcher asks, "Does anyone have to be in poverty?" In the United States, African Americans lead all other races in poverty with 18.8%, which is more than double White Americans.[5]

2.1.1 Types of Poverty

As stated previously, poverty has many dimensions, manifestations, and causes. The definition of poverty suggested by the United Nations Development Program tells us that one cannot measurement poverty by income as a single entity. The measurement process has to include a multicomponent method and consider quality of housing, the standard of living, electricity, access to clean water, sanitation, and education. Each of these factors contributes to the foundations of providing individuals and families to lead to an adequate lifestyle. We must understand that poverty can be broken down to include housing poverty, transportation poverty, energy poverty, and food insecurity poverty. The research will

2. Janofski, "What Is Poverty?"
3. Rajkumar, "Poverty," 1–49; Kimberlin, "Metrics Matter," 4–61.
4. US Census Bureau 2018, "Measures Poverty."
5. Creamer, "Poverty Rates."

discuss and explain how African Americans / Blacks are disproportionately impacted in housing, transportation, energy, and food insecurity poverty in Caddo and Bossier Parishes.

2.1.1.1 Housing Poverty: Living in impoverished conditions is not just limited or confined to cities, as many people think. Rural areas' poverty rates exceed urban areas' poverty rates in many cases. The number of low-income households around the globe is prevalent and exceeds the affordable housing units available for people. There are just thirty-five rental units, both affordable and available in the United States, for every one hundred households that are renters who are in the extremely low-income category. There is not one state in the United States where a worker making the prevailing state or federal minimum wage earnings can afford a two-bedroom apartment without paying above 30% of their monthly income. To be exact, a minimum wage worker must clock nearly 127 hours per week, more than three full-time jobs, to afford a two-bedroom rental, or 103 hours per week, more than two and a half full-time jobs, to afford a one-bedroom, according to the National Low Income Housing Coalition.[6]

Almost thirty-eight million US citizen households spend more than 30% of their income on housing. This cost forces families to make tough decisions about spending funds on balancing food, health, and transportation. Also, families considered severely cost-burdened and paying more than 50% of their income on housing are one in six in the United States. The researcher will cover this information in section 2.6.1, "Affordable Housing in Caddo-Bossier Parish." Lack of access to clean water and sanitation, energy, and fuel poverty can be included in housing poverty, although energy poverty can have its own category. For many people, the threat of eviction or insecure tenure is real. Insecure housing tenure can negatively impact individuals' and communities' economic, psychological, and physical well-being. On a daily basis, more than 20% of the earth's population struggle with living on land where they reside. Over 70% of the world's population resides in occupied homes without legal documentation to prove ownership or property rights.[7]

---

6. Habitat for Humanity, "Poverty and Housing."
7. Habitat for Humanity, "Poverty and Housing."

2.1.1.2 Transportation Poverty: Thirteen percent of household disburse-
ments for the average American go towards transportation. The cost of
transportation is not indistinguishable. Households of lower income pay
a larger amount of their spending on transportation. Once individuals
or households move up in income brackets, they pay a smaller amount
towards transportation. The larger portion of the transportation expenditure is the burden of the lower income households in the United States
and worldwide.[8] Even with America's transportation subsidies, the ex-
pense difference is evident among low-income earners. Transportation
expenses accounted for the fourth largest expenditure for US household
spending, with an average of $9,737 for each as the cost of transportation
in 2017. Americans are the owners of 2.28 vehicles on average. Furthermore, 35% of households in America own three or more vehicles. This
contributes to personal vehicles accounting for the larger scale of cost
for transportation expenditures, totaling $1.1 million in 2017, which was
close to 90% of expenditures of transportation.[9] The majority of this cost
is from the purchase of the vehicle ($4,001); the rest of the cost after that
($3,603) includes repairs, insurance, and other vehicle expenditures.
For personal vehicles, motor oil and fuel costs are $1,968 annually, ac-
counting for the smallest expenditure. Owning a vehicle in the United
States is an expensive endeavor, and Americans spend less on other
methods of travel than on vehicle ownership and maintenance. Vehicles
depreciate in value, so if a person sells their vehicle, the value is usually not regained during resale. Public transportation, ground, and local
transportation were under 5%. In the United States, $11,933 is the low-
est earning, which 20% of Americans made on average in 2016. They
also spend 29% ($3497) on transportation costs. Lower-income people
get the worst end of the transportation system due to lacking access to
affordable and reliable transportation. For Americans averaging about
$30,000 annually, their transportation spending was around 22%, and
the next quintile up spent 17%. In essence, for the US population that
moves from lower-income to higher-income, the expenditure portion
that is used for transportation decreases. US cities fail to provide enough
adequate transportation, so people must use personal vehicles. Personal
vehicles are not subsidized and are not cheap. Americans categorized in
the lower-income bracket possess fewer options. When US citizens began

8. Institute for Transportation and Development Policy, "High Cost of
Transportation."
9. Institute for Transportation and Development Policy, "High Cost of
Transportation."

to criticize public transportation, there was pushback with environmental concerns. However, transportation equity is in question, and the lack of public transportation is a burden financially due to citizens not having good options. Transportation inequity continues the cycle of poverty by making it hard to escape such a dire situation, as citizens have to make financial decisions on how to survive.[10] The researcher discusses transportation in section 2.8.1, "Transportation and Sprawl in Caddo/Bossier Central Business District" and section 2.8.3, "Transportation, Health Care Needs, and Renters."

2.1.1.3 Energy Poverty: Energy poverty is the lack of access to sustainable modern energy services and products, as defined by the World Economic Forum in 2010.[11] These services include heating and hot water, cooling, and lighting. Access to affordable and adequate energy is not equal in global distribution but is the engine of civilization. Energy poverty is noticeable where there is a deficiency of affordable, quality, adequate, reliable, safe, and environmentally sound energy services to reinforce development.

Social and economic development is solidly and constantly interwoven with the presence of energy, and due to this relationship, poorer countries' energy services are sub-standardly equipped. This contributes to unhealthy living conditions, limited access to employment, education, and malnourishment.[12] Not having proper energy can make manufacturing and the development of agriculture very difficult.

The United States continues to have inequalities in energy justice and poverty among Americans. A third of US households are having difficulties affording energy to cook and provide light for their residents, along with cooling and heating.[13]

2.1.1.4 Food Insecurity Poverty: The United States Department of Agriculture (USDA) defines food insecurity as a lack of consistent access to enough food for an active, healthy life. In 2020, thirty-eight million Americans (one in eight Americans), including nearly twelve million children, were categorized as food insecure. Food insecurity and hunger

10. Institute for Transportation and Development Policy, "High Cost of Transportation."

11. Habitat For Humanity, "Energy Poverty."

12. Habitat For Humanity, "Energy Poverty."

13. Reames, "Combating Energy Poverty."

are closely related and are easily understood concepts. Food insecurity is a lack of financial resources for food in the household, and hunger is a person's physical sensation of being uncomfortable or experiencing discomfort from a lack of food with the desire for food. There has been extensive research on food insecurity, an elaborate problem. Poverty and food insecurity are closely related. However, not everyone living beneath the line of poverty is experiencing food insecurity, and people that live above the line of poverty can experience food insecurity.[14]

The African American community, more than the White community in the United States, continues to face consistently higher rates of hunger due to African Americans' environmental, social, and economic challenges. Discriminatory practices and policies have contributed to Black people living in poverty, having fewer financial resources than Whites, and being more likely unemployed. These factors mentioned will lead people to experience a life of hunger. Due to the pandemic in 2020, 24% of African Americans experienced food insecurity, which was an increase. Compared to White children, Black children are three times as likely to be a part of a household that is food insecure.[15]

2.2 POVERTY IN LOUISIANA

Poverty in Louisiana is a tremendous concern to many of the state's residents. When some residents feel they have made economic progress, it blinds us to the fact that we face an inevitable conclusion that Louisiana still is in the rear of neighboring states in almost every measure of social and economic security and comfort. Louisiana's future conditions will not change unless maximum efforts are taken to bolster the economic and social conditions. This type of transformation requires a great deal of caring, to create awareness, and change, to diminish poverty and the extent or dimensions of poverty and its catastrophic repercussions. We have a huge gap to close before poverty is not in any description of Louisiana and its parishes.[16] There has been progress made in some areas of the South. However, the poverty bug has not loosened on Louisiana citizens, especially the African American community. From 1996 to 1998, 18.6% of Louisianians were poor, well above the national rate of just over 13%. Midway through this decade, virtually one-quarter of all families

14. Feeding America, "Hunger and Food Insecurity."
15. Feeding America, "Dedicated Response."
16. Council for a Better Louisiana, "Poverty Summary."

in the state earned less than $10,000—well below the federal poverty line of $15,150 for a family of four. There is a large gap in income disparity between the poorest citizens and the wealthiest citizens in Louisiana.

Louisiana has one of the widest gaps between its richest and poorest residents, according to the Washington, DC–based Center on Budget and Policy Priorities analysis released in December 2016. The report found that only Connecticut, California, and New York had a larger gap than Louisiana between average income from low-income households and the state's wealthiest.[17]

Leading the nation in child poverty is the state of Louisiana. The state of Louisiana has the largest proportion of children living in poverty, more than any other state in the United States. Many poor children are living in single-parent households in the state of Louisiana, and with the growing number of single women's birth rates, the amount will grow. In 1997, 43.9% of all infants were born to single women, well above the national average of 32.4%.

The Annie E. Casey Foundation released its annual KIDS COUNT report on child well-being in the United States, revealing that in 2013, 22% of all US children lived in poverty. Among them, the rate was 39% for African American children, compared to 14% for White children. In Louisiana, the numbers were even more stark: 48% of Black children and 13% of White children lived in poverty. Each year, the Casey Foundation, an organization dedicated to supporting disadvantaged children, publishes this KIDS COUNT report, evaluating every state based on sixteen indicators of child well-being across four categories. The categories are economic well-being (families' ability to meet children's basic needs), education (preschool enrollment, early learning, and graduation outcomes), health (factors such as birth weight, access to health insurance, mortality rates, and substance abuse), and family and community (parental stability and whether children live in high-poverty neighborhoods).[18]

17. Crisp, "Biggest Gaps."
18. Kotch, "Deepening Child Poverty."

Figure 1

Louisiana vs U.S. Child Poverty
Black vs White
2015

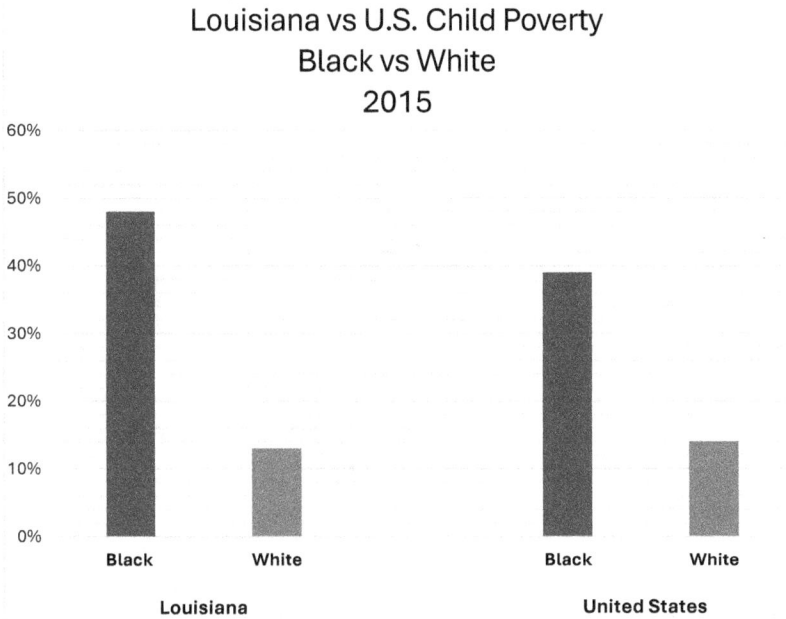

In 2015, with close to 46.4% of African American children living in poverty across the state, the outlook on their situation looked bleak, while White children living in poverty was 16.5%.[19]

Poverty is more than a person's status determined by an individual's income. The limited choices associated with poverty have devastating consequences passed on from parent to child in a continuing cycle of despair. Unfavorable conditions are the outcomes of limited opportunities that are associated with poverty being passed from generation to generation.

Poor health is one of the results associated with poverty. Children are vulnerable to poor health due to poverty. Being that Louisiana's birth rate is lower than any other state creates great concern due to African American children being the highest in poverty. These factors do not lessen as the children mature. As the children mature, the probability of these kids having health problems as adults is significant if the poverty continues throughout their lives.

19. Albares, "Poverty Gap."

Senior citizens that are in the low-income category have a greater chance of experiencing problems due to health, more than their middle-class and upper-class peers. Lower-income poor people also have limited access to health care.[20] Achievements through academics often evade low-income students, limiting how they can escape poverty and become self-sufficient when they achieve adulthood. Many times, low-income students, usually African American, are steered away from the courses that will best benefit them to succeed in future endeavors. Inadequate resources, ill-prepared teachers, low expectations, and today's rapidly changing economy make success challenging for African American students. This changing economy is one that values flexibility and critical thinking, and now labor-intensive, low-skill jobs that once were the staple of Louisiana's economy are being pushed to the back. The starkly evident value of postsecondary training is present when we consider individual income by educational achievement.

Louisiana has been called "one of the most dangerous states in the nation."[21] When there is high poverty, there is high crime because of a lack of income and resources in a community. A poor job market triggers criminal activity from those citizens who are unable to sustain gainful employment in the labor force. There is evidence that those with poor prospects in the job market are more likely to engage in criminal activity than those that can secure positions in the labor market. Those living in poverty are also more likely to be victims of crime because people who commit crimes usually prey on people near where they live.

Safe and secure housing continues to elude people that are poverty stricken. Homeownership is falling in Louisiana at a time while home-ownership rates are climbing in the United States. Middle- and upper-income citizens can afford safe and secure housing while homelessness increases in the state. People in poverty also face hunger, in which malnutrition in children is increasing, and they suffer from inadequate diets. For children that are incredibly young, cognitive development can be greatly interfered with due to hunger.

In 2015, nearly one in five Louisianians, which equates to 889,946 people or 19.6% of the population, lived in poverty. Those numbers were the third largest rate in the United States. That includes 300,000 children at 28.4%, which also is the third highest. Wages in Louisiana continue to trail behind the rest of the United States as well. The state of Louisiana's

---

20. Council for a Better Louisiana, "Poverty Summary."
21. Council for a Better Louisiana, "Poverty Summary."

household income was $45,727 in 2015 in comparison to the national median of $55,775. This income disparity placed Louisiana fourth highest in the states. The racial disparities are persistent and deep. The economic gap between Whites and African Americans is still severe and *substantial*. In 2015, one out of three Black Louisiana citizens lived below federal poverty. Compared to White Louisiana citizens at 13.2%, Black poverty was at 32.2%, which was almost two and a half times higher than that of Whites. In the labor force, the average White employee earned $56,093 compared to the Black employee's $27,537, more than twice the average compared to the African American employee.[22]

Louisiana has had a long tradition of devaluing education and the inadequate public education system that results in relatively depressed wage rates and dramatically unequal distribution of wealth, a generation of the "status quo" which makes it difficult to bring about change and for many people to improve their circumstances. Also, Louisiana has a history of public corruption, resulting in cynicism and cavalier and un-caring attitudes toward the poor and powerless, which sit the African American Louisianians at the bottom.[23]

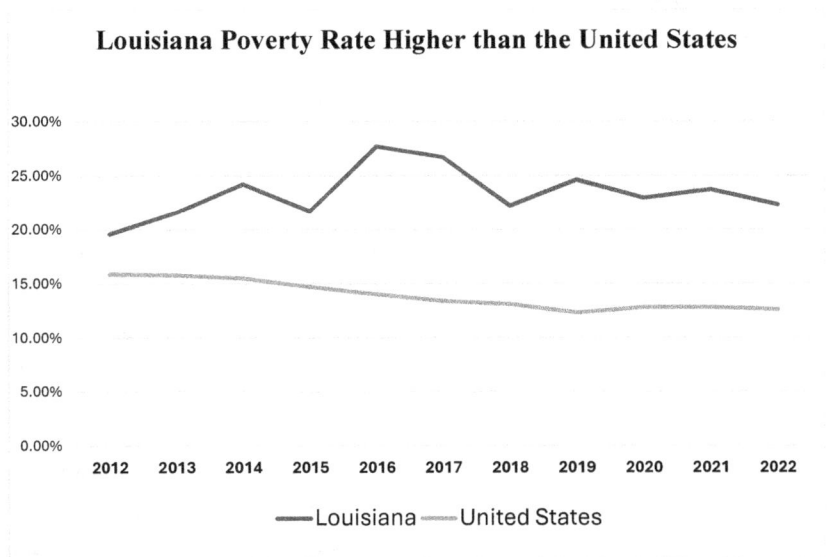

Louisiana Poverty Rate Higher than the United States

Figure 2: Louisiana Poverty vs. United States Poverty
Source: U. S. Census Bureau 2022

22. US Census Bureau 2018, "Measures Poverty"; Albares, "Poverty Gap."
23. Council for a Better Louisiana, "Poverty Summary."

2.3 PAST THIRTY YEARS POVERTY IN CADDO PARISH VS. BOSSIER PARISH, BLACK VS. WHITE

Poverty can be economical, marginalized, and the feeling of being dependent on someone or some entity. The basic definition of poverty is living without the basic necessities of life: water, housing, and food.[24] In the United States, poverty is calculated by the US Census Bureau set on a threshold. The United States numerical definition of poverty is a family of four with an income less than $69 per day and an individual with an income less than $34 per day.[25] The researcher's question is, "Does anyone have to be in poverty?"

The researcher decided to study the subject of poverty where he grew up, which is Shreveport, Louisiana, in Caddo Parish, Louisiana, the third-largest city in Louisiana. The researcher had resided in the largely African American communities of Allendale, Lakeside, and Queensborough. The researcher decided to study the last thirty years of African American poverty in Caddo Parish to see if there are any patterns. ALICE—which stands for Asset Limited, Income Constrained, Employed—represents a large segment of the population that earns above the federal poverty level but still struggles to afford basic household necessities. Every two years, a national report called the ALICE report is released by United For ALICE. United For ALICE researches and quantifies the cost of this "household survival budget" within the ALICE report. The ALICE Household Survival Budget breaks down the minimal cost of the five basic necessities for human living for different household sizes and locations, highlighting the financial strain on these families. These necessities include food, housing, childcare, health care, and transportation.[26] Also considered as basic necessities to live is technology, plus a contingency fund equal to 10% of the household budget and taxes. The minimum income level needed for a household's survival is represented by the ALICE Threshold and is attained from the Household Survival Budget.[27]

This report shows a huge population of hardworking residents who are having trouble making ends meet and are one emergency away from poverty because they have no savings for a safety net. According to the report, in Louisiana, 695,719 households, representing 40% of the state's

---

24. Rajkumar, "Poverty," 68–83; Kimberlin, "Metrics Matter," 4–61.

25. US Census Bureau 2018, "Measures Poverty."

26. Mcarty, "Poverty Numbers Climbing."

27. United Way ALICE Project, *ALICE*, 10.

total, cannot afford the basic cost of living, with conditions still lagging behind pre-recession levels. "In Northwest Louisiana, this statistic is higher than the state's total at 44%," said Sarah Berthelot, president/CEO of Louisiana Association of United Ways (LAUW).[28]

To place a smaller scope by focusing on a general area, the researcher will study the parish of Caddo to understand what and who is affecting poverty in this area. Caddo Parish received its name from the Caddo Native American tribe. Most of the tribe was removed from the area in the 1830s. The core of Caddo Parish was developed by the White owners of cotton plantations with thousands of enslaved African American who labored for them. For 2018, African American poverty in Louisiana was 29.4% statewide, 33.9% of Caddo African American residents were in poverty, and White Caddo Parish residents' poverty was 15.5%.[29] For 2020, Caddo Parish poverty was 34.01% for African Americans and 12.19% for Whites. The poverty rate of African American residents in Shreveport, Louisiana, the largest city in Caddo Parish, is dramatically higher than the national average of 25.2%. The percentage of African American / Black residents in Shreveport, Louisiana, who live below the poverty line is 35.6%. White residents' poverty in Shreveport is 16.5%. One out of every 3.9 Black / African American residents of Shreveport lives in poverty.[30] In Bossier Parish, Louisiana, African American / Black residents are 23.8% below the poverty level, and Whites are 17.6%.[31] For 2020, Bossier City poverty for Blacks is 33.05% poverty and for Whites 11.06%.[32]

According to research, the areas for which the poverty rate (population below poverty) reaches 20% encounter systemic issues that are more severe than in lower-poverty areas. A critical point of research and discussion in academic literature regarding the poverty rate of 20% is relevant for examining the social characteristics of low-poverty compared to high-poverty areas.[33] As the US Census Bureau, World Population Review, and other sources show, African American poverty has been over 30% for African Americans in Caddo Parish for many years.

---

28. Mcarty, "Poverty Numbers Climbing."
29. US Census Bureau 2018, "Measures Poverty."
30. World Population Review 2021, "Caddo Parish."
31. US Census Bureau 2020, "Bossier Parish."
32. World Population Review 2021, "Bossier Parish."
33. Dalakar, "10-20-30 Provision," 2–26.

There is a cost associated with being able to afford the basic necessities. Again, ALICE provides information on households that earn less than the basic cost of living in Louisiana but earn greater than the federal poverty level. The bare minimum household survival budget increased by 33% for a family and 16% for an individual with a low rate of inflation from the years 2010 to 2016.

According to the data, these numbers associated with this budget are still substantially higher than the $11,880 for a single-person adult and $24,300 for a family of four from the federal poverty level.[34] ALICE represents a growing number of individuals and families working but unable to afford the basic necessities of life, such as housing, food, health care, childcare, and transportation.

> These people living on the edge, they're not bums. They're hard-working people. We have this huge population that are working poor, who are living one emergency away from disaster, said Bruce Wilson, United Way chapter for Northwest Louisiana CEO.[35]

For these working poor people in Louisiana, buying healthy food, providing themselves with health care, and obtaining officially recognized childcare are basic needs forgone when disaster hits. People have to make decisions in Caddo and Bossier Parish.

When disaster strikes, ALICE families or individuals often choose to forgo health care, accredited childcare, or buying healthy food to make up the difference. Wilson also said,

> They have to make a choice. Do I take food off the table to pay for this extra thing? Do I not take my child to the doctor or the dentist? Do I make some other choice that has serious consequences?[36]

Northwest Louisiana has ten parishes, which include the parishes of Caddo and Bossier. This area has a high average of households living in poverty or at the ALICE Threshold of 44%. African Americans, other racial minorities, women, immigrants, those who have not completed high school or higher, and citizens with disabilities are in the ALICE population, according to this report.

---

34. United Way ALICE Project, *ALICE*, 10.
35. Talamo, "Struggling to Survive."
36. Talamo, "Struggling to Survive."

Job opportunities, community resources, and housing affordability are evaluated for economic viability in the ALICE report. In this report, Caddo received a ranking of "fair" for community resources and job opportunities and a "poor" ranking in the category of housing affordability. Bossier Parish received a "good" ranking for job opportunities and a "poor" ranking for community resources and housing affordability.[37]

Households on the ALICE report represent the hard workers in Caddo and Bossier Parish who play a crucial role in keeping the economic engine of Louisiana running. While these households play crucial roles, these people are not always sure they can provide for their basic needs. The ALICE report presents four main contributing factors that cause a struggling population in the parishes. These factors are a lack of affordable housing, private and public assistance that does not attain economic stability and low wages, and a cost of living that outpaces employee wages.

Between 2007 and 2013, employment paying less than $10 by the hour increased by 115% in the state of Louisiana, and employment paying $30 to $40 an hour decreased by 64%. An annual salary for one of the 70,820 cashier jobs in Louisiana is a base rate of $8.75 an hour. This rate will not bring a family to halfway on the survival budget threshold. The household survival budget—a bare-minimum budget that does not allow for any savings or luxuries—for a single adult in northwest Louisiana remained set at an estimated annual salary of $17,266. The survival budget for a family of four remained set at $41,480. A total of 33% of households in Bossier Parish could not attain these target incomes, and for Caddo Parish, the numbers rose to 44%.[38]

According to the ALICE report, households that live below the ALICE Threshold produce negative effects that extend to surrounding communities. This creates links between poverty and crime, from those who cannot afford housing to being homeless and not being able to afford certified childcare to putting children at risk. These types of issues will cause communities to be responsible for creating homeless shelters for the homeless, paying into the foster care system for the underage homeless, investing in social and educational services for children with inadequate childcare, and contributing to income for the unemployed.[39]

37. Talamo, "Struggling to Survive."
38. Talamo, "Struggling to Survive."
39. Talamo, "Struggling to Survive."

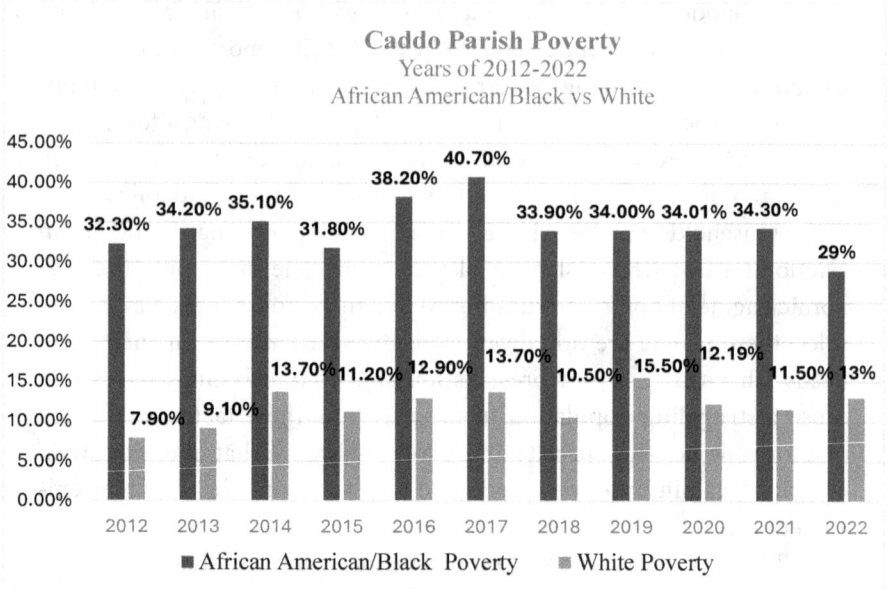

Caddo Parish Poverty
Years of 2012-2022
African American/Black vs White

Figure 3: Caddo Parish Poverty 2010–2022 Black vs. White
Source: U.S. Census Bureau (2022)

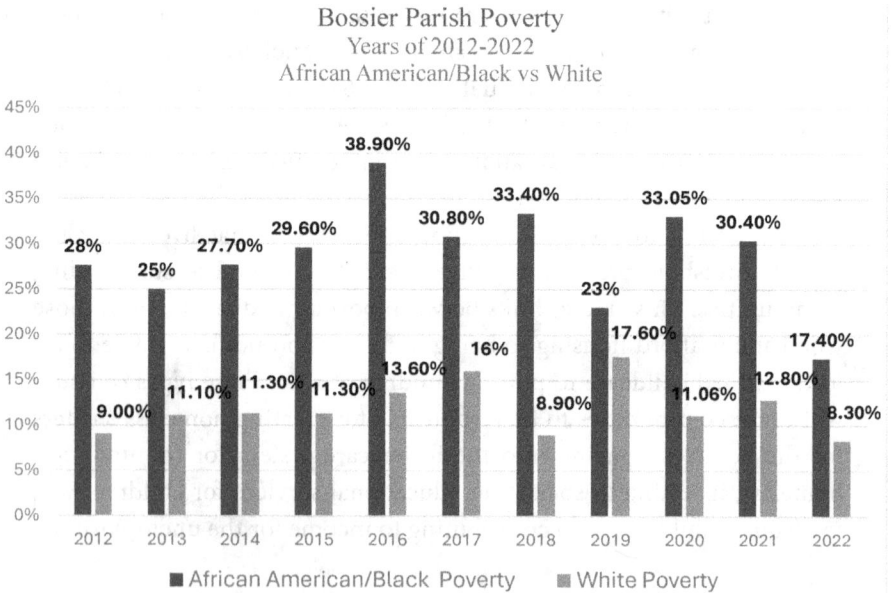

Bossier Parish Poverty
Years of 2012-2022
African American/Black vs White

Figure 4: Bossier Parish Poverty 2010–2022 Black vs. White
Source: U.S. Census Bureau (2022)

East Baton Rouge Parish Poverty
Years of 2010-2021
African Amercan vs White

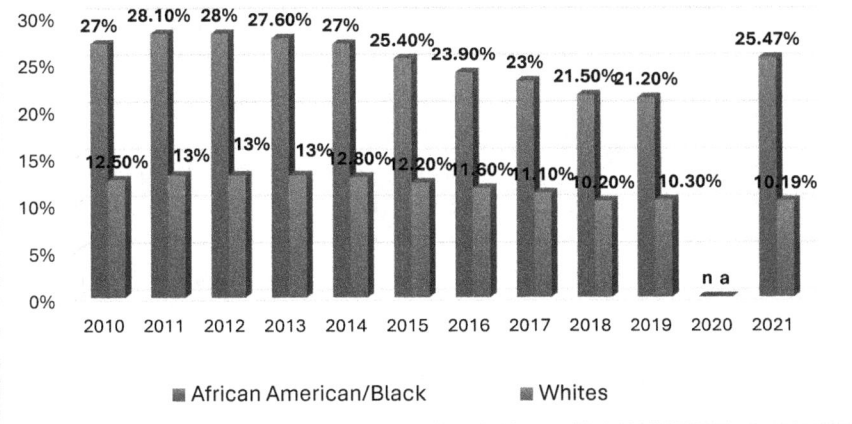

Figure 5: East Baton Rouge Parish Poverty 2010–2021 Black vs. White
Source: U.S. Census Bureau (2010) East Baton Rouge Parish, Louisiana population (2021)

In 2019, the US census shows that the population of East Baton Rouge Parish, Louisiana, was 47.2% African American and 45.9% White.[40] According to the World Population Review 2021, the East Baton Rouge Parish, Louisiana, population of African Americans was 46.10% and Whites 46.83%.

2.4 Caddo Parish Poverty Links to Institutional Racism and Study Areas

Wondering how African American people in Caddo Parish find themselves in a poverty-stricken situation linked to urbanization, politics, housing dilemmas, miseducation, unemployment, underemployment, and sprawl, one must understand the link to institutional racism. Some captured and sold Africans from the transatlantic trade found themselves in the Americas, some eventually making their way to Louisiana. At the start of the colonial era, Whites in the United States possessed socially sanctioned privileges, legally sanctioned privileges, and other rights. At the same time minorities, especially Africans, were denied the same

40. US Census Bureau, "East Baton Rouge."

rights. Americans of European descent were granted exclusive privileges in voting rights, criminal procedure, land acquisition, and education.[41] African Americans still face restrictions on their economic, social, and political freedom. The information given by this source states that racism is the systemic oppression of one race over another. In the United States, society has continued to experience high levels of racism and discrimination. One new phenomenon is the expulsion of sexual and racial minorities from America by the rise of the White nationalist in the "alt-right" movement. Racism consists of nine areas of human activity, which are economics, education, entertainment, labor, law, politics, religion, sex, and war.[42] From these "nine areas," the researcher will only use the areas of economics, education, labor, law, politics, and war in this research. The researcher will present information to show that Caddo Parish and Bossier Parish African American / Black residents are targeted in the areas of economics, education, labor, law, politics, and war by Racism White Supremacy. Urbanization and housing links to economics, labor links to employment and unemployment, and miseducation links to education. Laws maintain control in all areas, war is the act of racism or systemic oppression in the nine areas, and all can be intertwined directly or indirectly. Lastly, all areas directly link to politics. All the nine areas of human activity are controlled by Whites to keep Africans/Blacks all over the world confused, in poverty, and/or in a lower status than Whites on a collective basis.

2.4.1 White on Black Violence in Caddo and Bossier Parish

Violence in the Deep South caused significant population changes in the United States from the late 1800s until the 1970s. Lynchings were a tactical method used by Whites in the Americas to project fear, terror, and racial boundaries in the US, especially in the South. The lynchings, along with racial segregation, poor economic conditions, and discrimination, launched one of the largest and most rapid mass internal movements in history. This movement is called the Black Migration (also called the Great Migration or Great Northward Migration).[43] The Black Migration transitions from 1916 to 1970. Before 1890, the American South

---

41. Vandal, "Bloody Caddo."
42. Fuller, *United Independent Compensatory*, 150.
43. Vandal, "Bloody Caddo."

populated more than 90% of African Americans. By the end of the migration, just over 50% of African Americans populated the American South, according to the US census. When this migration occurred, urbanization occurred in other US cities. A slower reverse migration has occurred back to the South to states and cities, since the Civil Rights Movement, where economic opportunities are greater.[44] In the United States, 4,673 lynchings took place from 1882 to 1936. In Louisiana, there were 389 lynchings during this period, of which 333 were recorded to have happened to African Americans. For a time, the top four lynching counties in America were Ouachita, Caddo, Bossier, and Morehouse Parishes, all in north Louisiana.[45] After the American Civil War, there was no peace in Caddo Parish. There was little, if any, law years after the Civil War, and citizens in Caddo Parish observed some of the most heinous murders in recorded history.

Ironically, the very last city in the American South scheduled to officially take down its Confederate monument in October of 2017 was downtown Shreveport, Louisiana, in Caddo Parish at a seven to five vote.[46] The simple fact that Caddo had to take a vote on removing the monument shows that there is still a deep love for the old Confederate South. Not that the current concept of America is any better; it is just that the Confederate South is an overt type of racism. However, as of March 2022, the monument still stands.[47]

In Bossier Parish, after the Civil War, many intimidation factors were used by Whites to control Blacks. Sources present extremely violent situations to maintain supremacy over the newly freed enslaved Blacks.[48] Violence increased at the end of Reconstruction into the twentieth century. Conservative White Democrats attempted to keep power over the state, but it was a struggle. During the time of Reconstruction, 70% of the population in Caddo Parish was Black. Also, during this period of Reconstruction, there were 566 recorded homicides of Blacks. In Caddo Parish, 85% of the homicides happened against Blacks, and 80% of the perpetrators were presumed to be White. During this period of struggle, Bossier Parish recorded a total of twenty-six lynchings of African Americans by Whites. Many forms of tactics were used as a part of racial terrorism.

44. Themba-Nixon et al., *Persistence of White Privilege*, 7–71.

45. Finley, "Lynching."

46. Ferrell, "Migrating Shreveport Population."

47. Benn et al., "Caddo Confederate Monument."

48. Finley, "Lynching."

There were even records and evidence of mass murders by Whites on the Black population. For example, in October 1868, there were three reported mass murders. The first example was when nine Black people were taken to the Red River, told to swim, and shot at while swimming. All nine died. The second incident happened on the same night as the first. A report states that thirty Blacks were rounded up from around Shreveport, taken to the bank of the Red River, tied together with ropes, shot in their backs, and dumped in the river. The third incident happened when a group of White men took five Black men away from work, tied their hands, marched them to Red River, and shot them dead. Due to all of the murders and violence committed against Blacks in Shreveport and the rest of Caddo Parish, the parish received the nickname "Bloody Caddo."[49]

2.4.2 Six of the Nine Areas of Human Activity

As mentioned in the introduction, there are nine areas of human activity. To keep the system of Racism White Supremacy intact, White individuals who practice the system of institutional racism must control all nine areas of human activity. If White people who practice racism lose control over any one of the areas of human activity, then the whole system of racism could fall because the areas are linked together directly or indirectly. The nine areas of human activity are economics, education, entertainment, labor, law, politics, religion, sex, and war.[50] From these "nine areas," the researcher will only use the areas of economics, education, labor, law, politics, and war in this research, as stated before, because those areas are closely related to the researcher's purpose. Dr. Robert Bullard once said that

> racism plays a key factor in environmental planning and decision-making. Indeed, environmental planning racism is reinforced by government, legal, economic, political, and military institutions.[51]

Dr. Bullard mentioned the terms economics, legal, military, and political in his statement. Ironically those four words are mentioned in the nine areas of human activity that Neeley Fuller Jr. identifies. Legal as in

49. Vandal, "Bloody Caddo."
50. Fuller, *United Independent Compensatory*, 150.
51. Bullard, *Confronting Environmental Racism*, 16.

law, economics is the same, political as in politics, and military associated with war. Research and data have shown no progressive changes in many areas that could help African Americans obtain equity and equality in the United States since the Civil Rights Movement because these areas of human activities are still maintained and controlled by Racism White Supremacy.

2.4.2.1 *Economics:* Economics is the branch of knowledge that consists of production, consumption, and transfer of wealth. Economics is a social science involving producing, distributing, and consuming goods and services. It studies how individuals, businesses, governments, and nations make choices with allocating resources. Economics focuses on the actions of human beings, based on assumptions that humans act with rational behavior, seeking the most optimal level of benefit or utility. Alternatively, simplified, economics is the study of how people allocate scarce resources for production, distribution, and consumption, both individually and collectively.[52]

According to Neely Fuller Jr., economics is the correct distribution of and/or balance between all animals, persons, places, plants, etc. Economics, in the correct sense, is the sum of all the thought, speech, and/ or action used to produce maximum efficiency in revealing the truth in a manner that promotes the establishment of justice and correctness in all areas of activity. Economics also means using all things, thought, speech, and/or action with maximum efficiency with the objective of eliminating racism (White supremacy). Economics can be used constructively and successfully to manufacture correctness and justice through actions and speech.[53] The researcher argues that people with access to the most resources can control those resources and the world. The people who acquire smaller portions of the resources must use them wisely to change the predicament that they are in. In Caddo and Bossier Parish, African Americans have limited access or resources to change their economic status. In the Shreveport–Bossier City area, the casinos are major employers, and there are many unskilled workers that are employed there. Many African Americans in Caddo and Bossier Parish are unskilled laborers. Unskilled laborers are cheaper, have fewer technical skills, and are an

---

52. Hayes, "Economics Defined."
53. Fuller, *United Independent Compensatory,* 59.

inexpensive method for establishments to achieve their goals of services and products.[54] However, these unskilled laborers are not highly paid.

2.4.2.2 Education: Education is receiving or giving systematic instruction, especially at a school or university. The late Nelson Mandela, former president of South Africa, says,

> Education is the great engine of personal development. It is through education that the daughter of a peasant can become a doctor, that the son of a mineworker can become the head of the mine, that a child of farm workers can become the president of a great nation. It is what we make out of what we have, not what we are given, that separates one person from another.[55]

Kofi Annan, former UN secretary-general and Ghanaian diplomat, explains that "knowledge is power. Information is liberating. Education is the premise of progress, in every society, in every family. Literacy is a bridge from misery to hope. Education is a human right with immense power to transform. On its foundation rests the cornerstones of freedom, democracy, and sustainable human development."[56] Suppose education can give a person power, help a poor person become wealthy, be liberated, turn hope into misery, and help produce freedom. What happens if a race systemically oppresses another group of people from being properly educated, rather causing them to be miseducated, be purposely uneducated, and have education hidden from them? It seems that education is a tool of oppression as well as a tool of liberation and freedom.

Neely Fuller Jr. explains,

> Nearly all of the knowledge that non-White people receive while existing among or in contact with White people, has been presented to them by the Racist (White Supremacist) for the purpose of serving Racism (White Supremacy).[57]

White America controls the United States education system. America was created by White men, founded on Racism White Supremacy, and is still controlled by Racism White Supremacy. Therefore, African Americans in Caddo and Bossier Parish will only learn what the system of racism wants

---

54. Keilholtz, "Profit Margins."
55. Ellis, "Nelson Mandela."
56. Amanfo, "Interesting African Quotes."
57. Fuller, *United Independent Compensatory,* 101.

them to know at any given time. Also, in Caddo and Bossier Parish, there is a disparity of higher degree attainment with African Americans versus Whites, where African Americans are on the lower end of attainment. When individuals achieve higher degrees, they can acquire higher paying jobs.

2.4.2.3 *Labor*: Labor can be considered the amount of social, physical, and mental effort used to produce goods and services in an economy. To obtain a finished product, labor supplies the manpower, expertise, and services needed to turn raw materials into a completed service and/or product.[58] To produce goods and services, individuals must be in charge of accomplishing these goals by way of employees, supervisors or managers, owners, and producers.

Labor is any act of using energy and time to achieve an objective constructively. In a socio-material system controlled and dominated by a system of oppression called racism, all employment sustained and/or established by White folk is directly or indirectly controlled and dominated by White folk who practice Racism White Supremacy. If the last statement is true, this could explain why African American unemployment numbers are high in the United States, especially in the researcher's focus areas of Caddo and Bossier Parish. If African Americans are in a system of Racism White Supremacy, and the purpose of racism is to oppress African Americans / Blacks in the US, including Caddo and Bossier Parish, then it would make sense that employment is kept from African Americans directly or indirectly. To take it a step further, we could include education links to labor, for if African Americans are miseducated and do not achieve a high level of education, then African Americans will not be even considered for high salary/paying jobs, and the "lack of sufficient education" scenario makes it easier for ruling them out of higher salary/paying jobs.

2.4.2.4 *Law*: According to the Columbia Law Review, "Law is a rule of civil conduct prescribed by the supreme power in a state, commanding what is right and forbidding what is wrong."[59] According to Neely Fuller Jr.,

58. Amadeo, "Your Work Is Critical."
59. Bigelow, "Definition of Law," 1.

> It is important to know and understand that "Law" is not the same as "Justice," law is anything that is "done." In the system of Racism White Supremacy, do not expect the truth to be revealed or used in a manner that results in Justice and/or correctness through so-called law-making.[60]

Through the United States Constitution, Congress has designated duties of organizing the judicial and executive branches, a part in declarations of war, increasing revenue, and creating all laws required to execute these powers. The US Constitution was written in 1787 and placed into functioning in 1789. According to the US Constitution, the United States government exists to serve its citizens.[61] However, Blacks were not considered citizens but were treated as enslaved people since Christopher Columbus brought over Africans in the transatlantic slave trade in 1492. Furthermore, the enslavement of Black people was included in the US Constitution legally until ratified under the Fourteenth Amendment in the US Constitution in 1868.[62] After 1865, the southern states in the United States passed the Black Codes. The Black Codes were a series of laws to restrict and control the newly freed slaves' right to be free from bondage as humans.[63] Also, there are the Jim Crow laws that existed from the post–Civil War era through 1968. These particular collections of laws were to marginalize African Americans by refusing their rights to education, to be able to hold jobs, their right to vote, and/or other opportunities.[64] Some Jim Crow laws still exist today. Richard Nixon's War on Drug laws and Bill Clinton's 1994 Crime Bill laws were used to disproportionately jail and imprison Black people in the United States[65] Since the founding of the United States, both written and unwritten laws have been used as tools to oppress Black people. These laws are to keep Racism White Supremacy intact. Neely Fuller Jr. shares that "a law is a tool that can be used to produce and/or maintain justice or produce and/or maintain injustice."[66] In the United States, we have many injustices against people of color, especially African Americans / Blacks presently. The researcher will discuss more data and research regarding the creation

60. Fuller, *United Independent Compensatory*, 149.
61. United States Senate, "Thirteenth Amendment."
62. Jones, "14th Amendment's Promise."
63. Weatherspoon, *African American Males*, 8–74.
64. History.com Editors, "Jim Crow Laws."
65. Equal Justice Initiative, "Nixon Advisor"; Chung et al., "1994 Crime Bill."
66. Fuller, *United Independent Compensatory*, 150.

of criminals in America, Black incarceration, and Jim Crow laws in the 2.13 "Politics in Louisiana" section.

2.4.2.5 Politics: A simple definition of politics is the way groups of individuals interact with one another while making decisions and agreements as they live together in communities, neighborhoods, tribes, cities, states, and countries.[67]

During the existence of racism, the interactions between non-White people and White people and between non-White people and each other can be described as "terroristic, trashy, and/or tacky or The Tragic Arrangement"[68] as defined and described by Neely Fuller Jr. The meaning of Fuller's term "The Tragic Arrangement" is the total of all of the things that non-White people and White people think, say, and do in regard to their interactions with each other in all areas of activity which consist of economics, education, entertainment, labor, law, politics, religion, sex, and war. According to evidence and based on Fuller's Compensatory Counter-Racist Logic, the system of Racism White Supremacy has not been replaced with a system of justice which is a balance between people. This is because of the lack of White people's and non-White people's ability to come up with a better system, which keeps us in this state called "The Tragic Arrangement." This inability and the interactions between White racists and non-Whites are insanities since White racists require their victims of this system to promote insane ways of speaking, acting, and thinking. This control operates through politics. Politics can play a role in using humans as resources because if someone has power or control over you, then that person in power can use you through politics or by force.

The purpose behind the researcher using the definitions and terms of Neely Fuller Jr., Dr. Robert Bullard, and Dr. Frances Cress Welsing regarding racism is that the researcher postulates that racism or White supremacy is the cause of poverty, miseducation, poor political position, lack of homeownership, dictating population trends, lack of employment opportunities, high crime, miseducation, and overall poor social status and economics in the African American community in Caddo Parish, northwest Louisiana, and the entire United States. Racism White

---

67. Barker, *Politics of Aristotle*, 2–6.

68. Fuller, *United Independent Compensatory*, 167.

Supremacy is a global oppression system that plagues people of color worldwide.

2.4.2.6 War: War is defined as a state of usually open and declared armed hostile conflict between states or nations. Another definition provides that war should be understood as an *intentional, actual,* and *widespread* armed conflict between political communities.[69] The researcher sees war as a tool of racism. Neeley Fuller Jr. includes war in the nine areas of human activity controlled by Racism White Supremacy because he argues that White people have posed war on Black people in various manners, and Dr. Robert Bullard includes that military (the military is used in and for wars) solution is a key factor in racism.[70]

2.4.2.6.1 WARFARE ON BLACK PEOPLE: One can easily see that racism is war on Black / African American people and other minorities, with Black / African Americans being the primary target based on skin tone and genetics. Furthermore, it is evident White people who still practice racism are a dominant force in the world, especially in the United States. Dr. Frances Cress Welsing's research and studies presented that racism is a tool for White genetic survival. Dr. Welsing presented that the whiteness of the skin, or noncolored melanated skin, possessed by Caucasian people is a recessive genetic trait, a deficiency to produce color in the skin, and melanated skin people are genetically dominant, meaning that Black people have the most dominant trait.[71] Dr. Welsing concluded that it is a system for White genetic survival and is meant to prevent White genetic annihilation. If we fail to understand this, we don't understand what exactly is happening to the Black family, the attack on the Black family in general, and the attack very specifically on Black males as husbands and fathers. The White collective is not going to change because it is a survival system for a tiny minority of people on the planet.[72]

Another tactic of war is psychological warfare. Psychological warfare is the planned tactical use of noncombat techniques such as propaganda, threats, demoralization, intimidation, threats of war, and geopolitical

69. Long, "What Is War?"

70. Fuller, *United Independent Compensatory,* 158; Bullard, *Confronting Environmental Racism,* 16–18.

71. Bryan, "Frances Cress Welsing."

72. Welsing, "Cress Theory."

unrest to mislead, intimidate, demoralize, and/or influence the behavior or thinking of an enemy.[73] War and psychological warfare are tools used by Racism White Supremacy to keep non-White people oppressed, especially African/Black people. The researcher will go into more detail regarding this subject matter. Warfare on Africans/Blacks by Europeans/Whites has been going on for centuries, including recent history and the present. The harsh treatment of the enslaved in the Americas meant the Africans endured torture, rape, brainwashing, being experimented on medically and psychologically, long work days, and separation of families. The Jim Crow era included lynchings, no voting rights, unlawful incarceration, labor camps, segregation, and indentured servitude.[74] Other war tactics during the Jim Crow era included Whites destroying predominantly Black towns, communities, and neighborhoods in events such as the Rosewood Massacre, the Tulsa Race Massacre, and the Atlanta Race Massacre, to name only a few. Whites destroyed these places while killing Black people and injuring Black people for various reasons. During the Civil Rights era, Blacks dealt with police violence, segregation, voter suppression, and Black Civil Rights leader assassinations. Also, Blacks dealt with discrimination in employment, education, and housing practices.[75] Currently, there is less segregation in some areas, but segregation still exists, as well as unjust police killings. With regard to war tactics in environmental racism, African Americans deal with targeted issues in their communities, such as pollution dumping, housing discrimination, employment discrimination, and human health disparities. For example, in 2007, there was extraordinary evidence examined in the Toxic Waste and Race at Twenty report highlighting 413 nationally commercial hazardous waste facilities which were sited in neighborhoods that were disproportionately minority neighborhoods since 1965. In 2009, the Americans Changing Lives study presented that African Americans and people at lower education levels were more likely to reside within one mile of a pollution facility. People of color make up one-third of the US population, but the percentage of children of color who attend "sick schools" is 45%. "Sick schools" are typically comprised of low-income students living in a low-income community that are subject to living in poor and health-risk communities and attending schools that are older and poorly maintained. These schools have indoor environmental issues, indoor air

73. Longley, "Psychological Warfare."
74. History.com Editors, "Jim Crow Laws."
75. Bryan, "Frances Cress Welsing."

pollution, toxic pesticides, toxic chemicals, mold infestation, asbestos, radon, lead in paint, lead in drinking water, and other heavy metals. In Louisiana, the number of children of color in "sick schools" is 50%.[76] Water and air pollution cause health issues, shorter life spans, and death of people of color. The researcher presented the tactics and points in this section to show that White racism is a war on people of color, especially African Americans / Blacks.

2.4.2.6.2 PSYCHOLOGICAL WARFARE ON BLACK PEOPLE: Psychological warfare is the planned tactical use of noncombat techniques such as propaganda, threats, demoralization, intimidation, threats of war, and geopolitical unrest to mislead, intimidate, demoralize, and/or influence the behavior or thinking of an enemy, as stated before. Psychological warfare can assist with overcoming the enemy's will to fight back or uprise. Also, psychological warfare propaganda methods on the people are popular towards a target enemy.[77] For instance, White racists use propaganda on other Whites and other non-Black races to influence emotions, reasonings, motives, values, behaviors, and beliefs against Blacks / African Americans. To understand how psychological warfare was and is still used on Black people, the researcher will give a brief history in this section.

Psychological warfare tactics on Blacks were used since the transatlantic slave trade to the present time. Typical ways Whites use these tactics are to dehumanize and demonize Africans/Blacks. These tactics were the leeway of justification to mistreat, harm, enslave, keep in poverty, miseducate, and murder Black people. Other tactics included referring to Blacks as being less than Whites because of their skin color, lips, noses, hair, and inability to learn and be civilized.[78]

Whites steadily created ideologies and conducted studies meant to show that Blacks were inferior to Whites in the 1920s. This was mainly done by Whites drawing up tests and giving the tests to Blacks to take. When Black people did not perform well on a test, they were deemed less intelligent than Whites, who performed better. However, the test's validity was challenging because the test was given to Blacks that were not in a

---

76. Toxic Waste and Race at Twenty report, Americans Changing Lives study, and data on "sick schools" from Bullard et al., *Environmental Health*, 53–69.

77. Longley, "Psychological Warfare."

78. Adiele, *Popes*, 20–30.

good environment, were unfamiliar with testing items, had poor education opportunities, came from disadvantaged home conditions, and had
cultural barriers.[79] Nevertheless, the stigma on Black intelligence and
other psychological warfare strategies would continue for decades. African Americans still encounter these tactics in the workplace and schools.

For decades African Americans faced discrimination for wearing
their natural hair and/or naturally locked hair at work and school. For
many years, some African American natural hairstyles were deemed by
Whites to be unprofessional. However, here in recent times, there has
been a significant natural hair–wearing pushback by African Americans.
During the era of the United States slavery, in many instances enslaved
Black women had to cover their hair with wraps, and if they worked inside the enslaver's house, they had to put on wigs to imitate White wom-
en.[80] The tignon law was passed in 1786 by Governor Esteban Rodríguez
Miró in Louisiana and used to police Black people's hair.[81]

For years if Blacks did not conform to certain hairstyles as Whites
saw fit, they were and are still not allowed access to certain jobs, to play
in sports events, and to attend certain schools.[82] This was an attempt to
make Blacks feel their hair was not as good as White folk's hair, to make
Blacks feel inferior. Recently in 2010, Chastity Jones refused to cut off her
locks after accepting a job with Catastrophe Management Solutions, and
the company rescinded its job offer. In 2013, there was a filed suit by the
Equal Employment Opportunity Commission for Jones, but it was lost,
and in 2016 the Eleventh Circuit Court of Appeals upheld the district
court's ruling and dismissed the case.[83] Africans/Blacks had worn Afros,
braided hair, and locked hair for thousands of years before the transatlantic slave trade. Discoveries show Africans/Blacks to have been the first
humans on the planet by two hundred thousand years or more. Furthermore, it was also discovered through research that all races of humanity
derived from Africans/Blacks.[84]

79. Thomas, "Black Intellectuals' Critique."

80. Griffin, "Natural Black Hair."

81. Tadele, "Policing Black Women's Hair."

82. Cox, "Texas Teen Banned."

83. Griffin, "Natural Black Hair."

84. Stony Brook University, "Humans"; Zhongxi et al., "Chinese Descendants";
Coleman, "Humanity Is Born," 17.

Professor John Shea, PhD, of Stony Brook University links the earliest Africans to the first tool makers.[85] Professor Jin Li, a Chinese geneticist at the Research Center of Contemporary Anthropology at Shanghai Fudan University (RCCASFU), recently performed research that proved modern Chinese people originated from Black Africans, based on modern DNA testing techniques. Discoveries show the White race to be only as old as eight thousand to ten thousand years old.[86] If Blacks were the first race of people on the planet and are the fathers and mothers of humanity, why are there such despicable tactics being taken against Blacks on their hair, skin color, and other physical features?

Because Africans/Blacks were the first tool makers, they were the first race to build civilizations, including the pyramids in Egypt and Mesopotamia. Egypt consisted of all Black people for thousands of years, dating back from around 8000 BC to 10,000 BC. Lower Egypt was conquered for one hundred years by the Hyksos around 1640 BC, but the Africans took back control until being fully conquered by the Persians in 525 BC, the Greeks in 332 BC, and finally, the Romans in 30 BC.[87] Africans inhabited the continents first and maintained the world's lands and natural resources in good care. Also, Africans were the first to invent languages, astronomy, literature, philosophy, science, math, medicine, spirituality, metallurgy, and the arts.[88] Some of those inventions and discoveries were passed to the original Egyptians by African ancestors that predated Egypt.[89] In fact, the Greeks received language and literature from the Black Africans, and the Romans received literature form the Africans/Blacks as well.[90] Then there has to be a discussion regarding Africans being the first urban planners or city planners of the world and being the first explorers. Discoveries show that Africans began cultivating crops as far back as twelve thousand years ago and sailing boats since around 5000 BC.[91] Furthermore, the correlation between the architectural influences of ancient Egypt is seen in Rome, Greece, and Washington

85. Stony Brook University, "Humans."

86. Gibbons, "How Europeans Evolved."

87. Howard, "Ancient Egyptian Influences," 18–21; Finch, "Black Roots"; Walker, "100 Things," 1–4.

88. Finch, "Black Roots"; Howard, "Ancient Egyptian Influences," 13–15.

89. Walker, "100 Things," 1–4.

90. Coleman, "Humanity Is Born," 111–59; Burnett, "Ancient Egypt"; Joseph Smith Papers, "Egyptian Language," 2–33; Gardiner, "Egyptian Origin," 1.

91. Chimbiri, *Ancient Egypt*, 12–15.

DC.[92] Greeks were excellent record keepers. In his magnum opus, *A Lost Tradition: African Philosophy in World History*, Dr. Théophile Obenga quotes Aristotle ranking Egypt as

> the most ancient archeological reserve in the world and that is how the Egyptian, whom we (Greeks) considered as the most ancient of the human race.[93]

> The ancient Greeks traced all humans inventions to Egyptians from Calculus, Geometry, Astronomy, and Dice Games to Writing. . . . Since the time of Homer, Egyptian antiquity functioned strictly as a highly memorialized component of Greek history. Herodotus said it, Plato confirmed it, and Aristotle never denied it.[94]

Knowing and understanding this information, Black people can prove they are the fathers and mothers of mankind and are not inferior in intellect nor genetics but are in a physical and mental war waged by White people who practice racism. To keep African Americans from this information is part of psychological warfare because one of its tactics was to take away African Americans' rich history and teach Blacks that they come from enslaved people, making them think less of themselves and be easier to be controlled mentally. This tactic can be deemed as miseducation as well. African Americans do have notable great inventors, intellectuals, and awesome accomplishments in America despite being oppressed. The transatlantic slave trade assisted in interrupting Black history and endeavors.

To present more background on psychological warfare, the researcher will refer to another important event, the transatlantic slave trade. During the transatlantic slave trade, the Portuguese, British, Spanish, French, Dutch, and Danish, who are races of European descent, began the most horrific treatment of human beings. These White Europeans kidnapped and stole African people from the continent of Africa and shipped them across the ocean to multiple continents. Now, this is an act of war. Also, they purchased African indentured servants. African indentured servants usually only served anywhere from four to seven years of servitude and would be free of their serving after the terms were met. Indentured servants in Africa could own property, have

92. Browder, *Nile Valley Contributions*, 62.

93. Obenga, *Lost Tradition*, 45.

94. Obenga, *Lost Tradition*, 47.

their own indentured servants, go to school, and even marry.[95] Most importantly, African slavery never passed from one generation to another, and it lacked the racist notion that Whites were masters and Blacks were slaves.[96] The harsh treatment of slavery in the Americas would have the Africans endure rape (of women, men, and children), beatings, brainwashing, long workdays, etc.

Dr. John Henrik Clarke explained that there is only one race, the human race. The reason the race categories were created was to justify the transatlantic slave trade and colonialism.[97] Being that the Catholic Church had a history of slave masters and slaves authorized by Pope Nicholas V, the pope gave notice to Catholic kings and princes, along with Christopher Columbus, to pursue the transatlantic slave trade to help Europeans to take over the planet. The papal bull *Dum Diversas* was the first bull written by Pope Nicholas V on the issue of the Black/African enslavement together with the right of ownership granted to Portugal over West Africa.

Early stages of racism acted as a tool to separate humans by skin tone and to refer to them as subhuman or beast, and it justified the cause of the transatlantic slave trade. Also, the pope justified their slavery of Africans not only by saying they were a different race but by claiming and identifying Africans as inferior, pseudohuman, barbarous, lacking good morals, morally debased, untamed, and sexually lascivious. And the sexually lascivious label was placed on the African man, saying the sexual lasciviousness of the Black man was located in his sexual organ, which they portrayed to be similar in length and size with that of the devil. The English physician and surgeon Charles White (1728–1813) in 1799 concluded that the Black African was very hypersexual based on his long penis. Convinced of his clinical observations, he stated that "the penis of an African is larger than that of a European. So, the Black man was ruled a demon."[98] To make African lives even cheaper, they were also labeled as not having God in them, having no religion, lacking commonwealth, being without laws, being libidinous, and being beastly.[99]

95. Library of Congress, "Beginnings"; Public Broadcasting Service, "Africans in America."

96. Public Broadcasting Service, "Africans in America."

97. Clarke, "Race."

98. Adiele, *Popes*, 207.

99. Adiele, *Popes*, 207–8.

One last damaging tactic of psychological warfare during the transatlantic slave trade in American slavery was telling Blacks that there was something wrong with their skin and hair while simultaneously raping them, which in turn produced mixed-race children who were used as buffers between the lighter-skinned Blacks and darker-skinned Blacks. The mixed-race children were treated better than the darker-skinned Blacks and often helped police the dark-skinned Blacks. Even in the present time, darker-skinned Blacks and lighter-skinned Blacks still encounter competition, complexion battles, complexion issues, etc. between each other due to the psychological tactics of slavery. Whites still benefit from this because it can keep the focus off defeating racism. As we move into the twenty-first century, such psychological warfare tactics are pitting Black women and Black men against each other for the confusion and destruction of the Black race.

2.5 URBANIZATION

Urbanization refers to the mass movement of populations from rural to urban settings and how we adapt to the physical changes in urban settings through the movement.[100] There have been different observations and different views of the urbanization of the world's population. Many see it as a positive force in activity and development on an economic basis as economic activity moves away from agriculture to more remunerative activities.[101] Poverty reductions, distribution change, and economic growth have been viewed as a core part of population urbanization's leading process in many long-standing theories. If we look at urbanization from this view, then rural workers and homesteaders should be attracted by new economic opportunities in urbanized areas. However, in many instances, there has been a negative effect of urbanization that has ushered in new problems of poverty.[102] Negative effects of urbanization can be a lack of resources, poverty, unemployment, overcrowding, and crime.

2.5.0.1 Residential Land Uses: Residential land uses are for single- or two-family homes. Local jurisdictions can help increase the units of housing

100. Kuddus et al., "Urbanization," 1.

101. Ravallion, "Urbanization of Global Poverty," 8; Christiaensen, "Urbanization," 2–17.

102. DeJong, "Urbanization and Cities"; Christiaensen, "Urbanization," 2–17.

in parishes or counties, towns, and cities by modifying zoning policies which will also help with residential growth, higher density residential uses, and local jurisdictions.

2.5.0.2 *Rural Land Uses:* Rural lands include but are not limited to those generally developed to lower residential densities, timber harvesting, public or private recreation or open space, agricultural activities, resource conservation, and resource extraction. Rural lands can also include solid waste disposal sites, public services use, and institutional uses. Rural land uses are for rural residential subdivisions. They are usually clusters of residential development subdivided into parcels that are generally slightly larger or less than five acres. Neighborhood commercials use vacant parcels or can be used for rural residential subdivisions but are predominately developed with single-family homes.[103]

2.5.0.3 *Commercial and Industrial Land Uses:* Commercial areas include strip malls, supermarkets, hotels, hospitals, schools, churches, condominiums, gaming places, and office buildings. Industrial areas include chemical, petrochemical, and power plants, along with food processing or storage and manufacturing plants.[104] Commercial and industrial land uses typically are located near highways, roadways, and rail systems.

2.5.0.4 *Land Use:* Land use is an umbrella term for activities occurring on a given parcel of land, such as residential, retail, industrial, agricultural, or transportation uses.[105] We must understand that zoning is how government (local) regulates the different uses of parcels of land. Zoning and land use are not the same. To create an understanding regarding zoning and land use, the researcher will provide the details of how the two work together. As vacant land can be zoned for a use that has not yet developed, uses can be "grandfathered" or "nonconforming" (meaning that they existed before the land was zoned for different use), and zoning categories can permit more than one use—for example, an area zoned for industrial uses may also permit commercial uses, which may come to predominate in the area.

---

103. Robinson, "Land Use Behavior," 63–70.
104. Schmidt, "Commercial vs. Industrial."
105. Shreveport Metropolitan Planning Commission, "Population," 3–26.

2.5.0.5 Zoning and Ordinance: Zoning codes and ordinances give details and directions as to what type of development is allowed or permissible in each zoning district which includes residential, mixed-use, commercial, etc. Also, there are provisions for use of land within a district, down to each developed and used parcel. Zoning in residential areas and residential density is limited and managed regarding the number of housing units constructed in a particular land area. Parishes, counties, towns, and cities that are looking to add to their housing units may wish to revisit the zoning codes they have in place to facilitate growth by either researching and identifying possibilities in existing residential areas to add density and opening areas where residential development was not permitted at one point in time.[106]

2.5.1 Urbanization and Caddo Parish

Since the ending of the Black Migration during the period of 1916 to 1970, a slower reverse migration has occurred back to the southern states and cities. This reversal happened since the Civil Rights Movement when economic opportunities were greater in the South. In Caddo Parish, there was a decline in the population in the early 1990s, which was probably due to the loss of industries, high gang activity, murder, drugs, and criminal activity. After the casinos stabilized in the late 1990s and Hurricane Katrina's devastation happened, the population steadily increased in 2013, then the number started to decline again. The population in Shreveport is 182,616, in which the Black population is the largest with 57.09% outnumbering Whites at 38%. Blacks have the majority poverty rate in the city of Shreveport, which is the largest urbanized area in Caddo Parish and northern Louisiana.[107] The casino boom in Shreveport-Bossier happened in 1994. Shreveport City has three riverboats on its side of the Red River. The casinos are Eldorado, Sam's Town, and Cash Magic. Shreveport City's twin city, Bossier City, has four casinos, with now a total of seven between the twin cities. The first casino to open was Harrah's. After Harrah's opened in April of 1994, a month later Isle of Capri opened in May, and then a month after that Horseshoe opened in June. Not only would the casinos bring gambling, but they would also bring fine dining, buffets, hotels, entertainment, sponsorship

106. Local Housing Solutions, "Zoning Changes."
107. World Population Review, "Caddo Parish," 1.

opportunities, and tax dollars. Four more casinos opened directly on the Red River of Shreveport-Bossier, alongside the other three casinos. The gaming industry in Shreveport-Bossier quickly became recognized as the state's leader. Back in 2003, reports said that Shreveport-Bossier was the most prolific provider of revenue of the state.[108] However, the expectation of a foundation of a new economy in the Shreveport–Bossier City area was a wrong assumption. Other nearby states started in the gaming industry, and there came increased competition. As far as the worker's situation, the casino boom, in the beginning, became real for unskilled workers and for people who did not have advanced degrees. Unskilled and labor workers could work for the casinos and receive better pay than other jobs prior, but now it does not have much of an impact on them.

2.5.2 Housing Discrimination

To prevent a person from buying or renting housing because of race or color, national origin, family status, sex, religion, and/or disability by a housing provider is deemed housing discrimination. A real estate management company, landlord, or lending institution such as a bank is a housing provider.[109] Race still plays a significant part in distributing public benefits and public burdens associated with economic growth. The roots of discrimination are deep and have been difficult to eliminate. Housing discrimination contributes to the physical decay of inner-city neighborhoods. It denies a substantial segment of the African American community a basic form of wealth accumulation and investment through homeownership.[110]

Housing segregation and/or residential segregation and/or residential apartheid is the dominant housing pattern for most African Americans / Blacks, the most racially segregated group of people of color in America. Dr. Robert Bullard mentions that

> racism is and continues to be a conspicuous part of the American sociopolitical system, and as a result, Black people in particular, and ethnic and racial minority groups of color, find themselves at a disadvantage in contemporary society.[111]

108. Ferrell, "Gambling in Shreveport-Bossier."
109. US Government, "Housing Related Complaints."
110. Bullard, "Environmental Justice," 3.
111. Bullard, "Legacy of American Apartheid," 445.

A variety of White players that consisted of politicians, business elites, workers, merchants, shippers in the earlier stages, slaveholders, and slave owners created racial patterns in the cities of America since slavery. The Black ghettos being created and maintained by White racism, which was implicated in 1968 by the National Advisory Commission on Civil Disorders, continue the separate and unequal societies of Black and White. By way of lucid institutional practices, government policies, and private actions, a larger amount of White society will contain themselves from the nation's ghettos, reservations, and barrios, which are strategically kept isolated.

Housing discrimination is discrimination through tactical patterns that affect people's ability to purchase or rent housing units. This type of treatment, usually based on group characteristics, the housing market, and/or the area where people live, assists with the discrimination.[112] Many tactical measures can ensure racism is strategically ingrained in the housing market. Tactics such as housing discrimination, which includes redlining, house pricing discrimination, house buying exclusion, and White flight, are tools of racism used to cause home-buying issues and to prevent home buying and home maintaining in the Black community, which can bolster poverty and prevent African American wealth in the United States, including Caddo Parish. Housing discrimination denies a substantial segment of the African American community a basic form of wealth accumulation and investment through homeownership.[113]

> Even though the federal Fair Housing Act 1968 prohibited racial discrimination in housing, Blacks still do not receive equal treatment in the market or enjoy complete freedom of choice in housing.[114]

Nearly every major city in the US has established a fair housing division to implement and monitor fair housing policies, though the success of these agencies has varied and remains limited. There are alarming restrictions that Blacks encounter in the housing market regarding homeownership options. It denies them the benefit of long-term investments and tax savings due to institutional racism. Institutionalized racism can include such practices as coding records, threats, or acts of intimidation, refusing to lease or sell housing to Blacks, applications used to indicate

112. McCargo et al., *Building Black Homeownership*, 5–11.
113. Bullard et al., "Suburban Sprawl," 936–39.
114. Bullard, *Invisible Houston*, 50.

racial preferences of landlords, redlining (the act of lenders making policies not to create loans for homes in minority or low-income areas of the city), and racial steering (when agents in real estate present/show minority clients homes strictly in low-income or minority areas). A heavy burden that Blacks and other minorities take on, along with some other US citizens, is the spiral cost of housing. This is an addition to institutional and individual discrimination against Blacks and other minorities. The relevant discrimination in housing patterns in the United States is price discrimination and exclusion. Price discrimination refers to the act of charging one group a higher price than another group for identical housing. Exclusion refers to any technique designed to avoid selling or renting housing in a given location to a certain group of people.[115] In housing discrimination, Blacks pay more than Whites who make equal levels of income for identical housing because Blacks face a restricted housing supply. When this occurs, other social and economic costs get imposed on Blacks. Blacks having to pay more for housing (who are already making less income than Whites) and using most of their income to pay for housing costs leaves them less money for food, water, clothing, medical costs, etc. Black residents whose housing options are confined to the inner city often face the consequence of receiving less return on their tax dollars. The tax dollars for residential services such as street repair, fire and police protection, drainage systems, and so on vary remarkably according to neighborhood racial/ethnic makeup and location. There is racial discrimination in housing that arises independently of income level. A report stated that lending institutions had a higher percentage of minorities rejected for mortgage applications than nonminorities' applications despite income, according to US Department of Housing and Urban Development reports.[116]

If there were no discrimination, the percentage of African Americans / Blacks that own homes would be higher. The number of middle-class African Americans in the United States was only 59% in 2008, versus 74% of Whites.[117] The 1970 census showed that 42% of African Americans owned their own homes, and in 2017 there were 41% of African Americans who owned their own homes.[118]

115. Bullard, *Invisible Houston*, 50–53.
116. Bullard, *Invisible Houston*, 50–53.
117. Bullard, "Environmental Justice," 2–16.
118. Wake, "Shocking Truth."

2.5.2.0.1 SHREVEPORT/CADDO HOUSING DISCRIMINATION AND COM-
PLAINTS: The City of Shreveport Human Relations Commission, or
HRC, take complaints regarding discrimination in housing, public ac-
commodations, or employment against a protected group of people.[119]

2.5.2.1 *Redlining:* Redlining is the act of lenders making policies of not
creating loans for homes in minority and low-income areas of the city.[120]
In other words, redlining refers to discriminatory practices which deny
access to credit and insurance for borrowers in neighborhoods that are
economically disadvantaged and/or have high percentages of minorities.[121] Jim Crow laws were prevalent at one time in the United States,
mainly in the southern parts of the United States. However, redlining was
a common segregation tactic used in many parts of the US, even in places
Jim Crow laws were not commonly practiced.

The federal government was faced with housing shortages in 1933.
These shortages sparked the program created by the government to
overtly segregate and increase the US housing stock. The housing programs were created under the New Deal and were said to be virtually
the same as the state-sponsored system of segregation, according to author Richard Rothstein who proclaimed this in his book. Rothstein said,
"The government's efforts were primarily designed to provide housing to
white, middle-class, lower-middle-class families."[122] African Americans
and other people of color were left out of the new suburban communities and pushed into urban housing projects. This action furthered the
segregation efforts by refusing to insure mortgages in and near African
American neighborhoods. However, Rothstein's critics say that his ac-
cusations are not legitimate, and they respond by explaining that housing
segregation, like racism in general, has deep roots in American society. It
wasn't imposed by the federal government and certainly not by the New
Deal.[123] With both comments said, redlining did and still does exist.

---

119. City of Shreveport, *2019–2023 Consolidated Plan*, 25.
120. Bullard, *Invisible Houston*, 50.
121. Richardson et al., "Redlining."
122. Richardson et al., "Redlining."
123. Gross, "Forgotten History"; Walker, "What Was the New Deal?"

To explain, the New Deal was an endeavor by President Franklin D. Roosevelt to alleviate the anguish of the Great Depression when he took office in 1933. The New Dealers and President Roosevelt initiated various new programs to attack the issues hindering the country by creating jobs, supporting banks, investing in public works, bolstering wages, modernizing lagging regions, and giving a sense of hope to the US citizens.[124]

Redlining bolsters the evacuation of shopping centers in the inner city. Once these businesses leave the neighborhood and communities, replacements include liquor stores, fast-food operations, pawn shops, check cashing stations, and small food marts (mainly junk food). African Americans face discrimination from real estate brokers who show them limited options, mortgage companies, and banks, which reveals they do not have full access to saving institutions and lending banks, as their White counterparts do.[125]

2.5.2.2 *White Flight:* After the World War II era, there was a migration occurrence in the United States called "White flight." Many White residents in predominantly or "all-White" neighborhoods would pick up and leave as African Americans and/or other people of color moved into these neighborhoods. The White residents that left would resettle in newly built, overwhelmingly White suburbs.

Some have debated that White flight was an instinctive maneuver because of a decline in a neighborhood's property value and median household income that had been prone to happen in the past when there was an inundation of people of color and not because of racial attitudes or prejudices.[126] However, modern research shows that White flight happens in middle-class suburban areas where there is economic stability. White flight occurs as White folks move from one suburb to another as non-White people move into the suburbs of the neighborhoods Whites flee. Studies have shown that non-White people's neighborhood attraction ability is one that's integrated. In contrast, the average White person in the same study says they prefer predominantly White neighborhoods because they are more desirable than integrated neighborhoods. The suburbs aren't as White as they used to be, and as these suburbs get more diverse, the White flight phenomenon is repeating itself. Dr. Samuel Kye,

124. Walker, "What Was the New Deal?"
125. Bullard et al., "Suburban Sprawl," 945–47.
126. Kaul, "White Flight Didn't Disappear."

a sociologist, primarily studies racial inequality in metropolitan areas, micro-level data, and the US census to understand why and how residential segregation continues. In 2018, an analysis of the one hundred and fifty largest metro areas in the United States by Kye, who was pursuing his PhD in sociology at Indiana University, found White flight in recent years in 3,252 suburban US census tracts. He further found White flight in seven middle-class suburban neighborhoods in the county of Hennepin.[127]

2.5.2.3 *Renters Rights:* Between various states in the United States, it is common for tenant or landlord laws to differ. It is crucial for all parties involved to be knowledgeable concerning laws and rules in each state, and Louisiana is no different. In Louisiana, each person involved must do their own research.[128] When and if the rent is paid in a prompt/timely method in exchange for occupying a property, a landlord-tenant agreement is confirmed with or without a lease within the laws in Louisiana (per Code Title VIII).[129] Within this agreement, the renter/tenant has the right to a suitable residence and the proper due process before evictions, among others. According to Fair Housing laws, a tenant cannot be denied housing based on color, race, sex, age, religion, disability, national origin, or family status, sexual orientation, and marital status. Those individuals who are also protected are people that have a criminal record (unless they could be dangerous to other tenants or the rental) or who use Section 8 housing vouchers to pay rent. In essence, the criteria mentioned regarding the Fair Housing laws are reasons a prospective tenant can be accepted or denied. The landlord must decide on a prospective renter based on the information used in a formal screening procedure.[130] Receiving rental payments on time and the right to an eviction process after a violation of the rental agreement are the rights of the landlords.[131]

127. Kaul, "White Flight Didn't Disappear."
128. American Apartment Owners Association, "Louisiana Landlord."
129. iProperty Management, "Louisiana Landlord Tenant Laws."
130. Manolas, "Rental Housing," §2.
131. iProperty Management, "Louisiana Landlord Tenant Laws."

2.5.3 Caddo Parish and Bossier Parish Homeownership

The Louisiana Housing Census of 1990 shows Caddo Parish White homeownership was 64.8% and Black homeownership was 34.4%, with a gap of 30.4%.[132] The Louisiana Population and Housing Census of 2000 details a housing gap of 18.9%, with White homeownership at 58.3% and African American at 39.4%.[133] The Louisiana Population and Housing Census of 2010 show Whites at 53.2% in homeownership and African Americans at 43.6%, which puts the homeownership gap to 9.6%.[134]

CADDO PARISH
AFRICAN AMERICANS VS WHITES
HOME OWNERSHIP PERCENTAGES
1990-2022

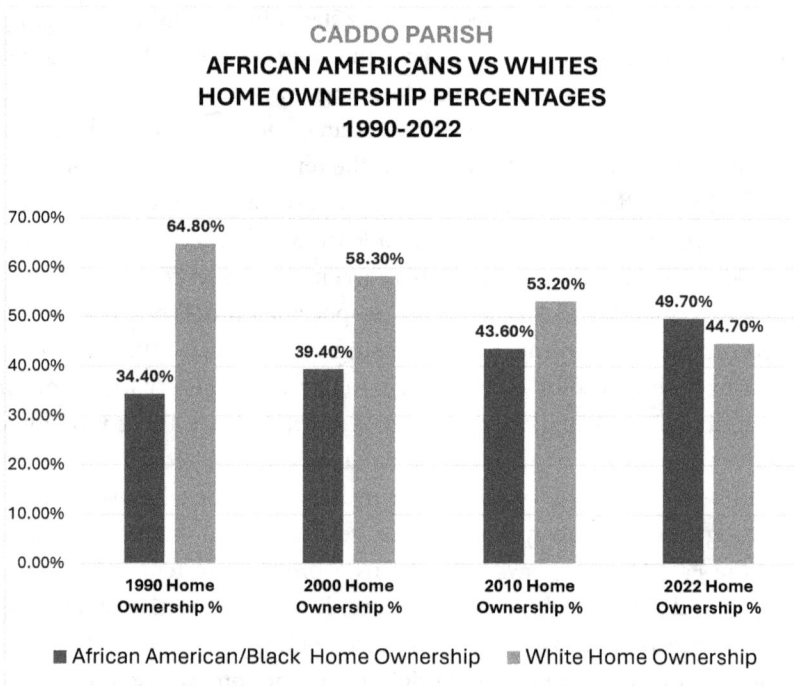

Figure 6: Caddo Parish Home Ownership 1990–2010 Black vs. White
Source: 1990 U.S. Census Louisiana Population and Housing, (1992), 2000 U.S. Census Louisiana Population and Housing, (2002), 2010 U.S. Census Louisiana Census Population and Housing, (2012) U.S. Census Bureau (2022)

132. US Census of Housing 1990, "Population and Housing," 220.

133. US Census of Population and Housing 2000, "Population and Housing," 96.

134. US Census of Population and Housing 2010, "Louisiana," 173; US Department of Housing and Urban Development, *Comprehensive Housing Market Analysis* (2012).

The current trend from 1990 to 2010 is that African American homeownership has increased by 9.2%, which is an improvement. White homeownership has decreased by 11.6% from 1990 to 2010. Looking at the increase in African American homeownership and decrease in White homeownership, it seems to be a positive trend for African Americans in Caddo Parish. Research also shows a trend in the population trend of Caddo Parish.

The Caddo Parish population in 1990 was 248,253 with Whites being 58.4% and Blacks 40%.[135] In 2000, the population was 252,161, the population of Whites was 52.2%, and Blacks were 45%.[136] Looking into the census year 2010, the total population was 255,543, the White population was 47.8%, and the Black population was 46.9%. The 2020 US census data showed a total population of 243,243, the Black population was 49.2%, and Whites were 44.3%. Judging by the decrease in the White population, the research can determine that this decrease is the reason for the White homeownership decrease in Caddo Parish. The increase in the African American population is the reason for the African American homeownership increase. Although the gap between them has closed, judging by the 2010 and 2020 population count, there is still a big homeownership gap between African Americans and Whites in homeownership. As of 2020, the Caddo Parish African American / Black population was 49.2% with only 43.6% homeownership, and White homeownership is 53.2% with 44.3% of the population, which shows a racial disadvantage.[137]

135. US Census of Housing 1990, "Population and Housing," 119.

136. US Census of Population and Housing 2000, "General Demographic Characteristics," 96.

137. US Census of Population and Housing 2010, "Louisiana," 6; US Department of Housing and Urban Development, *Comprehensive Housing Market Analysis* (2012); US Department of Housing and Urban Development, *Comprehensive Housing Market Analysis* (2021).

CADDO PARISH POPULATION AFRICAN AMERICAN/BLACK VS WHITE 1990-2020

■ African American/Black Population   ■ White Population

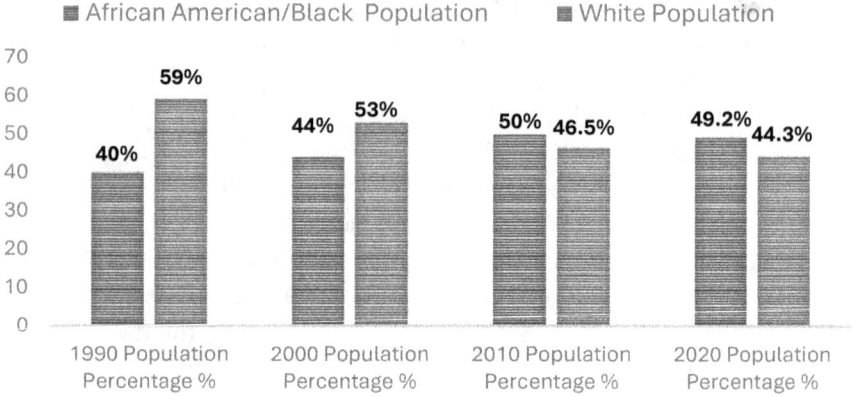

Figure 7: Caddo Parish Population Percentage 1990–2019 Black vs. White Source: 1990 U.S. Census Louisiana Population (1992), 2000 U.S. Census Louisiana Population (2002), 2010 U.S. Census Louisiana Population (2010) U.S. Census Bureau (2020)

To provide a comparison, it is fair to judge the same statistics in Caddo Parish with the neighboring parish, Bossier Parish. In the 1990 census in Bossier Parish, White homeownership was 79.9%, and African American homeownership was 17.4%, with a difference of 62.5%. The 2000 census reported White homeownership was 77.1% and Black homeownership was 18.9%, with a gap of 58.2%. In 2010, White homeownership was 75%, and Black homeownership 20%, which makes for a difference of 55%. In Bossier Parish, the White population is significantly larger than the Black population.

BOSSIER PARISH
AFRICAN AMERICAN/BLACK VS WHITE
HOME OWNERSHIP PERCENTAGES
1990-2022

■ African American/Black Home Ownership   ▥ White Home Ownership

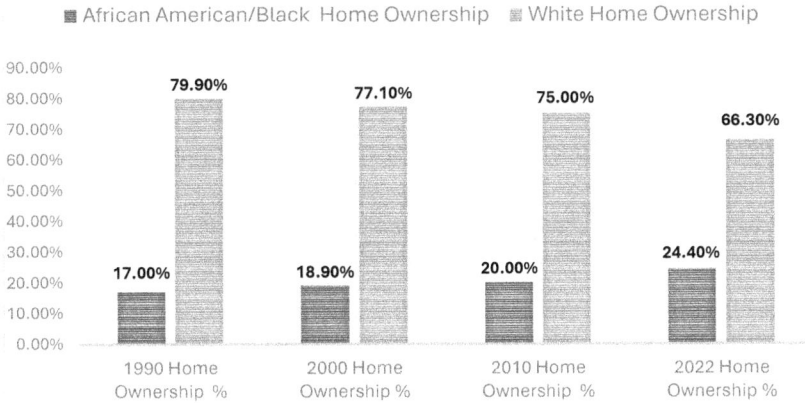

Figure 8: Bossier Parish Home Ownership 1990–2022 Black vs. White
Source: 1990 U.S. Census Louisiana Population and Housing (1992), 2000 U.S.
Census Louisiana Population and Housing (2002) 2010 U.S. Census Louisiana Census
Population and Housing (2012), U.S. Census Bureau (2022)

Reviewing the Bossier Parish population in 1990, Whites were 76.4% and African Americans were 20.02%, with a gap of 56.4%.[138] The following 2000 census showed the White population was 72.9% and African Americans made up 21%, with a difference of 51.9%.[139] In 2010, the White population was 69.2% and African Americans 23.1%, with a difference of 46.1%.[140] In the recent 2020 census, the population of Whites was 66.3% and that of African Americans was 23.3%, with a gap of 43%.[141] The White population is a large majority in Bossier Parish. The homeownership gap decreased between African Americans and Whites in Bossier Parish from 1990 to 2010 by 7.7%.

138. US Census 1990, *Population and Housing Caddo-Bossier*, 220.
139. US Census 2000, *Population and Housing Caddo-Bossier*, 96.
140. US Census 2010, *Population and Housing Caddo-Bossier*, 173.
141. US Census 2020, *Bossier Parish*, 1.

BOSSIER PARISH POPULATION
AFRICAN AMERICANS/BLACK VS WHITE
1990-2020

■ African American/Black Population   ■ White Home Population

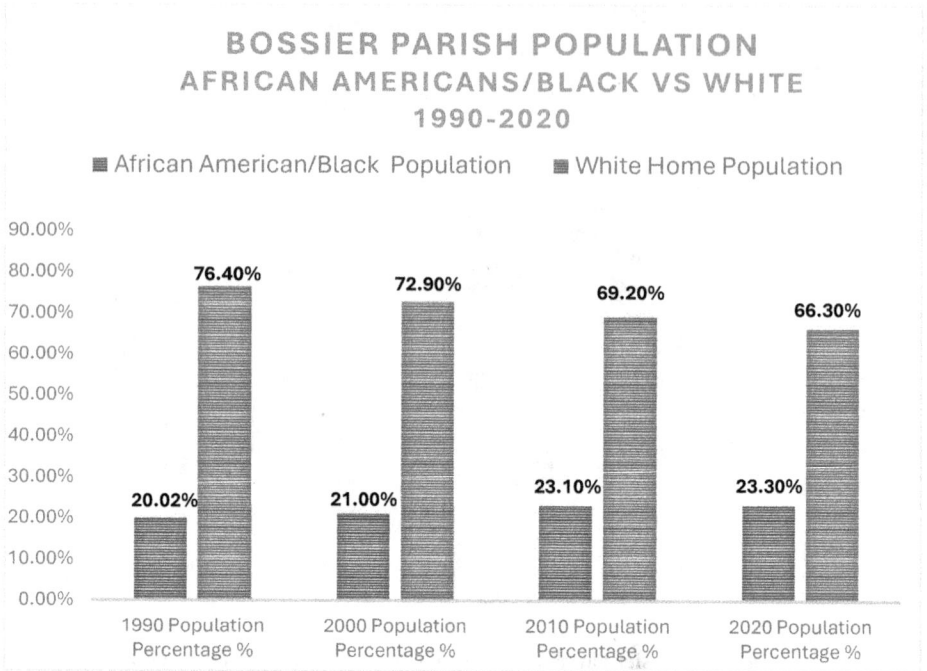

Figure 9: Bossier Parish Home Ownership 1990–2020 Black vs. White
Source: 1990 U.S. Census Louisiana Population (1992), 2000 U.S. Census Louisiana
Population (2002) 2010 U.S. Census Louisiana Population (2010), U.S. Census
Bureau (2020)

2.5.4 Caddo Parish and Bossier Parish Owners vs. Renters

In Caddo Parish's 1990 census on owners versus renters, there were
60,067 owner-occupied units and 33,181 renter units and a total of
93,248 units. Caddo Parish owners were 64.4% and renters were 35.5%.
The percentages of Black owners were 27.5%; Black renters, 52%; White
owners, 71.8%; and White renters, 52%. The Caddo Parish owners versus renters total statistics in 2000 was owners 63.8% and renters 36.2%.
Caddo Parish Blacks owners were 50.5%; Black renters, 49.5%; White
owners, 73.3%; and White renters, 26.7%. In 2010, the Caddo Parish
owners versus renters was owners at 61.4% and renters at 38.6%. Caddo
Parish Black owners made up 34.8%; Black renters, 56.5%; White owners,
63.2%; and White renters, 37.5%. In 2019, the Caddo Parish owners were

at 63.4% and renters at 36.6%. Caddo Parish Black owners were 40.2%; Black renters, 64.3%; White owners, 57.1%; and White renters, 32.7%.

In Bossier Parish's 1990 census on owners versus renters, there were 30,718 total housing units, of which 20,477 were owned units, and 10,241 were renters units. Bossier Parish had 66.7% owners and 33.3% renters. Bossier Parish Black owners comprised 13%, and Black renters were 26.4%. The White owners were 85.9%, and White renters were 71%. In 2000, Bossier Black owners were 48.2%, and Black renters were 51.8%. The White owners were 75%, and White renters, 25%. In the 2010 census, there were 65.7% owners and 34.3% renters. The Black owners were 13.9%, and Black renters were 36.4%. Whites owners were 83.6%, and White renters 60.3%. In the 2019 census, Bossier Parish's total owners were 66.7% and renters were 33.3%.[142]

Located in northwest Louisiana, Caddo Parish has a total estimated population of 245,831 with 49.2% Blacks, 46.2% Whites, 0.4% Native American / Alaska Native, 1.3% Asian, and 2.8 % Hispanic. Bossier Parish has an estimated population of 126,499 with 22.8% Blacks, 72% Whites, 6.6% Hispanic, 0.5% Native American / Alaska Native, and 1.9% Asian. The median age in Caddo Parish is 37.7 years of age, and the median age in Bossier Parish is 35.3 years of age. African American poverty in Louisiana is 29.4% statewide, and 33.9% of Caddo African American residents are in poverty. White Caddo Parish residents' poverty is 15.5%. The poverty rate of the Black residents in Shreveport, Louisiana, the largest city in Caddo Parish, is dramatically higher than the national average of 25.2%. A total of 35.19% of African American / Black residents in Shreveport live below the poverty line. White residents' poverty in Shreveport is 11.62%. One out of every 3.9 Black / African American residents of Shreveport lives in poverty. In Bossier Parish, Louisiana, Black / African American residents' poverty is 23.8%, and Whites were 17.6%. Bossier City poverty for Blacks was 33.05% and for Whites was 11.06%.[143]

Most Blacks in Caddo Parish have migrated to Shreveport. The population in Shreveport is 182,616, with the Black population being the

142. US Census of Housing 1990, "Population and Housing," 119; US Census of Population and Housing 2000, "Population and Housing," 96; US Census of Population and Housing 2010, "Louisiana," 6; US Census Bureau 2019, "Bossier Parish"; US Census Bureau 2020, "Bossier Parish"; US Census Bureau 2021, "Bossier Parish."

143. US Census Bureau 2019, "Caddo Parish"; US Census Bureau 2019, "Bossier Parish"; US Census Bureau 2020, "Caddo Parish"; US Census Bureau 2020, "Bossier Parish"; World Population Review 2021, "Caddo Parish"; World Population Review 2021, "Bossier Parish."

largest at 57.09%, Whites at 38%, Native American and Alaska Native at 0.04%, Asians at 1.67%, Native Hawaiian and other Pacific Islander at 0.06% and two or more races at 1.85%. Blacks have the majority poverty rate even in the city of Shreveport, which is the largest urbanized area in Caddo Parish and northern Louisiana. A total of 35.19% of African American / Black residents of Shreveport live below the poverty line. One out of every 3.9 residents of Shreveport lives in poverty. The poverty rate of Black residents in Shreveport is dramatically higher than the national average of 10.5% in 2019 by more than 25%. Approximately 55.7% of the total population of Shreveport is African American. The poverty rate of White residents in Shreveport is 11.62%. Approximately 36.5% of the total population of Shreveport is White. Bossier City African American / Black residents represent 27.89% and White 65.62%, Native American and Alaska Native 0.39%, Asians 2.39%, Native Hawaiian and other Pacific Islander 0.05%, and two or more races 2.52%. Black residents' poverty in Bossier City is 33.05%, and White residents' poverty is 11.06%.[144]

According to the Housing Census of 1990, African American homeownership was at 60,470, and Whites were at 93,248 in Caddo Parish. Bossier Parish African American homeownership was at 24,924 and Whites at 30,718. The Louisiana Housing Census of 1990 shows a huge gap of over 30,000 people in Caddo Parish. The Louisiana Housing Census of 2010 shows African American homeownership at 44,622 and Whites at 54,326. Bossier Parish African American homeownership was at 9,081 and Whites at 33,953. In Caddo Parish, the African American population outnumbers the White population by over 2.5%, yet the homeownership is greater by Whites. However, judging by the Louisiana Housing Census of 1990, the gap has decreased dramatically. In Shreveport, the largest urbanized city in Caddo Parish, Black or African American total homeowners is at 18,245, and White homeowners are at 25,260.[145]

---

144. World Population Review 2021, "Caddo Parish"; World Population Review 2021, "Bossier Parish."

145. US Census 1990, Population: *Social and Economic Characteristics*, 39.

COST OF RENTING

1,2, AND 3 BEDROOM
LOUISIANA, STUDY PARISHES AND LARGEST CITIES IN STUDY PARISHES
(2021)

Location	1 Bedroom Rent	2 Bedroom Rent	3 Bedroom Rent
Louisiana	$1,681	$1,278	$1,048
Baton Rouge	$1,137	$989	$765
East Baton Rouge Parish	$1,161	$917	$781
Bossier City	$1,067	$861	$725
Bossier Parish	$1,112	$897	$756
Shreveport	$1,064	$858	$723
Caddo Parish	$1,112	$897	$756

■ 3 Bedroom Rent   ■ 2 Bedroom Rent   ■ 1 Bedroom Rent

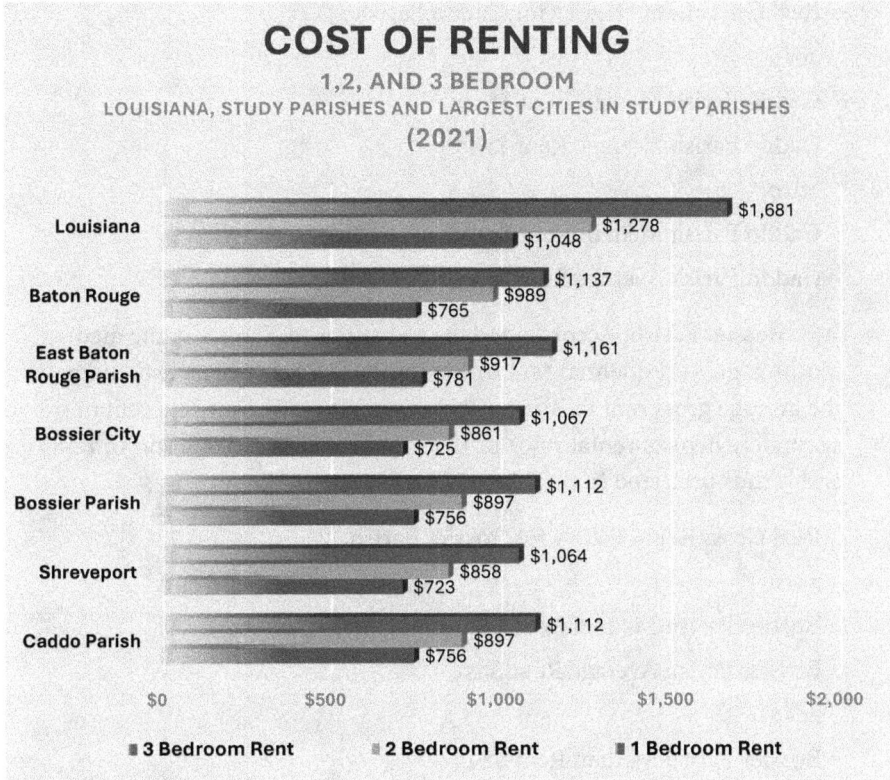

Figure 10: Renting Cost 1,2, and 3-Bedroom: LA, Study Parishes, and Largest Cities
Source: Best Places (2021)

Caddo Parish: The US census of 2000 reports that in Louisiana just over 24% of renter-occupied households and 6% of owner-occupied households have no vehicle available. In Caddo Parish, nearly 24% of renter-occupied households and nearly 7% of owner-occupied households are without vehicles. According to the Census of ACS in 2019, the median monthly gross residential rent in Caddo Parish was $810. Also, in 2019 the average gross rent in Caddo Parish was $780. The median rent more accurately depicts rental rates in the middle of the distribution of rents and is thus preferred in the analysis below.[146]

146. Louisiana Office of Public Health, *2005 Parish Health Profiles*, 164.

Real Gross Rent History for Caddo Parish

2019

Caddo Parish Median Rent $810

Caddo Parish Average Rent $780

2010

Caddo Parish Median Rent $753

Caddo Parish Average Rent $720

Bossier Parish: According to the Census of ACS in 2019, the median monthly gross residential rent in Bossier Parish was $983. Also, in 2019 the average gross rent in Bossier Parish was $956. The median rent more accurately depicts rental rates in the middle of the distribution of rents and is thus preferred in the analysis below.

Real Gross Rent History for Bossier Parish

2019

Bossier Parish Median Rent $983

Bossier Parish Average Rent $956

2010

Bossier Parish Median Rent $845

Bossier Parish Average Rent $868

East Baton Rouge Parish: According to the Census of ACS in 2019, the median monthly gross residential rent in East Baton Rouge Parish was $913. Also, in 2019 the average gross rent in East Baton Rouge Parish was $901. The median rent more accurately depicts rental rates in the middle of the distribution of rents and is thus preferred in the analysis below.

Real Gross Rent History for East Baton Rouge Parish

2019

East Baton Rouge Parish Median Rent $913

East Baton Rouge Parish Average Rent $901

2010

East Baton Rouge Parish Median Rent $849

East Baton Rouge Parish Average Rent $876[147]

147. Department of Numbers, "Caddo Parish"; Department of Numbers, "Bossier

Study Areas Cost of Living

Parishes Largest Cities in Louisiana

Year 2021

Shreveport	Bossier City	Baton Rouge
Median Home Price $290,786	Median Home Price $292,174	Median Home Price $302,584
Median Rent Monthly $910.91	Median Rent Monthly $915.25	Median Rent $947.86
Energy Bill Monthly $125.24	Energy Bill Monthly $131.45	Energy Bill Monthly $137.65
Phone Bill Monthly $133.50	Phone Bill Monthly $140.12	Phone Bill Monthly $146.73
Gas $2.44/Per Gallon	Gas $233/Per Gallon	Gas $2.42/Per Gallon
Doctor's Visit $104.62	Doctor's Visit $102.19	Doctor Visit $125.77
Dentist Visit $89.99	Dentist Visit $87.79	Dentist Visit $108.04

Figure 11: Cost of Living Cities of Study Area Parishes
Source: PayScale Shreveport (2021), PayScale Bossier City (2021), PayScale Baton Rouge (2021)

2.6 AFFORDABLE HOUSING

Affordable housing is having access to housing that the residents of a household can pay for while still having funds left over to afford needs such as meals, health care, and transportation. So, depending on a household's income determines affordability.[148]

Affordable housing is social rented, affordable rented, and intermediate housing provided to eligible households whose needs the market does not meet. Eligibility is determined by local incomes and local house prices. Affordable housing should include provisions to remain at an affordable price for future eligible households or for the subsidy recycled for alternative affordable housing provisions.[149] The term *affordable housing* refers only to publicly subsidized housing, such as those financed with Low-Income Housing Tax Credits, Section 8 vouchers, public housing funds, etc. Affordable housing does not necessarily mean living in government housing or project living.[150] Discussing affordable housing narrowly on publicly subsidized housing can be misleading because subsidized housing does not represent the majority of affordable housing. Most affordable housing is developed and operated without public

---

Parish"; Department of Numbers, "East Baton Rouge Parish."

148. Local Housing Solutions, "What Is Affordable Housing."

149. London.gov, "Affordable Housing."

150. Elkin, "Affordable Housing."

subsidy. This situation is naturally occurring affordable housing.[151] Affordable housing means a resident spends less than 30% on housing after post-tax income. If residents pay more than 30% on housing, they are cost-burdened.[152] We need to understand that affordable housing should be first affordable; then appealing; of good, sound quality; and adequate. To measure affordable housing, we must consider not only the simple cost of the mortgage payment or rent but all housing costs. All housing costs, such as payments related to the home, including insurance, taxes, utility associations dues, and phone service, should be included in housing affordability.[153]

2.6.1 Affordable Housing in Caddo-Bossier Parish

Affordable housing is a crisis nationwide, in the state of Louisiana, in Caddo Parish, and the Shreveport–Bossier City metro area. The most significant element in Shreveport that is affecting housing needs is residents being able to pay housing expenses or affordable housing. In Shreveport, households that have the lowest income earners have the least housing units to choose from and a lack of safe housing, which does not meet community needs. The options for those households earning below the 30% median income are mainly limited to rental properties. Also, with limited housing stock, the lower earnings tend to spend more on higher-priced rental housing. This situation forces the doubling-up of households together in one housing unit. The residents that have higher incomes have greater options for housing in the Shreveport area, and the economy is segregated heavily, especially in home values.[154]

According to data that was put together by Housing Louisiana in 2018 from numerous sources, one being the ACS, nearly 60% of the renters in the city of Shreveport-Bossier are not able to afford to live there.[155] The numbers presented signify that 40% of the population cannot afford to live in this area, and this percentage includes homeowners as well. A significant number of households in the Shreveport area are categorized

151. National Association for Latino Community Asset Builders, *State of Housing Affordability*, 4–39.

152. Elkin, "Affordable Housing."

153. Bossier City Metropolitan Planning Commission, "Proceedings," 10–13.

154. City of Shreveport, *2014–2018 Consolidated Plan*, 19–151; City of Shreveport, *2019–2023 Consolidated Plan*, 19–122.

155. Bayliss, "Nearly 60 Percent."

under extremely low income (under 30% median income), exceeding 13,500. Nearly three thousand of the extremely low-income households have one or more children six years of age and younger, and over three thousand are elderly. Data extracted from the ACS estimates that 31.5% of homeowners with a mortgage, 10.8% with no mortgage, and 58.3% of renters are cost burdened.

The Shreveport area has a severe cost burden issue when it comes to the lack of affordable housing for extremely low-income households. The number of homeowner households greater than 50% cost-burdened is 1,630; the renters above 50% cost-burdened, 5,715. Also, there are over 2,900 extremely low-income households with one or more children six years of age or younger. These numbers place cost-burdened and extremely low-income households at an approaching risk of becoming homeless.[156]

There is a large unmet demand or wait list for Section 8 and public housing for the Shreveport Housing Authority, with extraordinary demand for two- and three-bedroom housing. Habitat for Humanity presented data that showed one in six residents in the United States, roughly eighteen million households, spend more than half of their income on housing, which is deemed a severe cost burden. If a resident pays more than 30% of their gross income on housing, they are considered cost burdened, and if residents pay more than 50% of their income on housing expenses, then they are labeled in the severely cost burdened category. In the city of Shreveport, 71% of households earning below 30% of the median in the area are paying more than 30% of their income on housing expenses, in which 57% of that group is paying over 50% on their housing expenses. Of the residents that earn 30–50% of the median income, 65% of those residents are cost burdened, and 31% of that collective is severely cost burdened.

Of those residents that are earning 50–80% of the median income in the area, there are more than 41% that are labeled cost burdened. Residents with elderly members, fixed or limited incomes, and children are the most severely impacted by the cost burden. Also, owners and renters are both affected by the cost-burdened issue. In terms of sheer numbers, the Shreveport area's biggest housing problem is the cost-burdened households.

156. City of Shreveport, *2019–2023 Consolidated Plan*, 19–122.

In Shreveport, prices of homes are at their highest since 1980, and rent has gone up overall by 3.6% as of 2018. Rent is rising, which has contributed to the higher cost of housing, and this combination undercut the moderate gains in earnings. Cost-burdened homeowners and cost-burdened renters in the lower tier of income levels spend notably less on health care, retirement savings, transportation, and especially food than other households in their earning bracket who live in affordable housing.[157]

In 2017, though incomes varied throughout the city of Shreveport, the median income was $37,390. Even with the 2013–2017 ACS five-year estimates showing higher median incomes in Shreveport City, sometimes there were over 60% of renters and over 40% of homeowners who were cost burdened. Now based on 100% AMI (being the area median income), the 2015 CHAS (Comprehensive Housing Affordability Strategy) data showed that 3,620 homeowners and 7,310 renters were cost-burdened, spending was more than 30% of their income on housing, and this is not including the households who earned over 100% of the median income. If the households were included that earned over 100% of the median income, the numbers would be even worse. Near the central business district downtown, there is a high population of African Americans in older neighborhoods whose census tracts show that their income is 80% below the median income. These areas show there are poverty levels of over 37% in these population tracts.

Affordable housing differs from a household earning $30,000 a year to a household earning $120,000 a year. Both earning groups are looking for affordable housing, and both deserve affordable housing. In 2009, the median household in Bossier City was $47,057. For housing to be affordable for a household making the median income in Bossier City, all housing costs could not exceed $1,176. A household that earns 180% ($84,703) of the median could pay a bit more than $2,100 in housing expenses and still be in the affordable housing cost range. A household earning only 30% ($14,117) of the median income can only afford $353 of housing expenses. The chart below shows the Black versus Whites cost burden in the Shreveport City area. The cost-burdened Blacks of 30–50% exceed Whites by 3,000, and the Blacks who are greater than 50% cost-burdened

---

157. City of Shreveport, *2014–2018 Consolidated Plan*, 19–151; Bayliss, "Census 2020"; City of Shreveport, *2019–2023 Consolidated Plan*, 19–122.

exceed Whites by 4,735. In 2018, the Black / African American population in the Shreveport area was 56.8% and Whites 37%.[158]

Shreveport City Area Cost Burdened Black vs White

	Less Than 30%	30-50%	Greater Than 50%	No/ Negative Income (Not Computed)
African American/Black	22,670	7,500	8,230	1,730
White	25,650	4,500	3,495	410

Figure 12: Shreveport City Area Cost Burdened Black vs. White
Source: Shreveport Department of Community Development (2018)

2.6.2 Shreveport-Caddo Parish Housing Development

Single-family structures in Shreveport make up the majority of housing units at 72%, and renter households with two or fewer bedrooms represent 70% of renters. The residents who make the lowest of incomes will have the lesser options of housing stock to pick from, meaning the community needs are not met. So, typically rental properties become the only options for those residents who earn less than 30% of the median income in the area because there is no affordable housing priced for them. Owning a home is becoming less affordable, with a 53% increase in median home value. Some single-family structures tend to meet some larger housing unit needs for renters. However, there is a wide disparity between larger-unit owners' single-family housing units at 81% and renters' housing units at 30%. This gap shows there is a specific need for new housing development that should be targeted at larger households of renters needing three or more bedrooms. There is a growing senior population in Shreveport. This growth might put pressure on the market to provide new development of efficiencies, one-bedroom units, and senior apartment living. There are many land areas targeted for development that have deteriorating housing conditions and low homeownership. The HAPPI program gives families opportunities to purchase homes at

---

158. City of Shreveport, *2019–2023 Consolidated Plan*, 19–122; Bossier City Metropolitan Planning Commission, "Proceedings."

any location in the city. Shreveport is targeting small geographical areas to make them more visible and create a measurable impact. In 2000, Shreveport adopted its Revitalization Master Plan (RMP) in accordance with Parish Redevelopment Law (RS 33:4625). This Louisiana law gives local jurisdictions the authority to remove slum, blighted, and conditioned property and to requisition property to gain a clear title for the development of affordable housing.

To provide more affordable housing, the city-funded programs are providing programs for significantly low–income, low-income, and moderate-income households, which include one hundred and fifty down payment assistant projects, forty units of new construction provided by CHDOs (Community Housing Development Organizations), fifty new construction units, fifty additional units for homeownership, two hundred and fifty for rental, fifteen reconstruction projects, three hundred volunteer home repair projects, fifty accessibility projects, ten relocations for tenants living in substandard housing, and one hundred emergency repair projects.[159] The Consolidated Strategic Plan supports efforts to provide for homelessness prevention through a tenant-based mortgage, temporary assistants to prevent evictions through rental assistance programs, and permanent supportive housing, including for special needs populations. Also, for low-income homeowners, there is a plan to provide funding for reconstruction projects. Shreveport City and Bossier City downtown central business district are connected, and there has been planning for the potential of the development of housing in this urban area.

The Shreveport-Bossier metropolitan area has great potential to be a new urban neighborhood from a downtown planning outlook. All downtown neighborhoods can be affected positively with a concentrated mix of new types of housing if developed in and around this part of town.[160]

Furthermore, in the inner city and rural areas, chronic homelessness of individuals and families in shelters, transitional shelters, and of those who are unsheltered needs to be addressed immediately.[161]

159. City of Shreveport, *2014–2018 Consolidated Plan*, 19–151.
160. Shreveport Metropolitan Planning Commission, *Great Expectations*, 4–15.
161. City of Shreveport, *2014–2018 Consolidated Plan*, 19–151.

2.6.3 Bossier City-Bossier Parish Housing Development

The housing chapter of the Bossier City Comprehensive Plan is a purposeful agenda for the Bossier area to strategize how to have homes and neighborhoods satisfy present and future needs of residence requirements. In the plan, the neighborhoods in which affordable homes reside should offer curb appeal, dynamic character, a strong identity, proximity to amenities, and quality infrastructure.

The Bossier City Comprehensive Plan indicates residential developments located southwest of Barksdale Air Force Base and north of Interstate 220. This strategic planning is to have a central location of a residential development pattern, partnered with moderate density levels of the city, pushing a healthy development trend to counter sprawl, using important open space deemed a less efficient development pattern. The Department of Housing and Community Development is a source used to assist with several housing programs. It provides annual funding to the Community Development Block Grant fund utilized by the Bossier City Community Development department. Bossier City has the smallest average household size when compared to comparable nearby cities as well as Bossier Parish and the state of Louisiana. The average household in Bossier City is 2.43, Bossier Parish is 2.48, Shreveport is 2.48, and Louisiana is 2.61. This reflects that the twenty-five- to twenty-nine-year-old age group represents the larger age group by percentage and are often young families and working singles in Bossier City.[162] So, smaller housing is a part of the development plan to accommodate the residents. In Bossier, single-family units are the largest percentage of development, then apartments, followed by townhomes. Central Bossier City needs housing for the middle income and is encouraging housing diversity. There is a plan for lower-income housing and housing for young professionals. One plan is to renovate older homes and create mixed-use residential areas. Part of the development plan is to place condos and townhomes in and near the downtown and apartments in southern Bossier City while limiting mobile home use. Bossier City downtown area is connecting to the Shreveport City downtown area. Both are part of the Cross Bayou possible development plan to include a concentrated mix of new types of housing development in and around this part of town to revive the neighborhoods.[163]

162. Bossier City Metropolitan Planning Commission, "Proceedings."
163. Bossier City Metropolitan Planning Commission, "Proceedings"; Shreveport

2.7 SPRAWL

Sprawl is characterized by inadequate access to essential land uses such as housing, jobs, and public services like schools, hospitals, and mass transit. Sprawl development has sucked population, jobs, investment capital, and tax base from the urban core. Sprawl creates a situation where citizens need their own automobiles because of the scattered developments. These developments happen and create a situation where citizens without automobiles find it hard to gain access to the areas for jobs, adequate food, medical care, schools, and other public services. The citizens are affected by sprawl by way of urban decline, racial polarization, lack of affordable housing, suburban/city disparities in public education, erosion of community, water and air pollution, and disappearing farmland and wildlife habitat.[164]

2.7.1 Metropolitan Areas, Sprawl, and Spatial Mismatch

With the sprawl, there is a disconnect in the street network that very well hurts the African American community in Caddo Parish. As mentioned before, in the Shreveport-Bossier metropolitan area, there is a spatial mismatch between jobs and the labor force, including two of the top employers in the area, the LSU Health Services Center and Willis-Knighton Health System. However, these systems are not the only two employers in town. There are many employers and plenty of people who need to get to work, especially African Americans, who make up 57.09% of the population in Shreveport and 27.89% in Bossier City, not to mention people who are traveling to and from work from outside of the Shreveport-Bossier metropolitan area.[165] In 2000, an analysis of data was collected on jobs and people in metropolitan areas. Included in the data were job sprawl measures of employment decentralization for metropolitan areas. The findings revealed that Black residents living in metropolitan areas with higher levels of employment decentralization are at a greater spatial mismatch between them and job locations. The link between increased job sprawl and greater spatial mismatch disproportionately affects Black communities. While this issue is not as significant for White populations,

---

Metropolitan Planning Commission, *Great Expectations*, 4–15.

164. Bullard et al., "Suburban Sprawl," 936.

165. World Population Review 2021, "Shreveport"; World Population Review 2021, "Bossier City."

job sprawl has nearly twice the impact on spatial mismatch for Black individuals compared to Latinos overall.[166] There is a presence of more severe racial segregation between Blacks and Whites in metropolitan areas
characterized by higher job sprawls. The level of racial segregation is 15%
higher in high job sprawl areas than in low job sprawl areas on average,
with adjustments for metropolitan area size. The metropolitan job sprawl
is transferring into more spatial mismatch for Blacks, caused by Black
versus White segregation, among other factors. The results firmly imply
that job sprawl magnifies particular dimensions of racial inequalities in
the United States

2.7.2 Shreveport-Bossier Metropolitan Area Sprawl and Spatial Mismatch

The relationship between sprawl and the spatial mismatch between
Blacks and jobs is a constant factor in the United States. Location of jobs
from the residential areas of Blacks is a key factor in Black employment.
As of 2010, the census-delineated metropolitan statistical area (MSA)
that includes Caddo, Bossier, and DeSoto Parishes has been growing in
job creation, population, and relatively low unemployment. Compared
to other places in the United States, this area was doing well despite
the Great Recession of 2007–2009. However, there is still a major employment and income gap in the racial lines that consisted of African
Americans and Whites in this area. High levels of vacancy and blight are
characteristics of a shrinking city that Shreveport-Caddo seems to possess due to a decrease in population and land use. Continuing leapfrog
development, such as isolated subdivisions that are not easily accessible
to the city limits, could affect income, transportation, economic competitiveness, fiscal needs, cost, and quality of life in a negative way.[167] In
Caddo Parish, the central business district is in downtown Shreveport;
residents drive far to get to the CBD for jobs and drive back to the rural
areas or suburbs after work. Having a vehicle is essential for traveling
to schools, jobs, hospitals, churches, shopping, entertainment purposes,
etc. A spatial mismatch exists between jobs and the labor force in the
Shreveport-Bossier metropolitan area. LSU Health Services Center and

166. Stoll, "Spatial Mismatch Between Blacks and Jobs," 1–9.

167. Stoll, "Spatial Mismatch Between Blacks and Jobs," 1–9; Shreveport Metropolitan Planning Commission, "Population," 6.

Willis-Knighton Health System are two major employers in Shreveport-Bossier; however, there is a lack of quality housing near the two health care systems. Willis-Knighton Health System is the second highest ranked employer with 6,732 employees, and LSU Health Service Centers is the third highest with 2,762 employees in the Shreveport-Bossier metropolitan area.[168]

There is a way to measure urban sprawl globally, by way of the connectedness of the streets, called street-network sprawl. When sprawl is minimized, the streets are more connected, and they become more walkable. Cities' environmental footprint and livability are affected for decades by a street network because they are permanent and connected. Residents walk more and drive less in communities where the streets are more connected. Better outcomes for equity, social integration, health, sustainable consumption, and the environment are a result of a well-connected street network, not just sprawl reduction. Less-connected cities lead to more sprawl which equals a higher SNDi score for a city.

Out of 10,137 cities measured in the United States, half of the cities scored between 1.08 to 3.25, and the average score was 2.25. In 2014, Shreveport's score was 2.62 in the overall level of street-network sprawl and has risen. For development practices of street construction from 2001 to 2014 in Louisiana, Shreveport ranked second out of six cities in the most disconnected cities category and has held that same ranking since 1975. Compared to the United States, from 1991 to 2000, Shreveport ranked 95th out of 315 for most disconnected streets, and 56th from 2001–2014, steadily on the rise. As of 2015, out of 315 US cities, Shreveport is ranked 205th most disconnected.[169] Currently, there is a huge growth period in the entire Shreveport–Bossier City metropolitan area. Shreveport is growing in the west and the south, whereas Bossier City is growing mainly in the east and the north. This growth is triggering the two areas to grow away from one another, creating urban sprawl not experienced before. The result of urban sprawl is inner-city traffic pushed to the outer rim of the cities to the suburbs, which is creating a need for easier access to local freeways and the need for wider roads running north and south.[170] The US census of 2019 shows that transportation ownership of African Americans is at 39.7%, with Whites at 56.6%. The

168. Shreveport/Caddo Metropolitan Planning Commission, *Shreveport-Bossier*, 10; North Louisiana Economic Partnership, "Caddo Parish Competitive Advantages."

169. SNDi Trends, "Street-Network Sprawl."

170. Dimebag1980, "Shreveport City Profile."

US census data shows a consistent disparity in personal transportation that has been consistent from 2010 to 2019, with African Americans having less personal transportation than Whites in both Caddo and Bossier Parish (see figures in section 2.8.2).[171] African Americans not having their own transportation in a metropolitan area that has spatial mismatch and disconnected roads will make it difficult to get and maintain employment, especially in the CBDs. With African Americans being the majority renters in both parishes, and with less transportation, the renters in the suburbs and rural areas are at a higher disadvantage of getting to work (including to the CBD), financial institutions, hospitals, medical facilities, and shopping areas. Also, not having frequent and good-quality public transportation in the Shreveport-Bossier metro area is an issue. In some areas, there is an hour's wait for a bus, and some areas that needs public transportation experience no service.[172] SporTran is the public bus provider in the Shreveport-Bossier metropolitan area. There was a study in 2016 in which part of the research examines where the buses *should* go after they leave certain transit centers, which tells residents that the operators of SporTran do not even know where to pick up the residents.[173] The Shreveport-Bossier metropolitan area has a plague of urban sprawl, street-network sprawl, and spatial mismatch, making public transportation difficult for residents to use efficiently.

2.8 CADDO PARISH CENTRAL BUSINESS DISTRICT

Shreveport's Central Business District (CBD), or the Downtown Development District (DDD), is the downtown of the entire region and is the center of government, business, and courts for Caddo Parish. Every Monday through Friday, between twelve and fourteen thousand people travel into downtown Shreveport to work, and thousands more funnel into the city to attend events at the Shreveport Convention Center, play at the casinos or visit other downtown businesses or amenities, and enter the city center with business at Government Plaza or the courts.[174] Resi-

---

171. US Census Bureau 2019, "Caddo Parish"; US Census Bureau 2019, "Bossier Parish."

172. Burris, "Transportation Study."

173. Northwest Louisiana Council of Governments, "Public Transportation."

174. Streetscape, "Downtown Shreveport."

dents drive far to get to the CBD/DDD for jobs and then drive back to the rural areas or suburbs after work.

2.8.1 Transportation and Sprawl in Caddo/Bossier Central Business District

Transportation provides access to opportunity and serves as a key component in addressing poverty. In a day's time, transportation assists with getting people to school, work, church, visits to friends, and shopping.[175] Transportation also profoundly affects residential and industrial growth and physical and social mobility. Transportation decision-making— whether at the federal, regional, state, or local level—often mirrors the power arrangements of the dominant society and its institutions.[176] Transportation affects the growth of cities and towns by way of physical, social, mobile, and industrial growth. Public transit systems, freeways, and roads in the United States are subsidized and are built with the help of federal tax dollars. Essential services such as public transit systems offer livability and sustainability in any city or town. There are challenges faced with public transit, such as availability, punctual and consistent transit service, and/or reliable service. The citizens of Caddo Parish average about a 21.3-minute drive alone for the commute to work. Car ownership in Caddo Parish is the same as the national average, with about two vehicles per household. Being that sprawl is urbanization away from the CBD, it harms citizens who need their own transportation or a readily available transportation. There is a disproportionate number of Blacks versus Whites that have their own transportation to work, favoring the White citizens of Caddo Parish and Bossier Parish. When people do not have transportation to get to work, it can cause them to lose their salary, which can lead to more poverty. When a person does not have adequate transportation to grocery stores and healthy foods, it will eventually lead to health-associated problems. When people with health problems that do not have reliable transportation cannot get to hospitals and medical centers in an efficient manner, this can lead to death.[177]

Continuing leapfrog development, such as isolated subdivisions that are not easily accessible to the city limits, could affect income,

175. Bullard et al., *Highway Robbery*, 4.

176. Bullard et al., "Suburban Sprawl," 961–62.

177. Diab, "Urban Public Transportation," 19–21; US Census Bureau, "Caddo Parish"; Shreveport Metropolitan Planning Commission, "Population," 3–26.

transportation, access to employment, economic competitiveness, fiscal needs, cost, and quality of life in a negative way, to the point where it causes poverty for some. Smart development will assist in stopping this leapfrog development in the Shreveport–Bossier City area, which can otherwise easily cause poverty to people that have trouble accessing jobs.

The website for the Shreveport City public bus transportation, or SporTran, shows the operating hours are Monday through Friday between 6:00 a.m. and 6:30 p.m., and Saturday between 7:00 a.m. and 5:00 p.m. However, when the researcher called to verify this information, the customer service representative said that the hours of operation are Monday through Saturday, 6:00 a.m. to 11:45 p.m., and on Sundays from 6:00 a.m. to 6:00 p.m. If a person leaves work between 11:45 p.m. and 6:00 a.m., they cannot take public transportation to and from work. If these people do not have their own transportation, they will have to find alternative ways of transportation to work. Suppose they cannot rely on someone they know personally to provide them with a free ride. In that case, they will have to take a taxi, Uber, Lyft, etc., which usually costs more money. They will have difficulty maintaining a job, which keeps them in poverty, because it is difficult for them to obtain consistent transportation. Being that the SporTran website was not up to date, it could confuse potential riders. Furthermore, SporTran does not travel outside of the outer perimeter of the Shreveport–Bossier City area, which means people beyond that area who do not have their own transportation will find it difficult to get transportation to work and secure employment.[178] The researcher discovered that the main office buildings and substations are closed on the weekends and some weekdays. On the Bossier side, SporTran extends less than five miles east and less than three and a half miles north of downtown to the CBD.

2.8.2 Data on Car Ownership in Caddo Parish and Bossier Parish

Caddo Parish: The US census of 2019 shows that transportation ownership of African Americans is 39.7% and for Whites is 56.6%. The disadvantage of personal transportation has been consistent from 2010 to 2019.[179]

178. SporTran, "Public Transportation."
179. US Census Bureau 2019, "Caddo Parish."

With the data of renters showing less transportation than homeowners, the renters in the suburbs and rural areas are at a higher disadvantage of getting to work, hospitals, medical facilities, and shopping. Having a high percentage of African Americans in rural areas and suburbs in Caddo Parish with less access to their own and/or public transportation will put them at a greater risk of poverty.

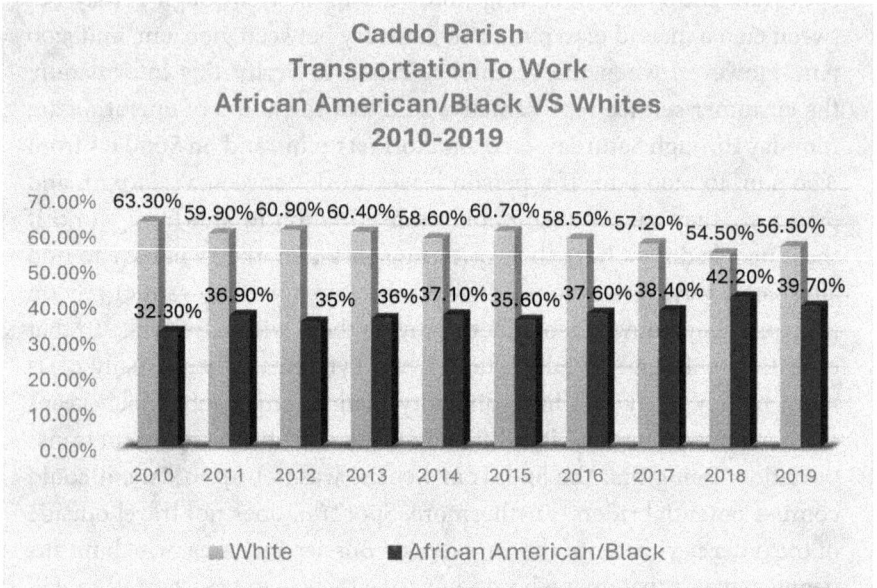

Caddo Parish Transportation To Work African American/Black VS Whites 2010-2019

Figure 13: Caddo Parish Owning Transportation Black vs. White 2010–2019
Source: U.S. Census (2019)

Bossier Parish: Bossier Parish showed a higher disparity in 2019, with African Americans at 27% versus Whites at 67.10% having their own transportation.[180]

---

180. US Census Bureau 2019, "Bossier Parish."

Bossier Parish
Transportation to Work
African American VS White
2010-2019

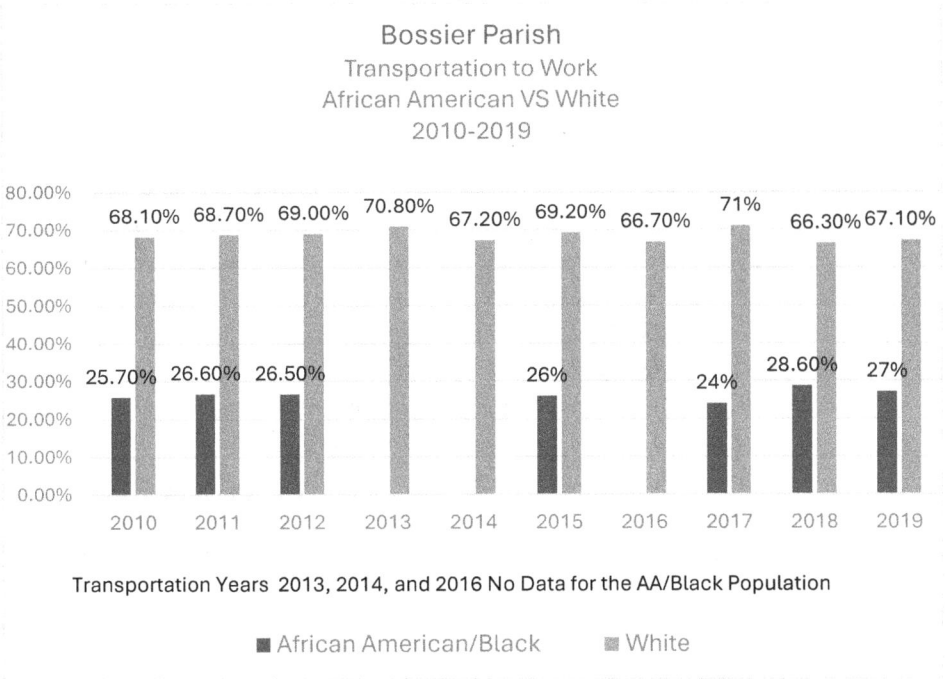

Transportation Years 2013, 2014, and 2016 No Data for the AA/Black Population

■ African American/Black   ▒ White

Figure 14: Bossier Parish Owning Transportation to Work Black vs. White 1010–2019
Source: U.S. Census Bureau (2019)

2.8.3 Transportation, Health Care Needs, and Renters

Not having affordable, available, and accessible transportation is a significant barrier for people in poverty. African Americans in the study area
with disabilities, who are elderly and not able to drive, and the poverty-
stricken, who are not able to purchase a vehicle, are at a disadvantage.
Limited access to affordable and reliable transportation, along with a lack
of available services in certain areas, are major barriers for people living in poverty. The majority of the people in poverty in Caddo Parish
are African American. The US census of 2000 reports that in Louisiana,
just over 24% of renter-occupied households and 6% of owner-occupied
households have no vehicle available. In Caddo Parish, nearly 24% of
renter-occupied households and nearly 7% of owner-occupied households are without vehicles.[181]

181. Louisiana Office of Public Health, *2005 Parish Health Profiles*, 130.

2.8.4 Caddo Parish Development Plans

To make the area a more attractive and dynamic location for corporate investments and expansion, there are plans for future Shreveport development that are part of the *Great Expectations* master plan. This plan modernizes the city's environmental sustainability, housing stock, neighborhoods, infrastructure, and transportation. Shreveport–Bossier City's plan for public transportation is to make SporTran more visible, increase the number of routes, run later routes, have more covered stops, increase the efficiency of service, provide technological advances, have newer buses, and change the location of certain terminals. Further plans include aiding with workforce training and business attraction through local organizations and in the city. Eliminating the cost-burdened and extreme cost-burdened residences and improving housing conditions for residents with housing maintenance issues are in the plan. The Cross Bayou plan is a plan for a concentration of mixed new housing types along with investment in the adaptive reuse of existing buildings and new products in the downtown area. Furthermore, there is a development plan to address the needs of inner-city and rural homelessness.

2.8.5 Bossier Parish Development Plans

The Bossier City Council along with the Bossier Police Jury adopted the Bossier City Comprehensive Plan. This plan is an official public document to assist with making a master plan for the physical development of the Bossier jurisdiction area. Under this plan, there is an objective to address the flooding and drainage issues along with the utilization and protection of Bossier's natural resources and beauty. Just like the Shreveport-Caddo side of downtown, Bossier City has it's contributing plan as well for the downtown area. This plan will create a new downtown and make use of brownfields for redevelopment and rehabilitation, manage growth patterns, mix-use housing, and manage community resources. Objectives for improving the Bossier multiple transportation network include improvement of automobile and truck traffic, water, rail, air, train, pedestrian safety, and adequate access to communities. Bossier's public transportation is included in the Shreveport–Bossier City plan for public transportation of SporTran to increase the number of routes, efficiency of service, newer buses, more covered stops, more visibility, later routes, technological advances, and to change location of certain terminals. There is a proposal for more business development for better economic opportunities which consists of a secure incentive program, designated opportunities, and a multitalented workforce to meet the needs of Bossier. The plan includes the Barksdale Air Force Base conservation and the surrounding Air Installations Compatible Use Zone. This is for the protection of both areas from the invasion by continuous new public parks and facilities, renovation, and/or redevelopment of existing and improving maintenance of the area.[182]

2.9 CADDO PARISH POPULATION AND BOSSIER PARISH POPULATION

The current estimated population of Caddo Parish is 237,848, of which African Americans / Blacks are the largest residents at 50.3%, outnumbering Whites at 43.6%, Native Americans and Alaska Natives at 0.5%, Asians at 1.4%, Native Hawaiians and other Pacific Islanders at 0.1%, and Hispanics 3.1%. Most Blacks in Caddo Parish have migrated to Shreveport. The population in Shreveport is 185,249, within which the Black population is the largest, making up 57.30%, outnumbering Whites at 37.17%. Blacks have the majority poverty rate, even in the city of Shreveport, which is the largest urbanized area in Caddo Parish and northern Louisiana.

The current estimated population of Bossier Parish is 128,746, of which Whites are the largest population at 64.4%, outnumbering African Americans at 24.1%, Native Americans and Alaska Natives at 0.7%, Asians at 1.9%, Native Hawaiians and other Pacific Islanders at 0.1%, and Hispanics at 7%. The population in Bossier City is 62,979, with the White population being the largest at 64.04%, outnumbering Blacks at 28.15%. Blacks have the majority poverty rate.[183]

182. Burris, "Transportation Study"; Bossier City Metropolitan Planning Commission, "Proceedings"; City of Shreveport, *2014–2018 Consolidated Plan*, 19–151.

183. US Census 2021, "Caddo Parish," 1; US Census 2021, "Bossier Parish," 1; World Population Review 2022, "Caddo Parish," 1; World Population Review 2022, "Bossier Parish," 1.

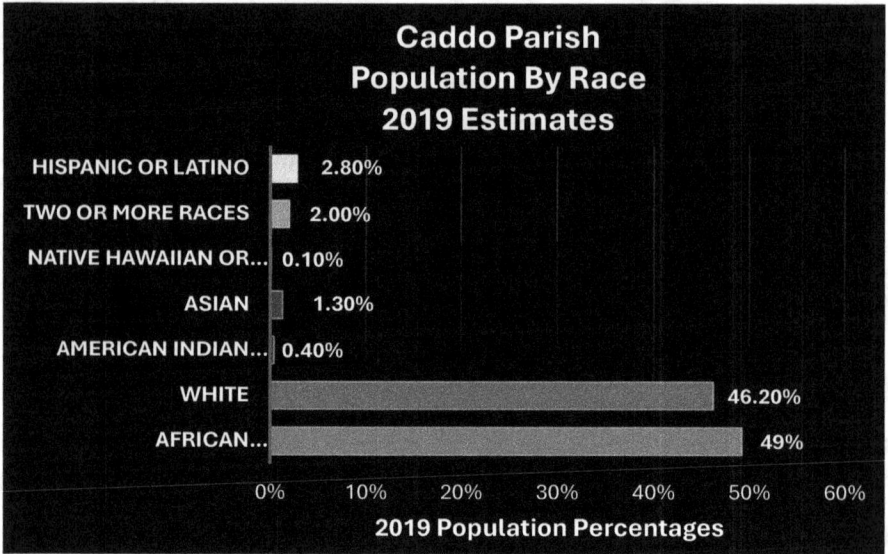

Figure 15: Caddo Parish Population Estimates by Race 2019
Source: U.S. Census Bureau (2019)

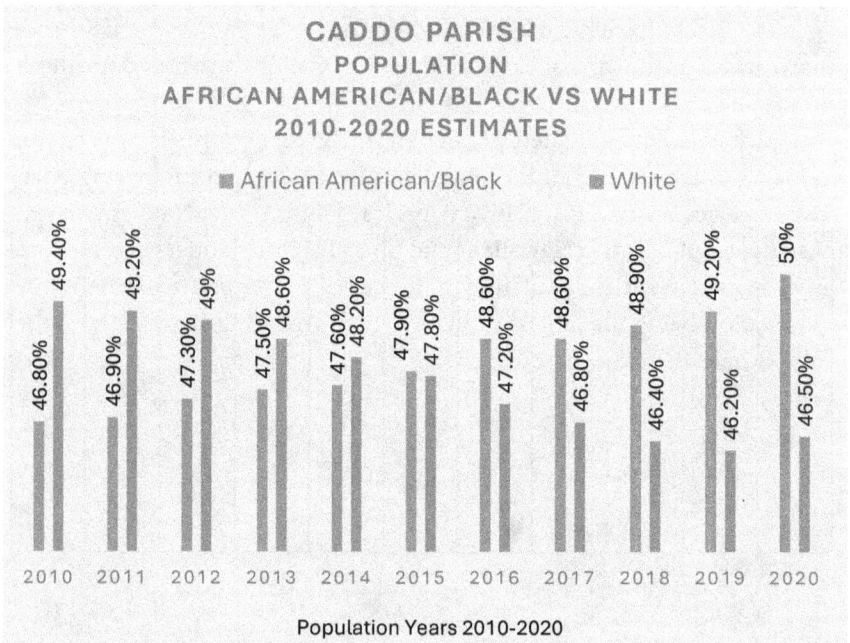

Figure 16: Caddo Parish Population Estimates Black vs. White 2010–2020
Source: U.S. Census Bureau (2021)

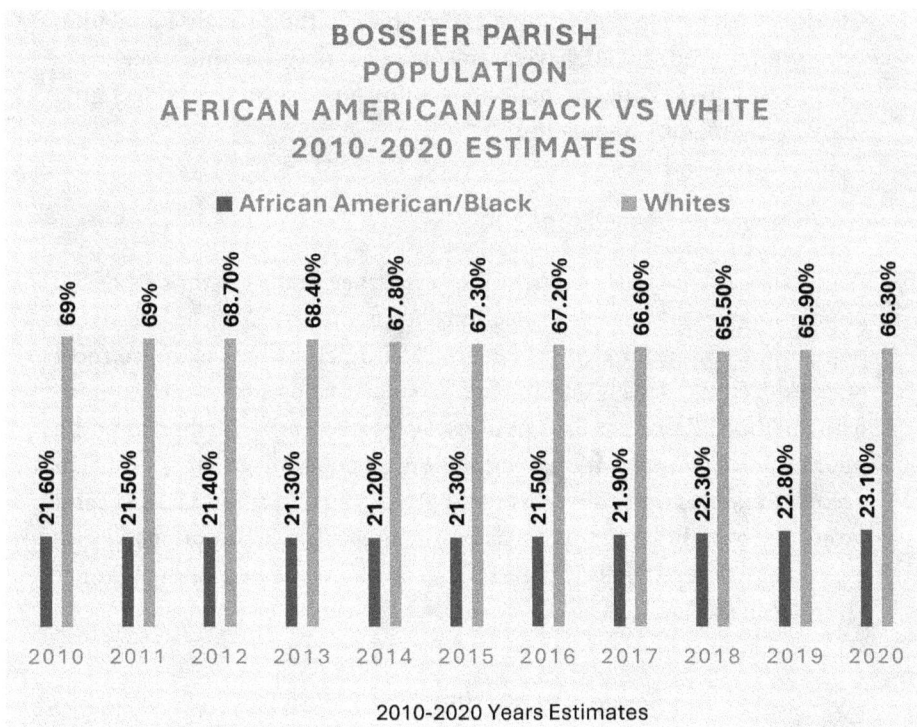

BOSSIER PARISH
POPULATION
AFRICAN AMERICAN/BLACK VS WHITE
2010-2020 ESTIMATES

■ African American/Black   ▩ Whites

Year	African American/Black	Whites
2010	21.60%	69%
2011	21.50%	69%
2012	21.40%	68.70%
2013	21.30%	68.40%
2014	21.20%	67.80%
2015	21.30%	67.30%
2016	21.50%	67.20%
2017	21.90%	66.60%
2018	22.30%	65.50%
2019	22.80%	65.90%
2020	23.10%	66.30%

2010-2020 Years Estimates

Figure 17: Bossier Parish Population Estimates Black vs. White 2010–2020
Source: U.S. Census Bureau (2021)

2.9.1 Population Trends

Urbanization refers to the mass movement of populations from rural to urban settings and how we adapt to the physical changes in urban settings through the movement.[184] Understanding the mass movements and trends of populations helps with urban planning. Like metropolitan populations all over the country, the population in Shreveport-Bossier metropolitan area has been growing older and more diverse, not just in race and ethnicity but also in household type, with fewer traditional families and more nonfamily households.

The current median age in Caddo is thirty-eight, an increase from thirty-six in 2009. Caddo Parish has particularly strong concentrations of employment in entertainment and recreation (which includes the casino industry), mining (oil and gas), arts, and health care. The Shreveport-Bossier region has grown in the last thirty years, but Shreveport and

184. Kuddus et al., "Urbanization," 1.

Caddo Parish have not maintained their share of this growth. Population trends in Shreveport City have been somewhat negative and, since 1980, have been experiencing a small net loss in population and a declining share of the region's population.[185]

2.9.2 Population Projections

Population projections will help the researcher predict estimates of the population for the future. Projections are made based on an estimated population. The estimated population will be consistent with the most recent decennial census and further produced using the cohort-component method. Based on assumptions of future deaths, births, domestic migration, and international migration population changes, we can predict possible courses by illustrated projections. In some cases, several projections might be produced based on alternative assumptions for life expectancy, future fertility, state-to-state or domestic migration, and net international migration.

2.9.3 Caddo and Bossier Parish Migration Trends

Data collected through research by the US census provides information regarding the increase and decrease in population in a parish/county. In the most recent collection, government officials in Shreveport–Bossier City expressed their concerns regarding making sure all residents are counted. The ultimate goal is to help researchers, communities, and businesses achieve an accurate and complete count. The count assists in determining such things as funding for school breakfast and lunch, where to open new shopping strips, where to build new police stations and fire stations, which services and products to offer, and population increase and decline.

There has been some population change in Shreveport and Bossier City, the two major cities in Caddo and Bossier Parish. Shreveport has seen a decline in population, and Bossier has seen an increase in population. Louisiana went through a depression in the 1980s due to the oil industry global crash. The depression equaled a substantial amount of job loss. Caddo and Bossier Parish were greatly affected by the 1980 recession, and Caddo Parish's declining population was the most visible

---

185. Shreveport Metropolitan Planning Commission, "Population," 7.

of the impacts. The 1980 recession presented Caddo Parish with its first population loss since the creation of the parish.[186]

From the 1990s and 2000s, a continued weak economy produced little growth, in Caddo Parish especially, more than in Bossier Parish. Bossier Parish grew more in the early 2000s because of a seventy-million-dollar bond to build three schools in 2004. Furthermore, the production of the schools led to the construction of the Louisiana Boardwalk (featuring Bass Pro Shops, several restaurants, outlet shopping, a bowling complex, and a fourteen-screen movie theater), Haynesville Shale, several casinos, Cyber Innovation Center, Millennium Studios, and StageWorks in Bossier. Even though Bossier Parish has seen some population gain since the 1990s, Caddo Parish still has a higher population.[187]

General Motors and AT&T/BellSouth both closed in the 2000s in Shreveport. AT&T/BellSouth closed in the early 2000s, which led to the loss of around seven thousand jobs. General Motors was closed in August 2012. The General Motors plant produced GMC Canyon, Isuzu I-Series, Chevrolet Colorado, and Hummer H3 series.[188]

According to the 2010 US census, Shreveport lost an estimated 8,848 residents, a 4.4% decline. An estimated population decline of 2,359 occurred in Shreveport from July 2016 to July 2017, a 1.21% decline from 194,394 to 192,036. The reason for the population decline is the result of the loss of higher paying jobs. Data collected by 24/7 Wall St. from June 2014 to June 2019 put Shreveport–Bossier City on the list of cities losing the most jobs with a −3.6% employment change (183,363 to 176,850).[189] The corporation 24/7 Wall St. provides information on financial news, such as the stock market, industries, and government policy on the economy. It created an index measuring eight categories which include housing, health education, economy, crime, infrastructure, and leisure. These categories were used to pinpoint the fifty worst cities to live in. In the United States, Shreveport made the top twenty-five out of the fifty cities with a ranking of twenty-one—just above Compton, California, at twenty. In this report, Shreveport's violent crime rate is more prevalent than in all of Louisiana. Louisiana's violent crime rate is 566 for every 100,000 residents, and Shreveport's violent crime rate was 959 for every

186. Bayliss, "Census 2020"; Shaw Environmental and Infrastructure, *Caddo Parish*, 12–21.

187. Shaw Environmental and Infrastructure, *Caddo Parish*, 12–21.

188. Listing Bidder, "Real Estate Commission"; Wendling, "US Election 2016."

189. Bayliss, "Census 2020."

100,000 residents, nearly double the state of Louisiana and fifth highest among the states in 2016.[190]

When there are substantially poor areas, violence is sure to follow. The financial hardships residents face in Shreveport are serious. There are 30.8% of residents who reside below the poverty line compared to the state population of Louisiana at 20.2% and the population of the United States at 14%. Shreveport is continuously losing residents. Within the last five years, the population fell by 3.7%, and the population in the United States grew by 3.7%.[191] Residents in Caddo Parish experience poverty due to factors such as lack of higher paying jobs, unemployment, and underemployment.

Many residents are moving out of the city of Shreveport into the rural country areas surrounding the city for more space and privacy. The flight from urban or downtown areas is part of the city's growth pattern. Shreveport City has seen migration to the south part of the city, north, and west, bordering Caddo Parish. This effect is also happening east across the Red River from Caddo Parish to Bossier Parish. There is new housing growth surrounding the Shreveport area. There is new home construction in the west, including the Greenwood area, new apartments to the north of the city, and multiple neighborhoods building up in the south along the Ellerbe Road corridor.[192]

According to an analysis done by 24/7 Wall St., between 2010 and 2018, the Shreveport–Bossier City area had the highest net migration decline among the metro areas in Louisiana.[193] The most recent migration is residents moving from Caddo Parish to the outer areas of Bossier Parish. This is a result of the employment of Haynesville Shale construction and natural gas, as well as the trend of affordable housing in northern Bossier Parish. The affordable housing trend in the parish of Bossier has assisted with an average net in-migration of three hundred residents yearly, migrating across the Red River from the Caddo submarket during the 2000s.[194]

A study from the 2015 ACS (updated 2019) showed which states the people from Louisiana are moving to when they leave Louisiana. The top ten states, along with the number of Louisiana migrants, are below.

190. Stebbins and Comen, "Worst Cities to Live In."
191. Stebbins and Comen, "Worst Cities to Live In."
192. Ferrell, "Migrating Shreveport Population."
193. The Center Square, "Shreveport–Bossier City."
194. US Department of Housing and Urban Development, *Shreveport–Bossier City* (2006), 9–12.

(1) Texas: 31,044; (2) Mississippi: 8,678; (3) Florida: 6,560;

(4) California: 6,324; (5) Virginia: 3,993; (6) Arkansas: 3,601;

(7) Georgia: 3,277; (8) Colorado: 3,007; (9) Tennessee: 2,784;

(10) North Carolina: 2,632.[195]

Texas is the closest state with a better economy than Louisiana and other neighboring states. Many of the researcher's friends and family have moved to Texas, with most of them living in Dallas, Houston, Austin, and San Antonio. The researcher moved from Caddo Parish and did not consider living anywhere else in northwest Louisiana. The researcher moved to southern Louisiana and then moved to Houston, Texas, because there were very limited employment opportunities for work in Caddo Parish and southern Louisiana. In terms of domestic migration, Louisiana is one of the least diverse states. In Louisiana, four out of five residents were born locally in the state, which shows there is little migration to the state.[196]

Immediately following Hurricane Katrina, on August 29, 2005, there was an influx of climate migrants that settled in the Shreveport–Bossier City area. The hurricane was the cause of twenty-five thousand migrants relocating to Caddo and Bossier Parish. However, less than a year later, those twenty-five thousand evacuees had dropped to ten thousand evacuees.[197] Most migration in Caddo and Bossier Parish is due to employment from casinos, Barksdale Air Force Base, and jobs in the medical field. Others move to northwest Louisiana for secondary education choices, including Southern University of Shreveport, LSU Medical School, LSU-Shreveport, and Centenary College, along with Louisiana Tech, Grambling State University, and Northwestern State University.

There is a compiled list of 2019's five-year estimates of immigrants who are foreign-born who moved to the Shreveport-Bossier metropolitan area for work and family. Listed below are the top ten countries and the number of immigrants from them.

(1) Mexico: 2,779; (2) Philippines: 904; (3) Vietnam: 746;

(4) Honduras: 704; (5) India: 602; (6) Germany: 450;

195. Larino, "Top 10 States."

196. Aisch et al., "Where We Came From."

197. US Department of Housing and Urban Development, *Shreveport–Bossier City* (2006), 9–12.

(7) United Kingdom: 381; (8) Pakistan: 323; (9) South Korea: 244; (10) China: 211.[198]

2.10 STUDY AREA EMPLOYMENT AND UNEMPLOYMENT

When a person or head of the household can take care of their family's basic needs and tackle unexpected costs, they feel financially secure. People being gainfully employed, fairly paid, secure, and having meaningful work is a sign of an inclusive economy. A city that struggles to provide a healthy economy will find it difficult to attract people to work, live, or play there. Not having a good health economy will make it difficult to create community well-being with sufficient resources for adequate schools, roads, parks, and other amenities to establish a thriving community. A person's mental and physical health can be affected negatively if a person is unemployed. Unemployment leads to negative behaviors such as physical inactivity, unhealthy diet, alcohol use, and smoking. Those factors mentioned are key to sustaining good health. People who are unemployed usually do not possess a steady stream of income, health care insurance, access to health services, or they even delay health care problems due to financial concerns. Premature deaths, a faster aging process, hopelessness, and intergenerational poverty result from financially insecure and unemployed people.[199]

2.10.1 Occupational Breakdown of the Labor Force in Study Areas

Below are charts of the occupational breakdown of the labor force in Caddo Parish, Bossier Parish, East Baton Rouge Parish, Shreveport–Bossier City metropolitan area, and Baton Rouge metropolitan area. The charts break down Whites versus minorities in the statistical data. In Caddo Parish, African Americans / Blacks are the majority. Caddo Parish minorities other than Blacks represent 3%. In Shreveport, minorities other than Blacks represented 4.91%. In Bossier Parish, minorities other than Blacks make up 5.3%. Bossier City minorities other than Black is 6.49%. East Baton Rouge Parish minorities other than Black is 7.07%. Baton Rouge minorities other than the Black population is 6.6%.[200]

198. Rizvi, "Immigrants to Shreveport."
199. Louisiana Office of Public Health, *2005 Parish Health Profiles*, 17–133.
200. US Census Bureau 2019, "Caddo Parish"; World Population Review 2020,

Table 1: Occupational Employment and Wages May 2020

Occupational Employment and Wages by Occupational Group

Shreveport Metropolitan Area (Including Bossier City)
Baton Rouge Metropolitan Area
United States

	% In Field Shreveport Metro	% In Field Baton Rouge Metro	Mean Shreveport Metro	Hourly Baton Rouge Metro	Wage U.S.
Total, All Occupations	100%	100%	$21.01	$23.68	$27.07
Management	4.50%	5.9	$45.60	$49.26	$60.81
Business and Financial Operation	3.4	5	$29.97	$29.67	$38.79
Computer and Mathematical	1.3	1.5	$33.39	$35.02	$46.53
Architecture and Engineering	0.08	2.4	$36.34	$43.50	$43.41
Life, Physical and Social Science	0.05	1.1	$34.76	$34.74	$38.15
Community and Social Service	1.3	1.3	$25.00	$23.98	$25.09
Legal	0.04	0.8	$34.94	$38.90	$54.00
Educational Instructional and Library	6.1	7.2	$21.71	$23.33	$28.75
Arts, Design, Entertainment, Sports, and Media	0.6	1	$22.00	$28.20	$30.96
Healthcare practitioners, and Technical	9.4	5.8	$35.21	$33.96	$41.30
Healthcare support	5.6	4	$12.77	$12.48	$15.50
Protective service	2.9	3.5	$20.46	$18.81	$25.11
Food preparation and serving Related	8.9	7.6	$10.31	$10.64	$13.30
Building and Grounds cleaning and Maintenance	3.6	2.5	$11.58	$12.78	$15.75
Personal care and Service	2.1	1.7	$13.59	$13.12	$15.68
Sales and Related	11.4	9.1	$15.99	$17.29	$22.00
Office and Administrative Support	14.5	11.8	$17.59	$18.07	$20.38
Farming, Fishing, and Forestry	NR	0.2	$17.35	$16.52	$16.02
Construction and Extraction	4.3	8.8	$20.88	$24.53	$25.93
Installation, Maintenance, and Repair	5.1	4.6	$23.06	$25.85	$25.17
Production	4.8	5.5	$22.05	$29.25	$20.08
Transportation and Material Moving	8.4	8.5	$16.40	$18.01	$19.08

Source: U.S. Bureau of Labor Statistics, (2021)

"Caddo Parish"; US Census Bureau 2019, "Bossier Parish"; World Population Review 2020, "Bossier Parish"; World Population Review 2021, "Baton Rouge."

2.10.2 Louisiana Government Employment

The following information reflects the demographics of the 70,518 employees of the Louisiana state government at the end of Fiscal Year 2019–2020. Data includes both classified and unclassified employees.

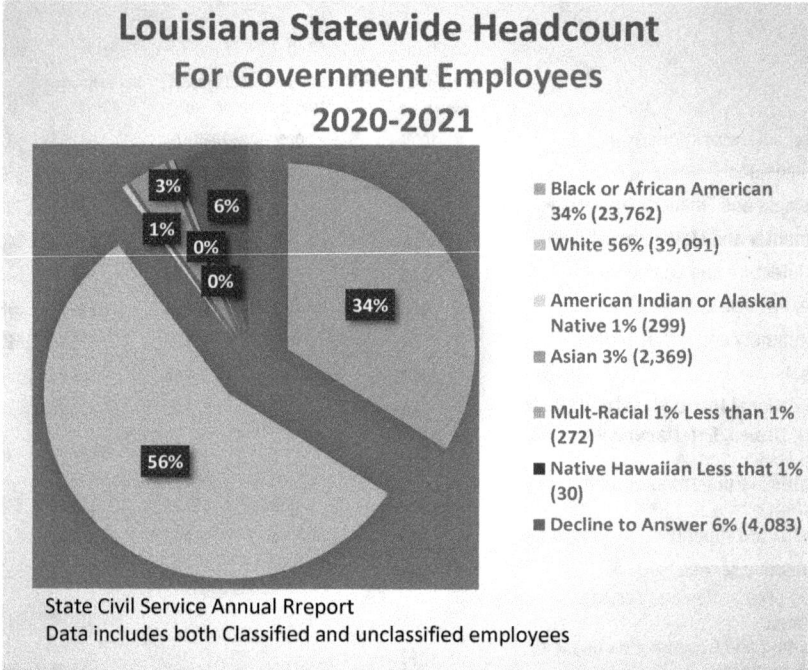

Louisiana Statewide Headcount
For Government Employees
2020-2021

3%
6%
1%
0%
0%
34%
56%

- Black or African American 34% (23,762)
- White 56% (39,091)
- American Indian or Alaskan Native 1% (299)
- Asian 3% (2,369)
- Mult-Racial 1% Less than 1% (272)
- Native Hawaiian Less that 1% (30)
- Decline to Answer 6% (4,083)

State Civil Service Annual Rreport
Data includes both Classified and unclassified employees

Figure 18: Louisiana Government Employee Headcount
Source: Louisiana State Civil Service (2022)

Caddo Parish:
2019 Government Workers: 15,874 at 16.5%
2019 Self-employed: 5,292 at 5.5%

Bossier Parish:
2019 Government Workers: 9,596 at 17.6%
2019 Self-employed: 3,219 at 5.9%[201]

---

201. Louisiana State Civil Service, *State Civil Service Annual Report*, 10.

2.10.3 African American Unemployment in Shreveport-Caddo Parish

The unemployment rate and income level in Caddo Parish is an issue. The Caddo Parish share of regional employment has been decreasing, and per capita income in Caddo Parish has declined slightly since 1999, with opposite trends in Bossier Parish. Caddo's master plan area shows a significant gap in income and employment between African Americans and Whites, in which African Americans are on the lower end of the spectrum. African Americans have a poverty rate almost four times as great as White residents; they are twice as likely as Whites to be unemployed, and their median earnings stand at less than two-thirds of White median earnings. The urbanization factor in Caddo Parish has seen most of the population migrate to Shreveport City, the largest city in Caddo Parish. African American unemployment rate in Caddo Parish was 11.6 in 2006–2008, and the White unemployment rate was 4.6. In 2008, African American median earnings were 59% of the White median, and the African American poverty rate was 32.9% compared to Whites at 8.4%. However, in most recent years, the African American unemployment rate has declined in Caddo Parish but is still twice as high as the Whites. High levels of vacancy and blight are characteristics of a shrinking city that Shreveport-Caddo Parish seems to have due to population and land use. Continuing leapfrog development, such as isolated subdivisions that are not easily accessible to the city limits, could negatively affect income, transportation, economic competitiveness, fiscal needs, cost, and quality of life.[202] In January 1990, Caddo Parish's unemployment rate was 9.2. In January 2000, it was 4.8. In January 2010, it was 7.8. In January 2020, it was 5.7.[203] In 2019, the US unemployment rate was 3.5.[204]

2.10.4 Unemployment Bossier City–Bossier Parish

In January 1990, Bossier Parish's unemployment rate was 6.9. In January 2000, it was 5.0. In January 2010, it was 6.0. In January 2020, it was 4.6. In reference to the 2008 ACS, Bossier City's unemployment rate is 4.8%, which was a bit higher than that of the state of Louisiana and Bossier Parish.[205]

202. Shreveport Metropolitan Planning Commission, "Population," 11.
203. Federal Reserve Economic Data, "Caddo Parish."
204. US Bureau of Labor Statistics, "Shreveport–Bossier City—May 2020."
205. Federal Reserve Economic Data, "Bossier Parish."

Caddo Parish vs Bossier Parish
Umeployment Rate
Years
1990, 2000, 2010, 2020

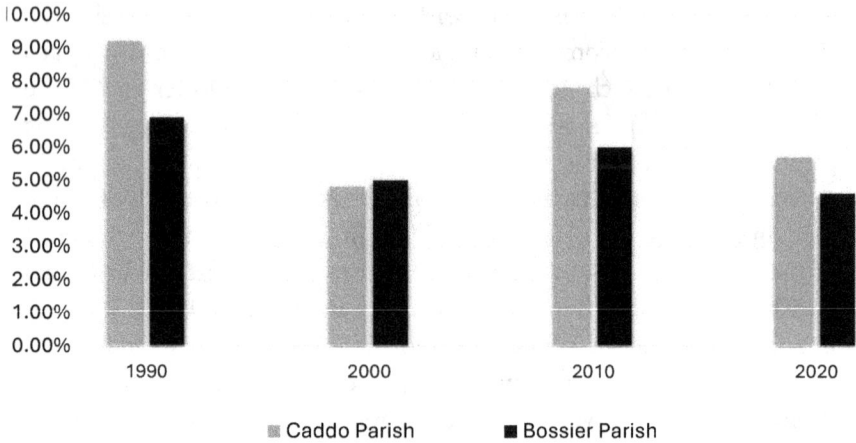

Caddo Parish   Bossier Parish

Figure 19: Unemployment Rate Caddo Parish vs. Bossier Parish 1990, 2000, 2010, 2020
Source: Fred Economic Data Bossier Parish (2021), Fred Economic Data Caddo Parish (2021)

CADDO PARISH
UNEMPLOYMENT RATE
AFRICAN AMERICAN VS WHITE

African American   White

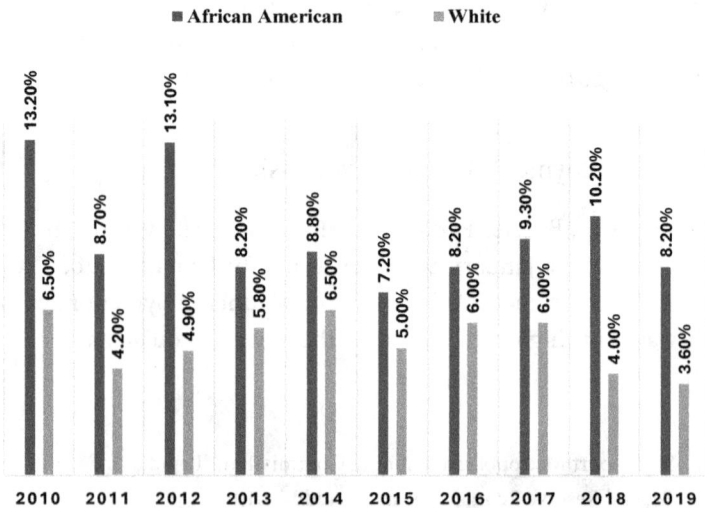

Figure 20: Caddo Parish Unemployment Rate Black vs. White 2010–2019
Source: U.S. Census (2019)

BOSSIER PARISH
UNEMPLOYMENT RATES
AFRICAN AMERICAN/BLACK VS WHITE
2010-2019

■ African American/Black   ▦ White

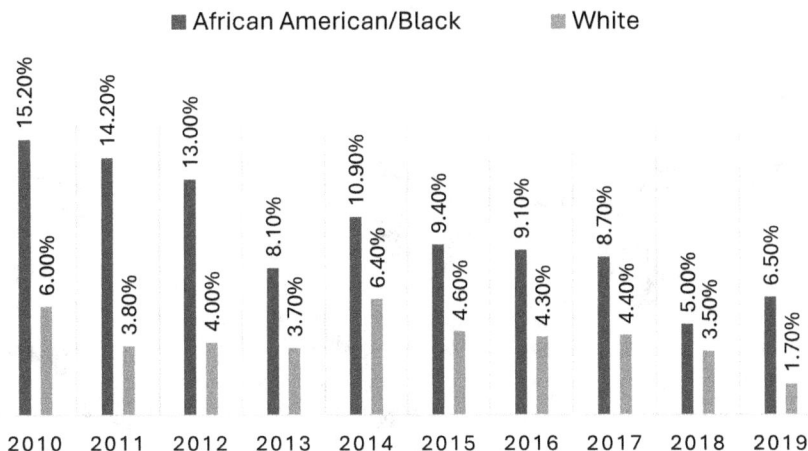

Figure 21: Bossier Parish Unemployment Rate Black vs. White 2010–2019
Source: U.S. Census (2019)

2.10.5 Local Business Ownership Study Area: African American vs. White

Local business owners can help a struggling community. Local business owners can create their income and their family's generational wealth and help employ other people locally. Business owners allow themselves an opportunity to make more money for the risk they take. One big entice-ment for business ownership is reaping the bigger financial rewards.[206] The research data that gives details on businesses owned by minorities will show a lack of Black business ownership. Black-owned businesses could provide jobs for Blacks, act as the main source of income for Blacks, and provide generational wealth for Black families. Understanding current and future business patterns is key to implementing planning strategies. The County Business Patterns is an annual series of local information that supplies subnational economic data by industry. This information also provides several establishments and employment quarterly. As of 2017, Caddo Parish had 3,761 White employer firms and 142 African

206. Leonard, "Owning Your Own Company."

American / Black employer firms. The White firms had a total of 42,745 employees with an annual payroll of $1,654,794; the African American firms had a total of 2,317 employees and an annual payroll of $38,757. Neighboring Bossier Parish, as of 2017, had 1,460 White employer firms and 46 African American / Black employer firms. The White firms have a total of 21,860 employees with an annual payroll of $768,426, and the African American firms had a total of 1,643 employees and an annual payroll of $24,235.[207]

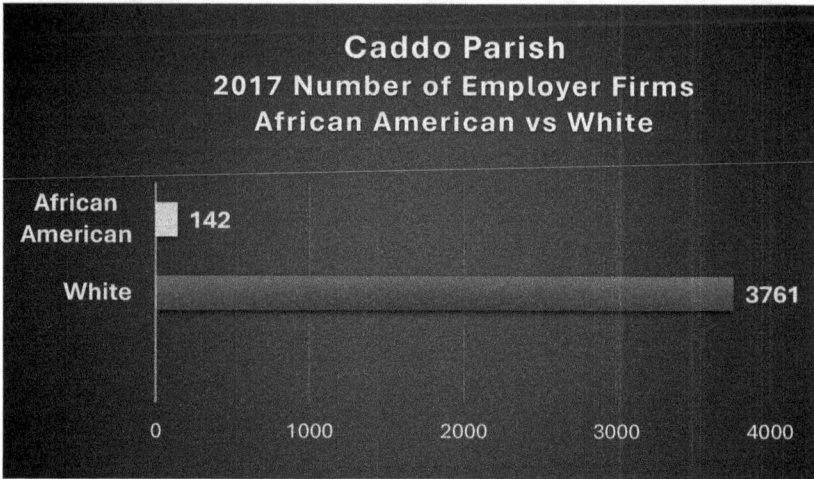

Figure 22: Caddo Parish Number of Employer Firms 2017
Source: Census Bureau (2020)

207. US Census Bureau 2017, "1-Year Estimates" (Caddo Parish); US Census Bureau 2017, "1-Year Estimates" (Bossier Parish).

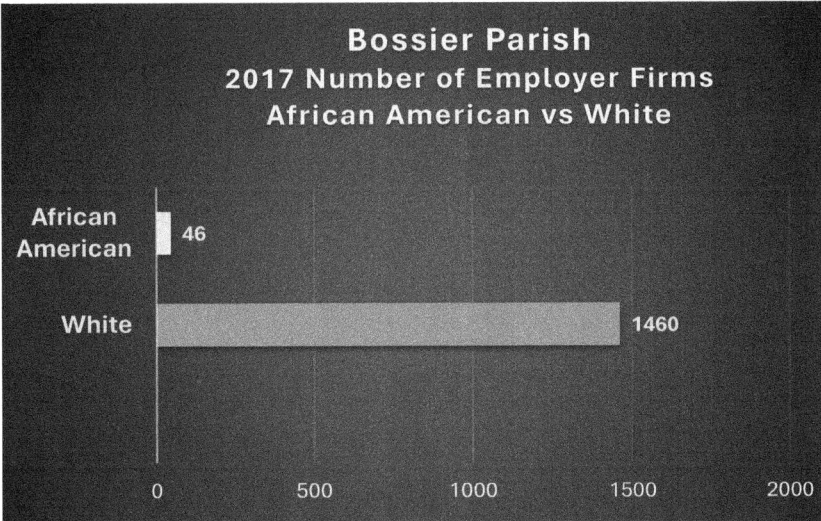

Figure 23: Bossier Parish Number of Employer Firms 2017
Source: Census Bureau (2020)

2.11 CADDO PARISH MEDIAN INCOME: BLACK VS. WHITE AND CLASSES

Listed below are the 2010–2019 estimated median income earnings for African Americans versus Whites and the 2012, 2015, and 2018 five-year ACS estimates for median income for African Americans versus Whites. This chart will show an income disparity between African Americans and Whites from 2010 to 2019. The disparities are present in the 2012 five-year ACS median income of $26,512, the 2015 five-year ACS median income difference of $28,622, and the 2018 report's gap of $29,016. The reports show that the median income gap is widening. The chart below shows the Caddo Parish median income statistics, with the following chart of Bossier Parish data for comparison.

Caddo Parish
Median Income
2010-2022
African Americans/Black VS White

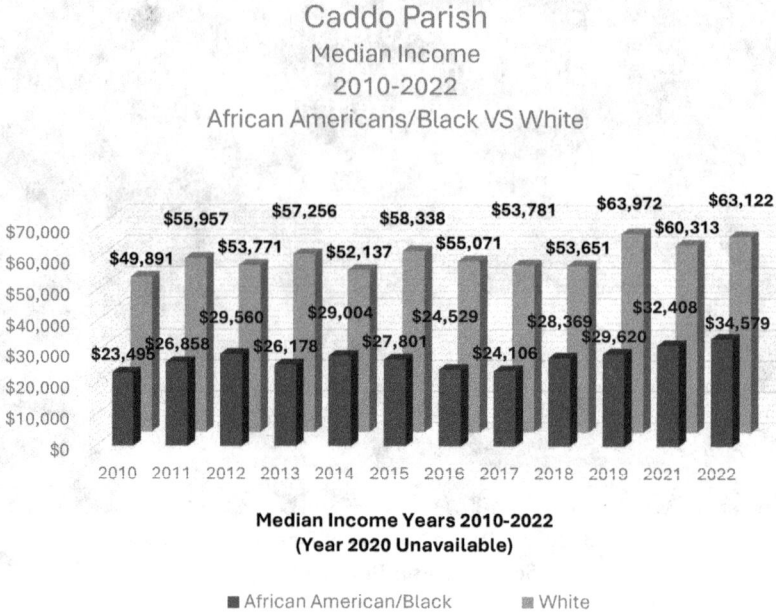

Median Income Years 2010-2022
(Year 2020 Unavailable)

■ African American/Black   ■ White

Figure 24: Caddo Parish 2010–2019 Median Income Black vs. White
Source: U.S. Census Bureau (2022)

Bossier Parish
Median Income
2010-2022
African American/Black VS Whites

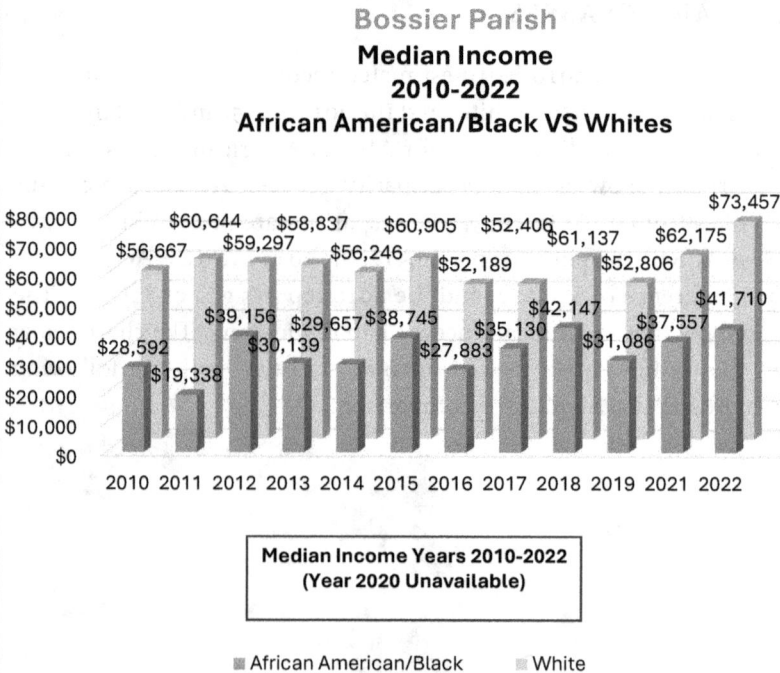

Median Income Years 2010-2022
(Year 2020 Unavailable)

■ African American/Black   ■ White

Figure 25: Bossier Parish 2010–2019 Median Income Black vs. White
Source: U.S. Census Bureau (2022)

2.11.1 Middle Class

Middle-class citizens are not considered rich people but instead considered a financially secure person or family. The middle class is made of those who are financially stable enough to take care of all of their needs, be able to save and invest for the next generation, have a good job, be able to provide themselves a safety net in case of an emergency, be able to afford health care, be secure enough to start a business, and/or be able to send children to college. The strength of a prosperous middle class and income inequality affects economic stability and economic growth. A strong middle class stimulates a well-educated population and human capital development. A strong middle-class population reinforces economic and political institutions influencing where the support of economic growth occurs. The strength of a prospering middle class breeds forthcoming generations of new entrepreneurs and stimulates communities. We will also witness a steady source of which goods and services are in demand as a result of a strong middle-class population. Middle-class America is not the only factor affecting economic growth and poverty, but it is indeed important.

Working together, human capital, skills, knowledge, and health are critical to growth. Using human capital is highly effective and must be commonly obtainable in a population. There must be avenues for children raised from low- to moderate-income backgrounds to be nursed along with their abilities and talents to match them to the most appropriate career. The strength of the middle class and inequity directly affects the use and access of human capital.

In the United States, the more the middle class exists and the less that inequality exists, the more the population is included in the government's political system. This maneuvers politics away from only answering to the economically powerful elite. The result would boost growth from the effects of providing a foundation for more inclusive economic institutions—meaning, incorporating effective governance that bolsters broad-based economic growth through initiating stable property rights and investing in public goods and quasi-public goods, such as infrastructure, education, and health. Accompanying these tangible things and level playing contains accountable, transparent, and regulatory structures.

Being in a strong middle-class family, or one that experiences less inequality or is not poverty stricken, enables a person to take more risks in becoming an entrepreneur. Living in the middle class gives entrepreneurs access to credit and financial security, allowing them time to foster ideas and take the risk of starting a business. A person in poverty or with low income would not have access to the same education that furnishes the skills and training to start a business as a middle-class person would, on average. Being subject to less inequality gives way to greater macro-economic security. Furthermore, it allows entrepreneurs to form knowledgeable investment decisions with more confidence concerning starting a business and its economic conditions. The existence of a strong middle class lets business investors know there is a marketplace for goods and services they are supplying to the population.

As more of the nation's economic gains go to those at the top of the income distribution—and if those families have a lower propensity to consume—this will pull down demand from potentially higher levels, given more equitable distribution.

Heightened inequality and a squeezed middle class leads families to either consume less, lowering demand, or put in place short-term coping strategies, such as borrowing more, which have long-term implications for growth and stability.[208]

2.11.2 Middle Class Study Area

Shreveport City experienced a decline during the 1980s due to the slow process of the downsizing of GE, the closure of General Motors, and a misguided K-12 educational system. Black and White graduates did not return to the Shreveport–Bossier City metropolitan area, and this caused a steady decrease in population. There were many losses in middle-class manufacturing jobs, with no replacement jobs as of yet. This event has left the city with 65% of the population living below the poverty line. Furthermore, many residents were no longer attracted to the area once the thirty-six-million-dollar economic development project was taken out of the bond. The project would have produced twelve hundred to twenty-four hundred new jobs resulting from the Citizen Bond Committee putting funds forward to create eight new industries. The project could have benefited African Americans, the area's largest population and impoverished group.[209]

---

208. Boushey and Hersh, "American Middle Class," 1–6.
209. Clark, "We're Better than This."

The Shreveport–Bossier City metropolitan area has seen a great out-migration of its population, especially its young and high-skilled workers, since the 1980s. With the incorporation of Webster Parish into the metropolitan statistical areas (MSA) and Bossier Parish's economic growth, the Shreveport–Bossier City MSA has seen some small gains in the last decade. The Shreveport-Bossier MSA situation of out-migration of its young skilled workers can support the economic stagnation or decline in this area.[210] The Shreveport–Bossier City metropolitan statistical area ranked fifth out of eleven comparable MSAs in population growth from 2008 to 2018. Still, it ranked last—eleventh out of eleven—in median household income in 2018.

2.11.3 Middle-Class and Higher Paying Jobs in Study Area

According to the US Bureau of Labor Statistics, the highest paying jobs in the Shreveport-City Bossier metropolitan are shown hourly in table 6 in section 2.10.1. The job sectors are management ($45.60); business and financial operations ($29.97); computer and mathematical ($33.39); architecture and engineering ($36.34); life, physical, and social science ($34.76); community and social services ($25.00); legal ($34.94); and health care practitioners, and technical ($35.21). Tables 1, 2, and 3 show hourly the 2018 labor force by ethnic group and sex (reflects 2017 data), which details the number of Whites and minorities employed in each occupation category in the study areas.[211] Though minorities get lumped into one racial group versus Whites, the majority of the population of the minorities in 2018 in each parish is African American or Black. According to the 2018 US census, the Caddo Parish African American or Black population was 44.5% and other minorities were 6.2%; Bossier Parish was African American 23.4% and other minorities were 11.2%; and Baton Rouge was African American 51.7% and other minorities were 9.7%.[212] In Caddo Parish and East Baton Rouge Parish, African American populations were greater than Whites. However, Whites have the majority of the higher paying jobs. I am proposing that Whites are unequally obtaining higher paying jobs than Blacks and/or unequally obtaining higher education to obtain higher paying jobs in the study area. It is

210. Norris and Norris, *Community Foundation*, 17.

211. Louisiana Workforce Information Review, *Department of Labor*, 6–106.

212. US Census Bureau 2019, "Caddo Parish"; US Census Bureau 2019, "Bossier Parish"; US Census Bureau 2019, "East Baton Rouge Parish."

essential to have higher paying jobs to obtain middle-class status for the African Americans in the study areas. As of November 2021, there were thirty-one thousand government jobs in the Shreveport–Bossier City metropolitan area, according to the Bureau of Labor Statistics.[213] Those jobs are included in the data on the Caddo and Bossier Parish labor force by ethnic group and sex, and didn't have a separate category for just government jobs' racial breakdown. It is essential to have higher paying jobs to obtain middle-class status for the African Americans in the study areas. The average annual salary for the federal government job category in Shreveport was $85,870 a year as of January 2022. The calculation equals $41.28 hourly, $1,651 weekly, and $7,156 monthly. These types of jobs definitely can put a person in the middle-class category. Judging by the labor force by ethnic group and sex figures, Whites in the study areas are likely employed in these positions.

2.11.4 Middle-Class Homeownership

Homeownership has allowed middle-class families to build wealth and generational wealth while simultaneously paying their housing costs. A wealth equalizer in the United States is homeownership. Because houses appreciate at rates that exceed inflation, housing is often an essential source of wealth accumulation for low- and middle-income families, which are generally not invested in stocks or other financial investments. A home's equity represents an average of 42% of an average family's wealth, which defines middle class. Middle-class families can build equity by owning a home. Historically, homeownership granted families the opportunity to keep in stride with the blooming value of financial investments held at the peak of the income distribution. Couples getting married and having children are generally lifecycle events that cause middle-class families to enter into homeownership. Their homes appreciate while simultaneously their mortgages are paid off. The family continuously accumulates the housing wealth needed to assist in financing themselves in retirement.[214]

---

213. US Bureau of Labor Statistics, "Shreveport–Bossier City—May 2022."
214. Clemens and Sabelhaus, "Middle-Age U.S. Homeownership."

2.11.5 Middle-Class Homeownership and Study Areas

The first figure in section 2.5.3 shows Caddo Parish homeownership from 1990–2010. It displays a disproportionate percentage of homeownership between African Americans and Whites in Caddo Parish. The most current US census of 2019 shows a reverse trend in the opposite direction from 2010 in homeownership gains for African Americans. African American homeownership is 40.2%, and White (alone) is 55.6%, according to the 2019 US census. In 2019, the African American population was 49.2% and Whites (alone) 44.3%.[215]

Another figure in section 2.5.3 shows Bossier Parish homeownership 1990–2010. In 2010, White homeownership was 75%, and Black homeownership was 20%, which makes a difference of 55%.[216] In 2019, the African American population was 23.2, and the White (alone) was 65.9%; the homeownership of African Americans was 21.2%, and Whites were 73.9%.[217] African American homeownership was down from 2010 by almost 1.2%. For comparison, the researcher included data from East Baton Rouge Parish. In 2019, the East Baton Rouge population consisted of 46.1% Blacks and 44.6% Whites, with homeownership for Blacks at 32.5% and for Whites (alone) at 62.5%.[218]

With the lack of homeownership in Caddo and Bossier Parish, African Americans cannot sustain a middle class nor accumulate wealth and generational wealth. And with the homeownership loss in both Caddo Parish and Bossier Parish, it is known that if an individual and/or family loses their home, they lose their class status. With African Americans in Caddo and Bossier Parishes being in high poverty and lacking high paying jobs, it is difficult to purchase a home in these conditions.

2.12 STUDY AREA BANKING DESERTS AND PAYDAY LOAN COMPANIES

A community or neighborhood without financial services or banking institutions is deemed a banking desert. When banking deserts occur, replacements are payday loan companies that charge high-interest rates

215. US Census 2019, "Caddo Parish," 1.

216. US Census of Population and Housing 2010, "Louisiana."

217. US Census 2019, "Bossier Parish," 1.

218. US Census 2019, "East Baton Rouge Parish," 1.

and more frequently generate a cycle of high-interest loans that are a struggle to pay off for borrowers of the loans. These borrowers continue to borrow even more funds to cope with overlapping debt and continue a cycle of poverty.[219] While payday lending has some restrictions, they are legal in Louisiana. In Louisiana, payday lender storefronts outnumber the number of McDonald's locations. A state audit in Louisiana shown to be severely critical discovered that state regulators managed the payday lending companies and failed to do their jobs. They should have exposed a magnificent range of tactics used to bypass maximize fees and state regulations charged per customer. Predatory lending has been targeting poor people, low-income communities, low-income elderly, and poor to low-income communities of color in the United States for years. This process continues to plague poor people, especially poor African American communities.[220] These banking deserts have developed in Caddo and Bossier Parish. Caddo Parish's population is around 50% African American / Black, an estimated 24.1% of households live below the poverty line, and the median household income is around $41,797—below the US median household income of around $68,703.

Cedar Grove, Mooretown, Forest Oak, Queensborough, Hollywood Heights, Allendale, Lakeside, Martin Luther King Jr. neighborhood, and other heavily African American–populated neighborhoods in Shreveport have been subject to banking deserts with payday loan companies, pawn shops, and liquor stores replacing financial institutions.[221]

In poor African American communities in Caddo Parish, high-interest rate loan promotions are frequent. Sign advertising for payday loans, income tax advance loans, or sometimes even holiday loans are often placed in poor communities of color, especially in poor African American communities in Shreveport. Technically, all signage without city approval on city streets is illegal in Shreveport, but the signs keep popping up anyway. Caddo Commissioner Steven Jackson says

> It creates a barrier for folks. If a person in the [predominantly black] MLK neighborhood had a new year's resolution to open a savings account, they'd have to drive ten minutes to [a bank] branch, but you can easily find a payday lending place over there.[222]

219. Smith, "Bank Deserts"; MacNeil, "Cedar Grove."
220. Abello, "Greater Shreveport."
221. Smith, "Bank Deserts"; MacNeil, "Cedar Grove."
222. Abello, "Greater Shreveport."

People in poor communities need help finding a financial empowerment center, a credit union, or a full-service bank to perform simple transactions such as making deposits, cashing checks, obtaining a mortgage, and securing a personal or small car loan. There has been a record of a local credit union designated as a community development financial institution being turned away from establishing themselves in bank desert communities in Shreveport / Caddo Parish, according to Caddo Commissioner Steven Jackson.[223] Why are full-service financial institutions turned away?

There is no specific credit score to acquire a payday loan in Louisiana. However, valid identification, bank account information, proof of regular income, and a person's Social Security number must be requirements. Borrowers can obtain payday loans even with no credit or poor credit. Payday lenders do not routinely check into borrowers' credit reports, but borrowers' credit can be harmed if they fail to make payments on time. Since there is no restriction on how often a person can apply for a payday loan or how many they can apply for, it can be risky for those who are already financially struggling. Payday lenders will convince individuals that payday loans will help borrowers, but in reality, these lenders are out to make a profit quickly. Not only do these payday loans not build credit, but the borrowers run the risk of hurting their credit. The maximum loan amount in the state of Louisiana is three hundred and fifty dollars, and the maximum finance charges are at 16.75%—or 391% APR. The term of the loan is limited to thirty days, and if the borrower fails to pay the total amount by the date due, there will be no rollover loans allowed.[224]

People who often use payday loans are African American and Latino families with children. These families' earnings are typically fifteen thousand to forty thousand dollars, they have poor credit, they are Social Security recipients, and they need extra cash for living expenses and different types of emergencies. Louisiana has 23% of residents who depend on predatory lending, the sixth largest in the United States The United States' percentage of residents that use predatory loans is 18%. There are around fifty-seven thousand Louisianian households that use payday loans yearly. In the United States, there are 20,600 payday loans compared to 12,800 McDonald's. In Louisiana, there are 936 payday loans compared to 230 McDonald's. There are 78 total payday loan lenders in

223. MacNeil, "Cedar Grove."
224. Sherris, "Online Payday Loans."

Shreveport / Bossier City. Individuals who take out payday loans are four times as likely to have filed for bankruptcy in the last five years and two times as likely to have filed for bankruptcy as individuals that were rejected for a payday loan. Section 4.6, "GIS Maps and Community Maps," has a map of the Shreveport-Bossier area showing bank branches (black map markers), low-income areas (polka-dotted areas), and minority populations (darker means a higher percentage), and the figure following shows the distribution of payday loan lenders.[225]

Table 2: United States Comparable Interest Rates to Payday Loan Rates

Interest Rates
Annual Percentage Rate (APR)

	Average	Up to
Student Loan	2%	8%
30-Year Mortgage	5%	8%
Subprime Mortgage	8%	15%
Credit Cards	15%	36%
PAYDAY LOANS	150%	782%

Source: News & Politics (2014), (Louisiana Budget Project 2016)

Table 3: Payday Loan Interest Calculations

How Payday Loans Carry Triple Digit APR's

Payday Loan Amount	$100
Interest	16.75%
Amount Owed	Equals $116.76

16.75%	X 26 Two-Weeks Periods
Two-Week Periods	1 Year
	Equals 436% APR.

Plus fees of $10 PER LOAN brings APR to 696%

Source: News & Politics (2014), (Louisiana Budget Project 2016)

---

225. News and Politics, "Payday Lending," 4–24; Louisiana Budget Project, "Payday Lending in Louisiana"; Abello, "Greater Shreveport."

2.13 POLITICS IN LOUISIANA

Just like the Reconstruction in 1867, the second Reconstruction did nothing to end economic inequalities that began in American slavery or stop reinforced years of Black/White segregation.[226] Many Blacks remain unemployed, and Black poverty remains far higher than that of Whites even though some Blacks entered middle-class, upper-middle-class, and affluent status. During this time, the southern Black communities mobilized and joined White allies politically to bring power to the Republican Party. Since 1980, Caddo Parish has voted for the overall national popular vote winner in presidential campaigns. However, fifty years after the Jim Crow era, nationwide Black homeownership in 1968 was 41.1% versus 41.2% in 2018, Black incarceration in 1968 was 604 (per 100,000) versus 1,730 (per 100,000) in 2018, and Black unemployment in 1968 was 6.75% versus 7.5% in 2018.[227] Not much has changed nationwide to favor Blacks, even with Blacks in political offices, electing a Black president, more Black millionaires, and Blacks switching political parties and views.

2.13.1 Politics in Caddo Parish

The current mayor of Shreveport is Mayor Andrew Perkins, who ran for United States Senate and experienced defeat in 2020.[228] All legislative powers accruing to the city under the city charter and the constitution and laws of the state of Louisiana are vested in and exercised by the council. Section 4.02 of the charter states that the council is composed of seven members, each elected from a separate city district. (The council holds regular meetings twice each month at city hall.) City council members include Tabatha Taylor (District A), LeVette Fuller (District B), John Nickelson (District C), Grayson Boucher (District D), James Flurry (District E), James Green (District F), and Jerry Bowman Jr. (District G).[229] Caddo Public Schools serves all of Caddo Parish and is a school district based in Shreveport. The district's founder was a Virginia native, Superintendent Clifton Ellis Byrd, who assumed the chief administrative position in 1907 and continued until he died in 1926. C. E. Byrd High School

226. Foner and Mahoney, "Americas Reconstruction."

227. Jan, "No Progress."

228. May, "Perkins Future as Mayor."

229. Shreveport Louisiana, "City Council," 1; these reflect the member appointments in 2021.

in Shreveport was named after the founding superintendent. There are
ten public high schools, seven middle schools, seven middle/elementary
schools, thirty-two elementary schools, and six unique schools in Caddo
Parish. Dr. Theodis Lamar Goree was appointed superintendent of Caddo
Parish Public Schools in Shreveport in December 2013. Superintendent
Goree serves over sixty-two schools, including three charter agreements
with forty thousand students.[230]

2.13.2 African American Incarceration and the US Political System

Scientists have discovered that Africans/Blacks originating in Africa were
the first humans dating back over two hundred thousand years before
other races.[231] African/Black people were the first to build civilizations
such as Nubia, Egypt (Kemet), and Mesopotamia.[232] The Ancient Egyptians, who were all African/Black before being conquered, began record-
keeping before 4,000 BC, gave other civilizations languages and literature,
including providing the Greek alphabet to the Greeks, color therapy,
philosophy, and art, to name a few early contributions.[233] Africans/Blacks
were also the first to arrive in the Americas, before Christopher Columbus and the Native Americans.[234] Many Africans were brought over in
the transatlantic slave trade. However, all Africans became subjugated to
systemic racism and oppression in the United States.

The Thirteenth Amendment to the United States Constitution provides that

> neither slavery nor involuntary servitude, except as a punish-
> ment for crime whereof the party shall have been duly con-
> victed, shall exist within the United States, or any place subject
> to their jurisdiction.[235]

The key words in the Constitution was that there was to be no slavery nor
involuntary servitude "except as a punishment for crime."

After 1865, the southern states in the US passed the Black Codes.
The Black Codes were a series of laws restricting and controlling the

230. Caddo Parish Public Schools, "About Caddo Parish."

231. Yong, "New Story."

232. Sertima, *They Came Before Columbus*, 4–11; Bradley and Clarke, *Iceman Inheritance*, 7–163.

233. Gaille, "Qualitative Research"; Rutherford, "Ancient Greek and Egyptian."

234. Sertima, *They Came Before Columbus*, 4–11; Imhotep, *First Americans*.

235. US Const. amend. XIII, §1.

newly freed slaves' right to be free from bondage as humans. After the American Civil War, the South lost free labor from the enslaved they had kept in bondage. The plantation owners looked to the local and state officials from the government to make a law or decree for ordinances and legislations that would allow a repeat in chaining Blacks to plantation life. Newly freed enslaved Black people had no power to restrict laws set on them, commonly in southern US states. Curfews, along with vagrancy laws, were passed for homelessness, roaming, and traveling, which also limited Blacks from leaving the plantations. Violating these laws resulted in fines because it was considered illegal to do so. If Blacks could not pay the fine, they would be forced to work on plantations to pay the fines off. The Black Codes denied African Americans equal education and freedom to travel leisurely. Furthermore, Blacks were treated badly by state sentencing laws, they were lynched, and they faced racist judges and prosecutors. Even today, African Americans experience racial profiling by authorities, which can lead to incarcerations and arrests, especially with African American males.[236]

In 1971, Richard Nixon declared a war on drugs, and the incarceration in US prisons and jails rose from 300,000 to 2.3 million. At the time, people of color represented two-thirds of half of those in federal prison jailed because of drug offenses. Convictions, sentencings, and arrests for drug offenses at a disproportionate rate have devastated Black communities in the United States. Between 1980 and 2011, African Americans were far more likely to be arrested for selling or possessing drugs than Whites, even though Whites use drugs at the same rate and are more likely to sell drugs, as the Washington Post reported.[237] The way that America dealt with drugs was not as a health issue; it was considered a crime issue. People could be sent to jail for low-level offenses, even possessing small amounts of marijuana. President Richard Nixon's plot to criminalize Black people by using the establishment of the war on drugs magnified the presumption of guilt against Black people. Nixon used political fear and anger to be tough on crime, which meant being tough on Black folks, and brought in a new political environment for every elected official afterward.[238] One primary strategy for Nixon's success was his Southern strategy plan. The plan entailed President Nixon recruiting

236. Weatherspoon, *African American Males*, 2–6.

237. Maxwell, "Southern Strategy."

238. Equal Justice Initiative, "Nixon Advisor."

southern states' White Democrats to become part of the Republican Party using racial fear.

President Nixon's chief domestic advisor, John Enrilichman, admitted that the "war on drugs" campaign was a plan to imprison Black people. Enrilichman said,

> The Nixon campaign in 1968, and the Nixon White House after that, had two enemies: the antiwar left and Black people. You understand what I'm saying. We knew we couldn't make it illegal to be either against the war or Black, but by getting the public to associate the hippies with marijuana and Blacks with heroin, and then criminalizing both heavily, we could disrupt those communities. We could arrest their leaders, raid their homes, break up their meetings, and vilify them night after night on the evening news. Did we know we were lying about the drugs? Of course, we did.[239]

Using segregation, economic inequality, and poverty to put Blacks in dire situations was and is indeed a tactic of systemic racism. To get fellow White Americans on board with criminalizing Blacks by using different terms was a tactic used by the campaign. President Nixon did this by using nonracial terms, crimes, and/or portraying certain strategies of the Civil Rights Movement as crimes against America. Ronald Reagan used some of these criminalization schemes with his war on drugs tactics. The criminalization of Blacks was amplified even more with Bill Clinton's 1994 Crime Bill, which was responsible for sending many Black people to jail, especially Black men, which helped destroy Black communities.[240] Even Ronald Reagan's campaign strategist, Lee Atwater, on a tape recorded interview, explained their Southern strategy on how to recruit other racists without sounding like a racist themselves, but sounding more political:

> You start out in 1954 by saying, Nigger, nigger, nigger. By 1968, you can't say nigger—that hurts you, backfires. So, you say stuff like, uh, forced busing, states' rights, and all that stuff, and you're getting so abstract. Now, you're talking about cutting taxes, and all these things you're talking about are totally economic things, and a byproduct of them is, Blacks get hurt worse than Whites. We want to cut this, is much more abstract than even the busing thing, uh, and a hell of a lot more abstract than Nigger, nigger.[241]

239. Drug Policy Alliance, "Top Advisor."
240. Chung et al., "1994 Crime Bill."
241. Perlstein, "Southern Strategy."

Black men raised in the top 1% by millionaires were as likely to be incarcerated as White men raised in households earning about thirty-six thousand dollars, explained a Chalkbeat article.[242] In 1968, Black incarceration was 604 per 100,000. In 2018, Black incarceration was 1,730 per 100,000, which shows that Black incarceration has nearly tripled in numbers. The unemployment rate for Blacks was 6.7% in 1968, and in 2018 it was 7.4%, an increase.[243] So, one must ask, as cities in the United States urbanize and sprawl, why did Black unemployment increase from 1968 to 2018? Lack of employment leads to poverty and contributes to people turning to a life of crime to be able to support themselves. Even if a Black people commit minor crimes and land themselves in jail, Blacks are finding it hard to be released from prison even if they are projecting good behavior.

2.13.3 Creation of Criminals in America

In the early years of America, people considered "White" were citizens who migrated from England, Scandinavian countries, Germany, and the Netherlands. When the Italian, Irish, Jewish, and Polish immigrants migrated to the United States in masses in the late 1800s and early 1900s, they were not considered part of the racially classified White race. These immigrants were known to have a racial classification below Whites but above Blacks, according to White supremacy logic. Not until years later, due to political strategy, racist reasoning, and being that Whites are the minority in numbers globally compared to non-White people, were they later adopted into the White race. By observation, one can tell the difference between Caucasoid and Negroid skin pigmentation, so this became an easy transition for the immigrants. Some arguments continue about whether the Irish were considered White or not from the moment they migrated to the United States. However, many early negative statements about the Irish say they were not considered White. Moreover, city authorities in the 1900s had looked at the Irish immigrants as the source of a serious crime problem. They were labeled by White American citizens as dirty, drunken, cruel, bloody, to be feared, blasphemers, swearers, rapists, and child murderers.[244]

242. Barnum, "Race."

243. Jan, "No Progress."

244. Harriot, "When the Irish Weren't White"; Starkey, "White Immigrants"; Gershon, "Stereotypes of the Irish"; Driscoll, "Black Maria."

The Italian, Irish, Jewish, and Polish immigrants began to make up the early twentieth-century urban ghettos. Because of poverty, no benefits, and low-income earnings, these people began forming crime syndicates and street gangs. They would become involved with extortion, running numbers, illicit schemes, counterfeiting, bootlegging, and drug dealing. Furthermore, we see the rise of the Italian, Jewish, and Irish mobs—hence, the creation of American-made criminals due to their poor living situations. New immigrants in many cities were more segregated than Black people were in the early twentieth century. In the 1950s, there was a change in new immigrants' segregation.

In 1911, Henry Pratt Fairchild, an influential American sociologist, made this statement regarding new immigrants:

> If he proves himself a man, and . . . acquires wealth and cleans himself up very well, we might receive him in a generation or two. But at present, he is far beneath us, and the burden of proof rests with him.[245]

After the 1940s, these immigrants' situation started to change. Once their transition into White status began, the immigrants were given gateways out of poverty and avenues to build wealth. These Irish immigrants migrated to the police force, fire department, and other service jobs. They commonly hired family members and countrymen once they could make hiring decisions. The Irish's history is commonly associated with Saint Patrick. Police vehicles in the early 1900s were called "Paddy Wagons" because they often contain Irishmen en route to jail. Ironically, now the people that were formerly considered criminals would dominate the New York Police Department.[246]

The Jews became included fully in the American mainstream and became part of mutual aid societies. In the political arena, Jews serve a healthy population at every level and branch of the US government, especially the US Supreme Court. The Polish, who were once thought of as the butt of American jokes with thoughts of being backward and uneducated simpletons, rose to white-collar labor market careers, formed labor unions, and benefited from the church.

Americans generally proclaimed that Italians were less skilled than the Jews and were more like the Irish. They were likely to be illiterate, had little urban experience, and became heavily involved with organized

245. Starkey, "White Immigrants."
246. Driscoll, "Black Maria."

crime. Once accepted into the White family, Italians had access to American public schools and, like the Irish, were given a stake in the police and fire departments. Italians also joined Jews in the labor unions.[247] These immigrants' melanin-less skin allowed them an opportunity to blend into the American White family, where Black people will never get, according to White racist logic.[248] These immigrants would observe how Whites mistreated Black people and then copy the behavior toward Blacks.[249]

Understanding that the mistreatment, poverty, and low wages led to a life of crime for the new immigrants in the late 1800s and early 1900s before becoming classified as White leads one to think how five hundred years of slavery, racism, rape, abuse, miseducation, Jim Crow laws, unemployment, underemployment, police brutality, being purposely diseased (Tuskegee Experiment), unfair housing practices, and more effected African Americans under the US political system.

2.13.4 African American Incarceration in Louisiana

The 2022 report Race and Wrongful Convictions in the United States examined the cases of 3,200 individuals exonerated nationwide since 1989. The researchers found that Black people were seven times more likely to be wrongfully convicted, faced higher rates of police misconduct, and typically spent longer periods in prison before being exonerated.

Black individuals were disproportionately represented across all categories of the 1,167 wrongful murder convictions documented in the Registry's database. They accounted for 56% (74/134) of death-sentenced exonerees, 55% (294/535) of wrongful murder convictions resulting in life sentences, and 54% (270/497) of wrongful murder convictions that led to fixed-term prison sentences.

There is a disproportionate incarceration rate for African Americans / Blacks versus Whites in the state of Louisiana and in Caddo Parish. Between the years of 2003 to 2012, researchers inspected data prosecuted by the Caddo Parish district attorneys from more than three hundred felony trials. They found that some individual prosecutors struck out Black prospective jurors at four and a half and five times the rate they struck out those who are not Black. Prosecutors in Caddo Parish, on an

---

247. Jones, "Polish Americans"; Burby, "Italian Immigration in NYC," 7.

248. Harriot, "When the Irish Weren't White."

249. Starkey, "White Immigrants."

overall basis, struck jurors of other races out at 15% and abruptly struck out Black jurors at 46%. With Caddo Parish being around 48% Black, the researchers found that there were less than four African American members in a standard twelve-member jury trial. Per capita, Caddo Parish sentenced to death more people than any other county/parish in the United States. Today, majority-White juries in Caddo Parish are sentencing mostly Black defendants to death (83% in the study).[250] These alarming rates are a pattern that reflects the parish's legacy as Louisiana's lynching capital and the site of the second highest number of racial terror lynchings in the South.

The state of Louisiana is known for its lengthy history of using captive labor or selling the labor of convicts to private companies. Even the Constitution outlawed this convict lease system in 1898. Louisiana State Penitentiary at Angola used prison labor without paying them well into the twentieth century. The convict lease system incentivizes the arrests of people for many insignificant offenses. In Louisiana, prison laborers typically work in cotton fields, sugar product companies, shrimp suppliers, and in oil and gas jobs, often dangerous tasks. The jobs pay from $0.86 to (for some offshore jobs) maybe up to $11.12 an hour.[251] Louisiana Sheriff Steve Prator of Caddo Parish unwittingly admitted to modern-day slavery in October of 2017 when he objected to the releasing of a certain number of nonviolent prisoners because of a new law. The sheriff was not against releasing prisoners because he thought they would be repeat offenders. Rather, he wanted those good-behavior prisoners to stay in jail to maintain vehicles, cook in the kitchen, and detail cars for free, which presents modern-day slavery.[252]

2.13.4.1 Existing Jim Crow Laws in Louisiana: After the American Civil War and the abolishment of slavery, there were still laws that existed to oppress Black people in America. These laws were the Jim Crow laws. These laws were an assembly of the local and state governments' legalized segregation statutes. These laws existed for a hundred years. However, there are some Jim Crow laws that are still in existence in Louisiana. From the post–Civil War era through 1968, these particular collections of laws intended to marginalize African Americans by refusing their

250. Equal Justice Initiative, "Illegal Racial Discrimination."
251. Berlin, "Louisiana's Oil and Gas"; Arresting Inequality, "Jim Crow."
252. Bromwich, "Louisiana Sheriff's Remarks."

rights to education, hold jobs, vote, and other opportunities. People would face stiff penalties if they attempted to break these Jim Crow laws. The lawbreakers would face violence, arrest, jail sentencing, fines, and possibly death.[253] In 2019, Louisiana moved to change the Jim Crow law that allowed a jury to convict a person with a split-verdict decision. In 2020, the United States Supreme Court deemed this particular law unconstitutional.[254] A person in Louisiana could receive a "life without the possibility of parole" sentence with a verdict of ten to two or eleven to one from a twelve-person jury. Louisiana was the only state in the nation with this law, which put a stop to the 138-year-old Jim Crow practices. A unanimous decision is required for a conviction now, and this could help change mass incarceration rates in Louisiana, especially for African Americans.[255] Black inmates make up four in five of the over fifteen hundred inmates serving time under the Jim Crow split-decision law in Louisiana. Black inmates are more than one in four of those who have served at least twenty years in prison already, and the longest serving person under this same law has been incarcerated since 1967. There have been 1,543 verified split verdicts through appeals, court files, and transcripts, with the possibility of others joining the pile. There was a six-year research of jury trial data by *The Advocate* in 2018. The research was performed across Louisiana parishes. The report found that a split jury convicted 80% of Black inmates, a notably higher rate than the broader Black prison population, which was 67.5%. Furthermore, *The Advocate* found that Black defendants were 30% more likely to be convicted by split juries than White defendants and that twelve-member juries were divided with guilty verdicts 40% of the time.[256] In Louisiana, Jim Crow jury convictions are responsible for 80% of Black men and Black women still in prison, with 62% of these Black men and Black women serving life sentences without parole possibilities.[257] One factor that assisted the Jim Crow laws in the courtroom was the illegal racial discrimination in jury selections that has been documented and has plagued the Caddo Parish courtrooms.[258] Listed below are the incarceration statistics for the United States, Louisiana, and Caddo Parish.

253. History.com Editors, "Jim Crow Laws."

254. Simerman, "1,500 Louisiana Inmates."

255. Drouaillet, "Louisiana Strikes Down."

256. Simerman, "1,500 Louisiana Inmates."

257. Allen, "Jim Crow Jury Verdicts."

258. Equal Justice Initiative, "Illegal Racial Discrimination."

Incarceration Rates Comparing Louisiana And Founding NATO Countries

Country	Rate
ICELAND	36
NORWAY	54
NETHERLANDS	65
DENMARK	69
LUUXEMBOURG	109
ITALY	97
BELGIUM	105
FRANCE	107
CANADA	109
PORTUGAL	116
UNITED KINGDON	144
UNITED STATES	614
LOUISIANA	1067

Incarceration Rates Per 1000,000 Population
In all countries with a total populaion of at least 500,000

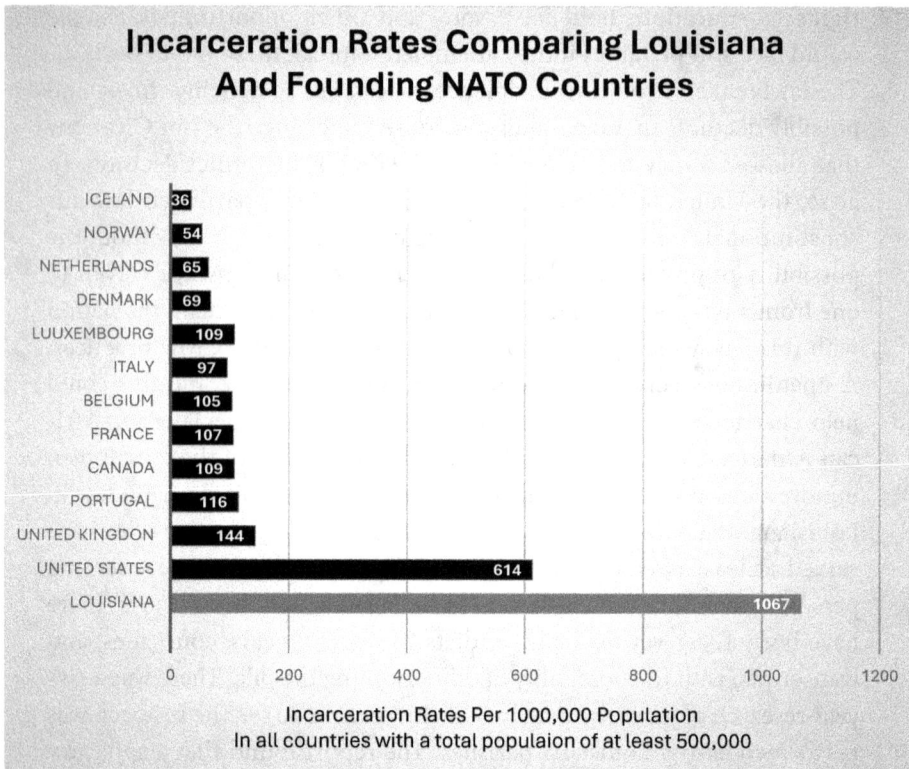

Figure 26: Incarceration in Louisiana vs. other NATO Countries
Source: Prison Policy Initiative 2024

Racial Disparities in Louisiana Prison and Jail Incarceration Rates

People in state prisons and local jails, per 100,000 state residents in each race or ethnicity category

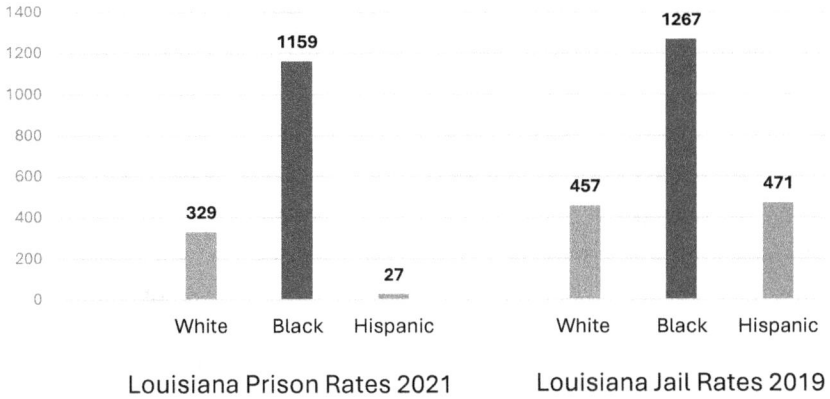

Louisiana Prison Rates 2021   Louisiana Jail Rates 2019

Figure 27: Louisiana Prison and Jail Rates by Race
Source: Prison Policy Initiative 2021

Caddo Parish
2000 and 2010
Incarceration Population
Black vs White

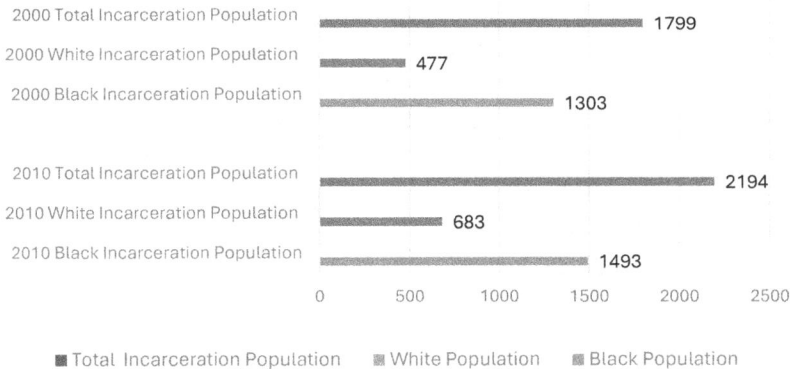

2000 Total Incarceration Population — 1799
2000 White Incarceration Population — 477
2000 Black Incarceration Population — 1303

2010 Total Incarceration Population — 2194
2010 White Incarceration Population — 683
2010 Black Incarceration Population — 1493

■ Total Incarceration Population   ▨ White Population   ▨ Black Population

Figure 28: 2000 and 2010 Caddo Parish Incarceration Black vs. White
Source: Prison Policy Initiative 2018

2.14 IRS INEQUALITIES

The researcher will present information about the Internal Revenue Service (IRS) on how the tax system burdens Black taxpayers and benefits White taxpayers. The researcher will show how this system intends to preserve wealth inequality and racial disparities.

There are a few other insights to focus on besides income alone when referring to income inequalities. For one, it is crucial to focus on wealth because it presents long-term systemic dynamics. Tax expenditures are skillful deception financial tactics for government benefits. Secondly, the receivers of such advantages generally do not perceive themselves as receiving benefits. It is essential to recognize and label advantages, as it is socially common to name disadvantages when race is involved.

Third, the federal tax code is not the only contributor to inequality. While federal tax receipts were 65% of total tax revenues in 2016, states accounted for 20%, and local governmental units accounted for the remaining 15%. Furthermore, local and state governments pay a large share of education, which is a critical factor in the inequality equation. As with the federal tax system, state and local tax systems have exhibited a distinct and systemic shift away from income tax and progressivity towards consumption-based taxes.[259]

There have been links to taxes and inequality according to race. There is a history of racism in the United States and how it connects to wealth. There has been research to support the IRC (Internal Revenue Code) and more notable corroboration in a survey of state tax systems. Many state tax codes, along with the IRC, perform candidly to intensify prior historically based racial wealth imbalance and expand wealth inequality. The Jobs Act of 2017 and recent tax cuts help inflate these effects. Author Richard Reeves references the inequalities between the 20% wealthy in the US and the rest of the population. In this case, the top percentile benefits unequally from many policies from the federal government. These policies helped the top percentile build wealth and pass it on through generations of their families. The wealth passing works with pensions that alleviate offspring of costs associated with caring for parents as they enter senior status, such as tax-preferred 401(k) pensions. Not only do these pensions relieve children of costs associated with caring for aging parents, but they can also use the 529 college tax-deferred accounts to subsidize investment of the human capital of those same offspring. All

259. Strand and Mirkay, "Racialized Tax Inequity," 280–83.

the while, those able to purchase houses in high-class communities with good schools are supported with home interest mortgage deductions purchased with tax-subsidized local property taxes. Tax policy affects the amount of wealth higher-income earners can stockpile yearly and add to their wealth, which causes overall wealth inequality. High-income taxpayers benefit from earning potential disparities, the income adds up over time, and this conclusively affects their accumulation of wealth. For example, with private income such as dividends, earnings, and other incomes, the top 10% of households increased their income from 1963 to 2016 by 90%. The families in the bottom 10% increased their income by less than 10% during the same period. The mass of income among wealthy taxpayers is evident across every state in the United States. The top 5% of households' average income exceeds that of the bottom 20% of households by at least ten times.[260] These numbers give an advantage to high-income taxpayers. According to the US Census Bureau data, Blacks are the only people encountering a median income decrease since 2000. The other races, including Hispanics, Asians, and Whites, experience income gains. The value of tax breaks or tax expenditures grows as household income increases. Higher-income taxpayers are usually not likely to need tax incentives or tax expenditures; however, they are considerably more available to high-income households. These incentives help promote retirement savings, homeownership, and funds for college. On the other spectrum, low-income and moderate-income households receive significantly smaller benefits from tax expenditures for engaging in the same activities. The IRC creates a realized-based system for wealth and income disparities at a greater level. The income gained from higher-income taxpayers enables them to make certain financial investments such as in stocks, bonds, second homes, artwork, and other assets that increase value. These types of capital gains or unrealized gains assist with making contributions to the wealth gap. More than $584 billion (69%) of these unrealized capital gains from investment properties, investment funds, stocks, and businesses were owned by the top 1% of income earners in 2018. Such assets can be held on to by the wealthy if they wish, and the assets increase in value while being protected from taxation. Some commentators have noted,

> America's tax code no longer adheres to the core principle of ability to pay—the idea that taxes should be based on a person's

260. Strand and Mirkay, "Racialized Tax Inequity," 280–83.

capacity to pay taxes. Instead, today's tax code turns that prin-
ciple on its head by letting the wealthiest of the wealthy pay
virtually nothing on their gains.[261]

Recent studies have shown that the Tax Cuts and Jobs Act (TCJA)
has assisted with continuing the increase of the racial wealth divide and
inequality. The TCJA was supposed to reduce tax bills and promote
economic stimulus for middle-income taxpayers but has provided little
benefit instead. However, the TCJA has yielded more considerable tax
benefits for the wealthy. Numerous vital state taxes were administered
in the early twentieth century when Blacks in the South were banned
from casting votes and urban regions were not represented well in various state legislatures. State codes still consequentially affect middle- and
low-income households paying a sizeable share of their income taxes
compared to wealthy households.

States rely heavily on consumption taxes, especially sales tax. Consumption taxes are a significant reason for the inequality in states, which
disproportionately affects low-income families because they spend most
of their income on consumables instead of investments or savings. Since
1970, states have doubled their sales tax, strengthening the inequality
and property taxes, disproportionately affecting middle- and low-income
families versus high-income families.[262]

2.14.1 Blacks/Minorities and Social Security in the United States

African Americans / Blacks and other minorities fare differently under
Social Security versus Whites. Blacks and other minorities have fewer
retirement resources, such as assets and pensions, than Whites. Although Blacks have lower income earnings and shorter life spans, some
benefit from a progressive formula through disability and survivor's
benefits enough to stay above the poverty line.[263] Black citizens' retirement income is mainly received from Social Security because they lack
income-producing assets and other income sources, unlike their White
counterparts. Workers that earn lower wages have a difficult time creating sufficient savings. Compared to African American families in 2016,
White families average about six times more liquid retirement savings.

---

261. Strand and Mirkay, "Racialized Tax Inequity," 283.

262. Strand and Mirkay, "Racialized Tax Inequity," 280–83.

263. Hendley and Bilimoria, "Minorities and Social Security."

Over a lifetime, the average Black man earns $1.8 million, while the average White man averages $2.7 million.[264]

2.14.1.1 Free Labor of Enslaved and Enslaved Life Insurance Policies: The American slave trade gave White Americans over a four hundred–year jump start on obtaining riches and generational wealth for themselves, creating policies to create generational wealth from the deaths of the enslaved Blacks in which White American laws against Blacks made it all possible. There is no cost for services when there is free labor, so Whites built America off of the free labor of Blacks and passed the earnings through generations.

Research indicates that at least sixty other companies were involved in the business at the time. Nearly all of those companies went out of business and/or do not have records detailing their history. In the earliest stage of New York Life's history, the company (named Nautilus Insurance at the time) sold policies on enslaved persons' lives between 1846 to 1848. Two policies were sold in 1849 after the trustees' vote, possibly due to challenges in communicating the decision nationwide.[265] According to Howard Dodson, director of Schomburg Center, some other companies were in this type of business for a much more extended period.[266]

In their archives, Aetna researchers found four such policies dating to the 1850s, as well as a reference to the practice in the company history compiled in 1956.

> "They were insurance policies that were purchased by owners of slaves. If something happened to those slaves, the owner was reimbursed. We're not defending this in any way, please understand, but it was legal at the time," Laberge said.[267]

AIG, Ace USA, and Manhattan Life had ties to insuring enslaved people. One report shows more than four hundred slave owners insuring their enslaved people, and the report detailed an enslaved person being worth twenty thousand dollars in the year 1850.[268] Slave owners were known to torture, mutilate, and kill enslaved people for various reasons

264. National Committee to Preserve Social Security and Medicare, "Black Americans."

265. New York Life, "Common Questions."

266. Morian, "Slave Owners."

267. Slevin, "Aetna's Past."

268. Morian, "Slave Owners."

and to intimidate other enslaved people. This information shows slave owners could collect insurance from the death of the enslaved that they murdered.

2.14.2 Progressive Benefit Formula

Social Security is critical to African Americans / Blacks; its importance presents itself through percentages of poverty rates. Current poverty rates emphasize the importance of Social Security to people of color. Without Social Security, 50.5% of Black Americans would live in poverty; with it, that rate drops to 18.8%. African Americans earn lower incomes than Whites over a lifetime on average. The current progressive formula benefits lower-income earnings, but only a little.[269]

2.14.3 Disability

African Americans / Blacks usually receive Social Security Disability Insurance (DI) benefits because they have a higher rate of disability. The higher benefits-received-to-taxes-paid ratio is received by workers with a higher probability of becoming disabled. Recipients of Social Security DI benefits stop paying payroll taxes earlier than those not receiving DI because their disability benefits automatically turn to retirement benefits when the individual reaches full retirement age. Once this conversion occurs, the individual is treated as a retirement beneficiary, and the payroll tax requirements change accordingly.

Although DI recipients may not be actively employed, Social Security still considers them as part of the workforce. As a result, they continue contributing to Social Security and Medicare through payroll taxes while receiving DI benefits—until those benefits convert to retirement benefits at full retirement age (typically sixty-seven for individuals born in 1960 or later). DI beneficiaries begin to receive benefits before workers who are not disabled. Social Security DI benefits can be paid to both disabled workers and families as well.

269. National Committee to Preserve Social Security and Medicare, "Black Americans."

2.14.4 Life Expectancy

Since African Americans / Blacks have shorter life expectancies, they receive benefits for fewer years than Whites, with regards to workers who live to the age of retirement. African American families are more likely to receive survivor benefits for Social Security because African Americans have a higher chance of living fewer years after retiring or dying before retirement. However, the benefits are not enough to create wealth. African American males receive reduced benefits compared to White males because they are more likely to take early retirement at age sixty-two.[270]

2.14.5 Health in Louisiana and Caddo Parish

According to the United Health Foundation's State Health Rankings for 2004, Louisiana was ranked as the least healthy state in the nation for a combined measure of identified health outcomes and risk factors—a ranking Louisiana has held for fourteen of the last fifteen years.[271]

The inequities in health care include many barriers that hinder access to such care. The included barriers are in the categories of financial, organizational, and sociocultural. Affordability and cost of health care are financial barriers to equity and access. These barriers are prevalent for the unemployed as well as for the employed, and for the uninsured as well as the insured. Being insured is not equivalent to being adequately insured and does not ensure that an individual will receive adequate health care.[272] Medicare, Medicaid, and LaCHIP are government-sponsored insurance programs that target a specific population segment with certain eligibility requirements. Eligible families, adults, and, most importantly, children are commonly not enrolled since they cannot get to a health care provider or find one or properly navigate the health care system, so services become unused. The health issues that people have might start as low-cost preventative care but have the possibility of becoming profoundly serious and expensive before they can access insurance. The most vulnerable are the children dependent on their parents or guardians. In Louisiana, including Caddo Parish, African Americans and their

---

270. National Committee to Preserve Social Security and Medicare, "Black Americans."

271. Louisiana Department of Health, "State Health Rankings."

272. Louisiana Office of Public Health, *2005 Parish Health Profiles*, 122–23.

children are the most vulnerable because of poverty, lower income, education, and lack of ready transportation.

A 2005 survey in Louisiana identified that 21.6% of Louisiana's population was uninsured, including 29.4% of African Americans and 18.1% of Whites. Employed citizens were the most uninsured because of the high cost of health insurance. In 2003, Louisiana had an estimated 11.1% (135,400) uninsured children under nineteen years of age. For Region 7, including Caddo Parish, 15.2% (22,700) are uninsured children and 21.6% (65,300) are uninsured adults. An estimated 14.6% (10,396) of children in Caddo Parish alone were uninsured. In Region 7, 18,600 of 22,700 children were 200% below the federal poverty level. These estimates signify that these children are likely to qualify for either LaCHIP or Medicaid. By facilitating and identifying children's enrollment in the appropriate program, access to health care for these children could increase. For adults in Region 7, 50,000 of 65,000 were below the 200% federal poverty level. This group cannot afford private company insurance or employee-sponsored insurance. In Louisiana's rural residences, for every 4,187 persons, there was only one physician.

Organizational issues include a shortage of primary care providers, adequate capacity, medical specialists, or other health care professionals. Other issues also include lack of facilities such as nursing homes, assisted living centers, and hospitals. Other barriers include transportation and childcare. Transportation can act as a barrier linked to poverty status and income level. Childcare is included because of affordability and availability to bring children to medical appointments.[273]

The inequities that can lead to health care disparities are social-cultural issues constituted by the problem of equity. Barriers that cause confusion can lead to not being treated for a medical condition. Examples of confusion are when to seek care, where to go, not understanding what to do, and ignorance of the health care system. Other barriers that are associated with social-cultural factors are discrimination and confidentiality. Such barriers exist due to race, occupation, spiritual and cultural differences, income disparities, and miscommunication because of language barriers among staff and providers. Moving constantly, lack adequate transportation, not having a phone, having many children, having

273. Louisiana Office of Public Health, *2005 Parish Health Profiles*, 4–165.

disabilities, pregnancy, and having multiple jobs make it difficult to seek preventive medical attention in time.[274]

2.14.6 Birth Numbers in Caddo Parish

Families make up a community, and how healthy the family is will be due to the community's health. Family is a major factor in the social unity of a community, so it is vital that families are kept healthy. To ensure that the communities and families are healthy, they must achieve the goal of preventing low birth rates, infant death, and preterm birth. A mother's poor health or a high-risk pregnancy can negatively affect the weight of a baby. Population growth is a component measured by the birth rate. Planners in communities use birth rates to measure present and future needs of health, childcare, and education.

In Louisiana, the low birth rate percentage for African American infants is twice that of White infants, which also impacts the infant mortality rates in those populations. From 2000 to 2002, 12.2% of babies born in Caddo Parish were of low birth weight, compared to 10.5% in the state and 7.7% nationally.[275] African American births in Caddo Parish were relatively high compared to Whites. After the 3,043 African American births in 2010, in 2011 African American births dropped by more than half of that number, and White birth numbers rose. In the following years, African American births in Caddo Parish never reached numbers in the three thousands nor the two thousands, and White births remained steady.[276] These figures are below.

274. Louisiana Office of Public Health, *2005 Parish Health Profiles*, 4–165.

275. Louisiana Office of Public Health, *2005 Parish Health Profiles*, 130.

276. US Census 2020, "Caddo Parish," 1.

CADDO PARISH
WOMEN'S BIRTH NUMBERS
2010-2019
AFRICAN AMERICAN/BLACK VS WHITE

■ African American/Black   ■ White

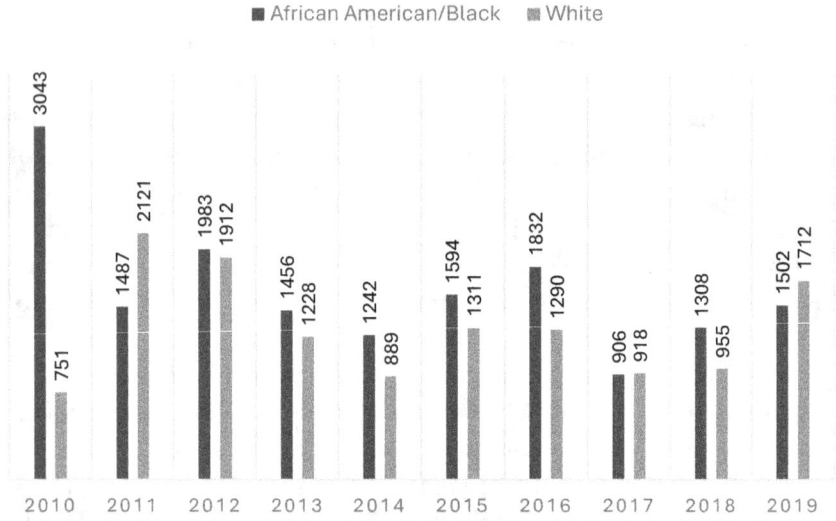

Figure 29: Caddo Parish Women's Numbers Black vs. White 2010-2019
Source: U.S. Census Bureau (2020)

BOSSIER PARISH
WOMEN'S BIRTH NUMBERS
2010-2019
AFRICAN AMERICANS/BLACKS VS WHITES

■ African American/Black   ■ White

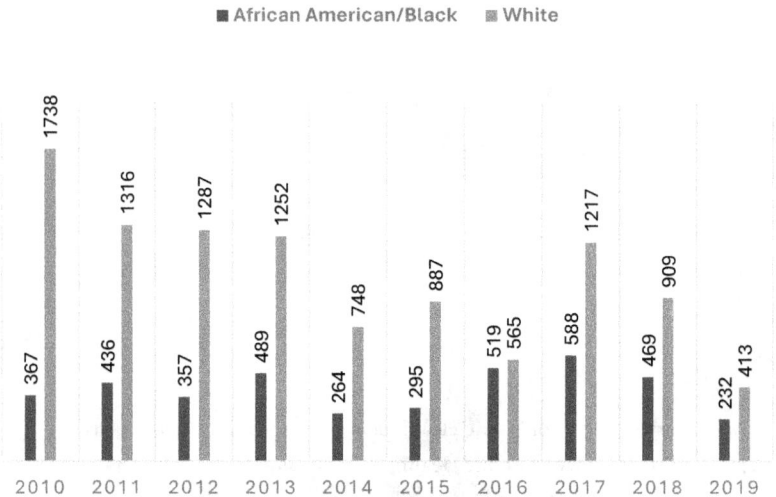

Figure 30: Bossier Parish Women's Birth Black vs. White 2010-2019
Source: U.S. Census Bureau (2020)

2.14.7 Infant Mortality Rate in Caddo Parish

The measurement of deaths within the first year of each one thousand infants who are born in a single year provides the infant mortality rate. A clear indicator of the well-being and health of mothers and children is the mortality rate of infants. In Louisiana, in 2002, the infant mortality rate was 10.2 per 1,000 live births. In Caddo Parish, the rate was 13.5 per 1,000 live births. Infant mortality rates differ by race. In Louisiana, in 2002, the Black infant mortality rate was just over two times the rate for White infants.[277] Between the years of 2015 to 2017 (on average), the infant mortality rate (per 1,000 live births) in Louisiana was highest for Black infants at 11.0, followed by Asian or Pacific Islanders at 5.3 and Whites at 5.2. During the first year of life between 2015 to 2017, Black infants were two times as likely to die.[278]

Louisiana
Infant Mortality Rate By Race 2015-2017 Average
(Rates Per 1,000 Population)

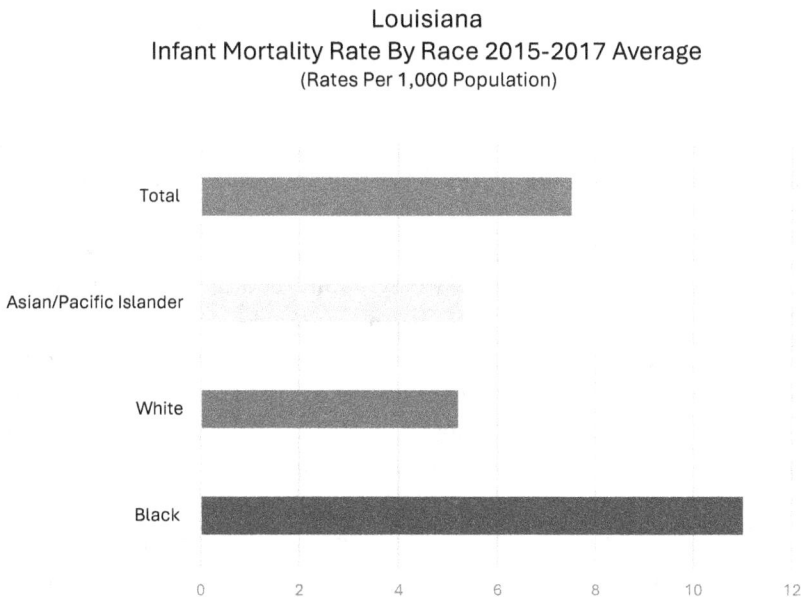

**Figure 31: Louisiana Infant Mortality Rate by Race Average 2015–2017
Source: March of Dimes, Louisiana (2020)**

277. Louisiana Office of Public Health, *2005 Parish Health Profiles*, 130.
278. March of Dimes, "Louisiana Infant Mortality."

2.15 The Black Education Experience in the United States and Louisiana

"Race, Not Just Poverty, Shapes Who Graduates in America" is an article by Matt Barnum. Barnum's studies showed that poverty is not a proxy for race when it comes to academic outcomes. Research shows that White men earn significantly more than Black men, even when Black men come from families that make the same income. Black males who come from wealth are more likely to become poor adults than to stay wealthy, and Black males who start out as poor are more likely to remain in a poor status. There was a study performed in the United States using data on millions of US citizens that were born between the years of 1978 and 1983 called the Equality of Opportunity Project. The project looked at the educational and economic outcomes of the people, and it showed that the impact of racism on Black males was apparent. The study revealed that schools and education policies affecting Black students were associated with significantly lower college attendance rates among this group. The studies highlighted that 78% of White males that were poor graduated high school, and 70% of Black males graduated though their families had the same income as the White graduates'. There were differences in the women too, but not as great as the men.[279]

According to a 2017 article that presented data from a survey from WalletHub, Louisiana has the worst public education system in the United States. It is ranked fifty-first in state rankings for school safety. For reading and math scores, Louisiana was ranked forty-eighth in the nation, and it was ranked forty-third for the highest percentage of injured or threatened high school students.[280] Rankings include several factors: graduation rates, reading test scores, math test scores, dropout rates, schools' inclusion in the US News and World Report list, pupil-teacher ratios, number of certified teachers, advanced placement scores, and ACT and SAT scores. The researchers also pulled data on students' access to illegal drugs, discipline, youth incarcerations, participation in violence, and high school students not attending school because of safety concerns, being threatened, or injured.

Stereotypes and/or attitudes are implicit biases that can affect people's decisions, understanding, and actions unconsciously. Understanding how institutional racism is strengthened by implicit racial bias and

279. Barnum, "Race."
280. McElfresh, "Louisiana's Education."

how other biases determine outcomes in the educational experiences of students in implicit racial bias can help us to better understand how institutional racism and other forms of bias affect the educational experiences of students from disparaged communities. White flight and privatized education have been contributing to the students of color taking over as the majority in the public school system since 2014, and these demographic trends will continue. Currently, schools are now more segregated. Racial achievement gaps continue, and after high school, students of color graduate at a lower percentage from college than White students.[281]

When crimes are broadcasted and reported, the media uses positive photos of the White suspects and incriminating and negative photos of Black citizens. Representation in an unequal manner affects how the masses of society view African American / Black adolescents. There is a terrible underrepresentation of African American students in academic programs of rigor. Only 9% of African American students are in gifted and talented programs, but 16% of African Americans are in the public school system. A third of high schools with the largest percentage of Blacks and Latinos do not offer chemistry courses, and a quarter do not offer Algebra 2. These students obviously will find themselves at a great disadvantage in succeeding in academia. Disciplinary actions in schools get disproportionately placed upon students of color. Disciplinary actions result in in-school detention, suspension, and expulsion, causing students to miss classroom time and fall further behind in their studies. Black children represent 18% of preschool enrollment, and 48% receive more than just one suspension out of school. In grades K–12, African American / Black students are nearly twice as likely to be expelled from school and four times as likely to be put through suspension as White students. White boys received out-of-school suspensions at a rate of 6%, while Black boys received a rate of out-of-school suspension at 20%, which is three times that much as White boys. White girls received out-of-school suspension at a 2% rate while Black girls received out-of-school suspension at 12%, six times as much as White girls.[282]

Researchers have found that there are physiological effects of racism on African American / Black students. The development and learning of Black students get impeded by implicit and explicit bias, as well as open and observable racism. The gaps in academic performance of

281. Johns, "Disrupting Implicit Racial Bias," 2–12.
282. Johns, "Disrupting Implicit Racial Bias," 2–12.

Black students compared to White peers can also explain the stress of racial discrimination. Perceived discrimination and stereotype threats are two sources of race-based stressors of physiological responses that researchers found to lead the body to pump out more stress hormones. Researchers have found that these stressors pump out more into Black and Latino students. Perceived discrimination is the perception that one will be treated differently or unfairly because of race. Stereotype threats relate to the stress of confirming negative expectations about one's racial or ethnic group. Coping mechanisms or psychological responses are biological reactions of students who get impeded by race-based stress. These responses tend to lessen the stress of Black students when undergoing race-based stress. Even though these strategies help reduce race-based stress, these strategies have consequences for academic success. Students tend to cope by devaluing the importance of performing well in school and or the significance as part of their makeup or identity, which then affects academic performance.[283] These same hindrances affect students in Caddo Parish, Louisiana.

Representation of Black teachers for Black students is an issue in the education system. Also, the representation of Black male teachers is very low in the public school system. Females are the majority of teachers in the public school system in the United States. To be more specific, 76% of public school teachers were female, and only 24% were male from 2017 to 2018. Furthermore, only 11% of elementary school teachers in the public school system were male. Regarding race-specific demographics, from 2017 to 2018, 79% of teachers in the public school system were White, which was down from 1999 to 2000 when 86% of teachers were White. From 1999 to 2000 the percentage of Black teachers was 8%, and from 2017 to 2018, it was 7%. The Hispanic percentage slightly rose from 6% in 1999 to 2000 to 9% from 2017 to 2018.[284]

Researchers discovered that Black and Hispanic students show remarkable positive results when having teachers that match their ethnicity and race. In this situation, Black and Hispanic students showed more positive attitudes, higher test scores, higher college attendance, greater graduation rates, and better attendance. These minority teachers also fueled other gains by students of color because teachers of color held their students to expectations of a higher standard. "Representation absolutely

283. Johns, "Disrupting Implicit Racial Bias," 2–12.

284. National Center for Education Statistics, "Public-School Teachers."

matters, and it matters for almost every educational outcome you can think of," said Seth Gershenson, a public policy professor at American University.[285]

According to federal data, there are high turnover rates among Black teachers in the US Federal data further showed that 85% of White teachers return to the school they were in the year before, but in the case of Blacks, the numbers were 78% and for Hispanics, 79%. Experts say that retention among Black and Hispanic teachers is lower because they usually work in urban area schools. Typically, these students are more in need, and teachers become burned out.[286] However, the researcher suggests that the high turnover rate of Black teachers is more than just being burned out due to needy students.

2.15.1 The Black Education Experience in Caddo Parish

To keep a certain group of people in an institutionalized system of racism, Whites must make sure they are not educated properly, or are miseducated. Education is a key element in controlling someone's mind and thought process. Education can be a process of learning something constructive or nonconstructive, and depending on who is teaching a person, it can mean a great deal to someone's thought process. In Caddo Parish, there is a racial divide in the education system. Advanced placement courses and gifted programs are a less likely option for Black students versus their White peers. Blacks are more likely to be expelled or suspended from school. In Caddo Parish, 43% of students in AP courses are Black, and 53% are White. Of students selected for gifted and talented composition, 20% are Black and 67% are White. Of students who receive out-of-school suspension, 80% are Black students and 16% are White students. Of students who receive expulsion, 82% are Black and 15% are White.[287] Black students are also known to be denied certain schools because of their race in Caddo/Bossier Parishes. A case in point was Lemon v. Bossier Parish School Board in Shreveport City Court. The case consisted of Black / African American children who were stationed at Barksdale Air Force Base. The children attended all-Black schools in Bossier Parish and were eligible to attend Bossier Parish public schools. The students lived closer

285. Meckler and Rabinowitz, "America's Schools."
286. Meckler and Rabinowitz, "America's Schools."
287. Groeger et al., "Miseducation."

to the predominantly all-White schools and claimed they were denied admittance to White schools because of race and had to attend school further away. "They allege their applications were denied solely because of their race and the policy, *712 custom and practice of defendants in maintaining segregated schools."[288] Out of all the students in the United States school system, the students who rank the highest for suspensions, expulsions, being kicked out of school, choosing to leave school, having low GPAs, scoring poorly on tests, and having high rates of referral and placement in special education is Black males.[289] Such instances can lead Black students to be unsuccessful, turning toward a life of crime and poverty in their immediate or near future.

Caddo Parish
Advance Placement Courses
African American vs White
2018

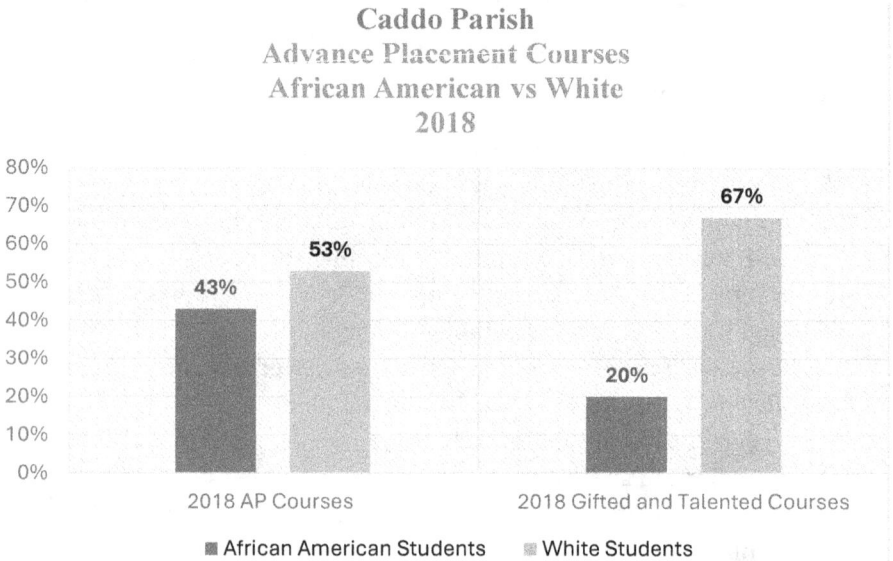

Figure 32: Caddo Parish Advanced Placement African American vs. White
Source: Groeger, Waldman, & Eads, (2018)

288. Lemon v. Bossier Parish School Board, 240 F. Supp. 709 (W. D. La. 1965). https://law.justia.com/cases/federal/district-courts/FSupp/240/709/2145273/.

289. Wyatt, "Black Males in Special Education," 5–12.

Caddo Parish
Suspension and Expulsion Percentage
African American vs White
2018

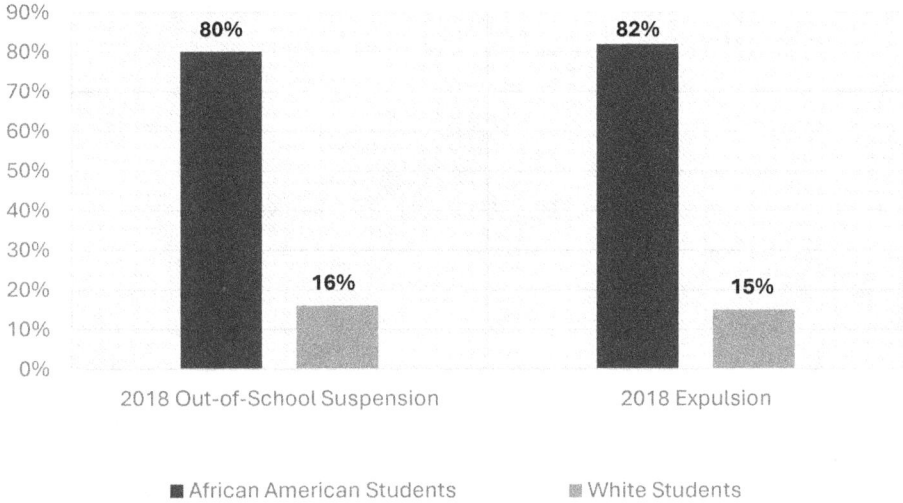

**Figure 33: Caddo Parish Suspension and Expulsion African American vs. White
Source: Groeger, Waldman, & Eads, (2018)**

2.15.2 Education Levels in Caddo Parish

Education levels are important factors depending on what kind of job opportunities and industries will be attracted to a certain area. The proportion of adults with post-secondary degrees, increasingly recognized as the key to obtaining living wage jobs, is below the national average. Disparities between African Americans, 15% of whom hold a post-secondary degree, and Whites, 27.1%, are significant in 2017.[290] In 2019, the disparity was even more significant, with Blacks at 15.4% and Whites at 31.6%. Below are charts showing Caddo and Bossier Parish's 2015–2019 education attainment estimates and the 2015 and 2018 five-year education estimates of African Americans / Blacks versus Whites. The 2015 ACS five-year estimate of education attainment of high school or higher in Caddo Parish for African Americans was 59,538 and for

---

290. Shreveport Metropolitan Planning Commission, "Population," 11.

Whites, 80,338. For bachelor's degree or higher it was 10,906 of African Americans, while Whites were at 27,465. According to the 2018 ACS five-year estimate of education attainment of high school or higher in Caddo Parish, African Americans were 61,543 and Whites were 77,608. For bachelor's degree or higher, African Americans were 10,692 while Whites were 26,684.

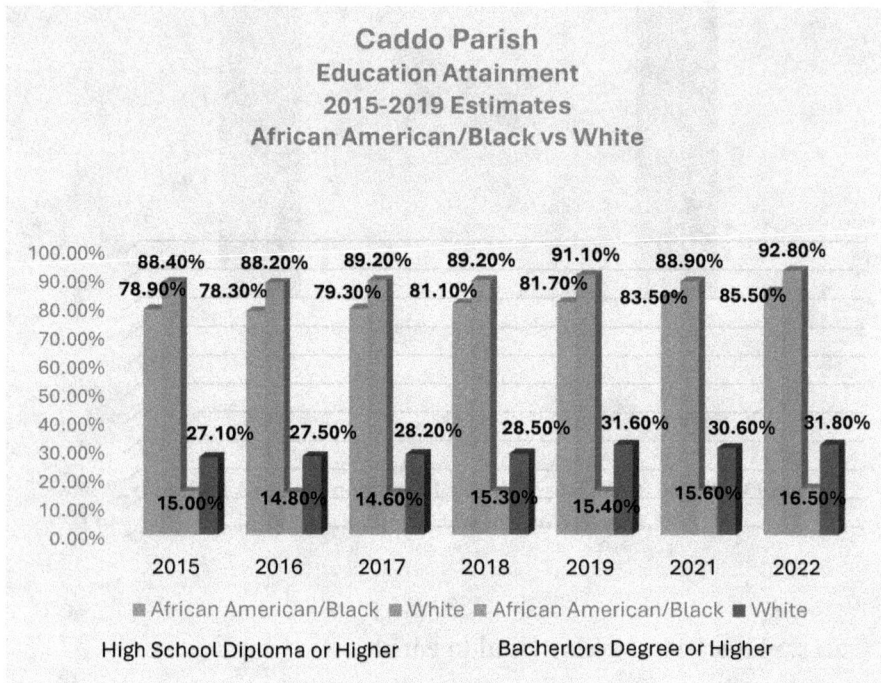

Caddo Parish
Education Attainment
2015-2019 Estimates
African American/Black vs White

High School Diploma or Higher   Bacherlors Degree or Higher

Figure 34

CADDO PARISH
EDUCATION ATTAINMENT
AFRICAN AMERICAN VS WHITE
2015 AND 2018
ACS 5-YEAR ESTIMATES

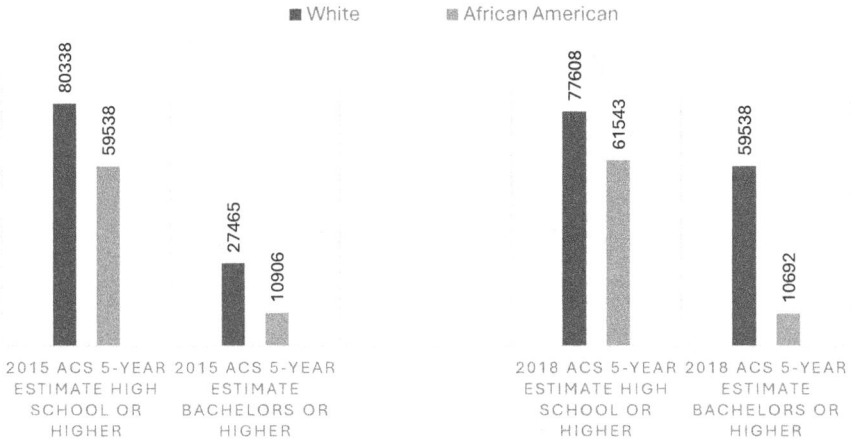

■ White   ▨ African American

80338 59538   27465 10906   77608 61543   59538 10692

| 2015 ACS 5-YEAR ESTIMATE HIGH SCHOOL OR HIGHER | 2015 ACS 5-YEAR ESTIMATE BACHELORS OR HIGHER | 2018 ACS 5-YEAR ESTIMATE HIGH SCHOOL OR HIGHER | 2018 ACS 5-YEAR ESTIMATE BACHELORS OR HIGHER |

Figure 35: 2015 and 2018 5-Year Estimates Caddo Parish Education Attainment
Source: U.S. Census Bureau, (2020)

To have a comparison, the researcher compares the Caddo Parish data to Bossier Parish data from the 2010 to 2019 education attainment estimates and the ACS five-year education attainment estimates. According to the 2015 ACS five-year estimate of education attainment of high school or higher in Bossier Parish, African Americans were at 12,749 and Whites were 55,036. For the bachelor's degree or higher, African Americans were at 2,746 while Whites were 16,804. According to the 2018 ACS five-year estimate of education attainment of high school or higher in Bossier Parish, African Americans were 14,271 and Whites were 56,595. Bachelor's degree or higher for African Americans was 3,343 while Whites were 16,095.

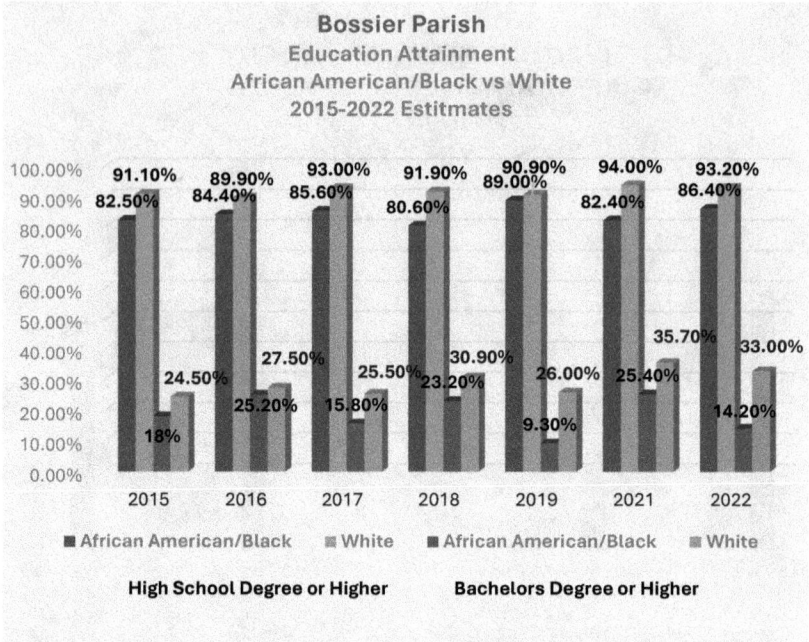

Figure 36: Bossier Parish Education Attainment Black vs. White 2015–2019
Source: U.S. Census Bureau, (2020)

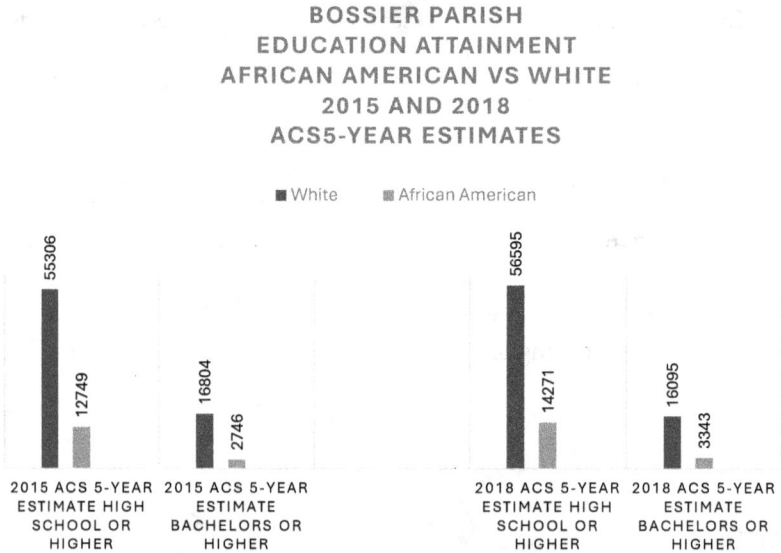

Figure 37: 2015 and 2018 5-Year Estimates Bossier Parish Education Attainment
Source: U.S. Census Bureau, (2020)

CHAPTER 3

Methodology and Research Design

3.1 RESEARCH METHODOLOGY

POVERTY IS AN UNACCEPTABLY low-standard way of life that is a complex human phenomenon. It has multiple causes, manifestations, and dimensions. This chapter outlines the methodology implemented in my study of Caddo Parish. The researcher will investigate the spatial relationships with the factors affecting African American / Black poverty in Caddo Parish and compare those relationships with neighboring Bossier Parish. Analyzing poverty from many disciplines results in a steady pattern of forming questions regarding this issue. Sometimes the questions asked are out of curiosity and being puzzled, but quite frequently, questions are to find solutions to the poverty issue. Qualitative research is good for gathering social science data/research and physical observation of the study area. That is why the researcher wanted to use this method. Qualitative methods can pose as complementary and or alternatives to quantitative methods or approaches. Although this is a qualitative study, quantitative data will be in the secondary data findings provided. The quantitative method data will provide geographical visualizations, descriptive statistics, and the use of GIS (Geographic Information Systems) for spatial and statistical analysis. Quantitative methods help present answers only to certain questions regarding poverty and will only provide partial information about poverty. The researcher thinks that a single approach to appraising poverty can capture all the necessary aspects of the poverty phenomenon.[1] Providing quantitative data in this qualitative research method through data analysis would help strengthen a useful comprehension and firmer understanding of poverty, particularly in Caddo Parish. This chapter will detail the research methods of the researcher's choice and the rationale behind them. It will explain using spatial analysis data for the research and the researcher's quantitative methods. Both methods will help the researcher and readers comprehend and relate. It will help validate the study and improve its reliability.

3.2 STUDY AREA

The parish of Caddo (French: *Paroisse de Caddo*) is in the northwest area of the state of Louisiana with the coordinates of latitude 32°34'48.00" N and longitude −93°52'48.00" W.[2] Caddo Parish received its name from the Caddo Native Americans who once populated the area. However, most of them experienced removal from the area in the 1830s. The parish was established on January 18, 1838, carved from Natchitoches Parish.[3] The researcher will compare variables in Caddo Parish to Bossier Parish, the neighboring parish, with African Americans and White Americans in these parishes. Shreveport City and Bossier City are the two largest cities in both parishes, referred to as the "Twin Cities" because they are two cities in neighboring parishes separated by the Red River but connected by numerous bridges. The data will be gathered from census tracts and downloaded from the share file from the US Census Bureau that will concentrate on Caddo and Bossier Parish. There are sixty-four census tracts in the parishes highlighted in GIS mapping. Caddo Parish is the fourth largest populated parish in Louisiana. The core of Caddo Parish, developed by planters of cotton plantations with thousands of African American enslaved people who labored them, borders Texas and Arkansas. During the American Civil War, Shreveport was the capital of Louisiana from 1863 to 1865.[4] Caddo Parish's population in 1990 was 248,253 and has shrunk to 240,204.[5] According to the US Census Bureau, Caddo

1. Odhiambo et al., *Quantitative and Qualitative Methods*, 15–54.
2. Latitude, "Caddo Parish."
3. FamilySearch, "Caddo Parish."
4. Joiner and Tripp, "Major Confederate Capital."
5. US Census of Housing 1990, "Population and Housing," 220; SuburbanStats, "Caddo Parish Louisiana Population."

Parish has a total area of 937 square miles (2,430 km²), of which 978 square miles (2,530 km²) is land and 58 square miles (150 km²) is water (6.2%). The parish of Caddo covers 852 square miles, with its borders being Arkansas to the north, the Red River to the east, Texas to the west, and DeSoto Parish to the south in the northwest area of Louisiana. Part of the Red River National Wildlife Refuge is in this parish.[6]

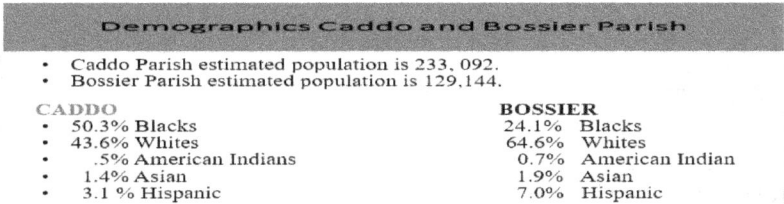

Demographics Caddo and Bossier Parish

- Caddo Parish estimated population is 233,092.
- Bossier Parish estimated population is 129,144.

CADDO		BOSSIER	
•	50.3% Blacks	24.1%	Blacks
•	43.6% Whites	64.6%	Whites
•	.5% American Indians	0.7%	American Indian
•	1.4% Asian	1.9%	Asian
•	3.1 % Hispanic	7.0%	Hispanic

Figure 38: 2021 Demographics Caddo and Bossier Parish
Source: U.S. Census Bureau, (2021)

6. E-Reference Desk, "Caddo Parish."

Demographics			
	2010 Census	2019 Estimate	2024 Estimate
Population	254,969	243,505	239,627
Households	102,139	99,201	98,185
Median Age (2019)	37.6		
5-Year Population Growth Projection (2024)	(1.59%)		
Race (2019 Estimate)			
White	45.54%		
African American	49.71%		
American Indian or Alaska Native	0.45%		
Asian	1.35%		
Other	2.95%		
Income (2019 Estimate)			
Median Household Income	$39,177		
Average Household Income	$61,399		
Educational Attainment (2019 Estimate)			
Some High School, No Diploma	9.80%		
High School Graduate	34.20%		
Some College or Associate Degree	29.37%		
Bachelor's Degree	13.99%		
Master's, Professional or Doctorate	8.57%		
Average Weekly Wage (Q1 2019)			
Average Weekly Wage	$859		

Figure 39: Socio-Demographic Characteristics of Caddo Parish
Source: NLEP, (2019)

Caddo Parish, LA Detailed Education Attainment Breakout by Race (Age 25+)

Education	White	Black	American Indian	Asian	Native Hawaiian	Hispanic
Bachelor's degree or higher	31.3%	14.2%	19.2%	49.7%	9.6%	22.0%
High school graduate or GED	29.0%	39.2%	39.1%	15.6%	16.4%	29.0%
Less than high school diploma	8.9%	18.2%	8.2%	17.1%	50.7%	25.7%
Some college or associate's degree	30.8%	28.4%	33.6%	17.6%	23.3%	23.2%

Figure 40: Education Attainment by Race
Source: (Town Charts, n.d.)

3.2.1 Analysis of Caddo Parish

Caddo Parish communities consist of Belcher, Blanchard, Dixie, Gilliam, Greenwood, Hosston, Ida, Mooringsport, Oil City, Rodessa, Shreveport-Parish Seat, and Vivian. Caddo Parish is connected globally by air service, interstates, rails, a multimodal transportation system of ports and US highways. Major interstates are I-20, I-49, I-220, and (planned) I-69. Major highways are US 71, US 79, US 80, US 171, LA 1, and LA 2. The ports consist of the Port of Shreveport-Bossier (five miles), Red River Port (forty-eight miles), Natchitoches Port (seventy miles), and Ouachita Terminals (ninety-nine miles). Caddo's Class 1 railroads are Kansas City Railroad (KCS), Union Parish (UP), Burlington Northern and Santa Fe (BNSF; uses UP tracks), and its air service Shreveport Regional Airport (8.2 miles).[7]

The Bureau of Labor Statistics (BLS) conducts the Quarterly Census of Employment and Wages (QCEW) for each parish (county) and state in the country. The number of retail businesses in Caddo Parish consisted of 1,197. The total number of restaurants is 384. Supermarkets and other grocery stores are at 35. Caddo and Bossier combined had 53 multi-tenant retail centers in 2015, which include regional malls, community shopping centers, neighborhood shopping centers, specialty shopping centers, strip and convenience shopping centers, and a total of 57 in 2018.[8] In the Shreveport area, which includes the Bossier City area, there are 40 different banks, three dozen credit unions, and various financial institutions. Some of the most notable banks are Regions Bank, Farmers Bank & Trust, Guaranty Bank & Trust, Barksdale Federal Credit Union, JP Morgan Chase Bank, Citizens National Bank, Sabine State Bank, and Trust Company. In the Shreveport area, which includes Bossier City, there are approximately 520 branches from 45 credit unions and 90 banks, including various financial institutions. One of the longest-standing banks in Caddo Parish is the Texas Heritage National Bank, established in 1892. Shreveport City has 69 bank branches. The most popular is Regions Bank, with 10 banks. JP Morgan Chase, National Association, and Capital One have 9.[9]

---

7. North Louisiana Economic Partnership, "North Louisiana."

8. TMG Consulting, "Commercial Market Assessment," 4; Stirling Properties, *Retail Market Survey* (2015), 2–21; Stirling Properties, *Retail Market Survey* (2018), 3–20.

9. Shreveport Area, "Banking."

In Caddo Parish, the most common sectors of employment are health care and social assistance, mining (oil and gas), retail, casino entertainment, and accommodations and food services. Some residents that live in Caddo Parish may work in another city because Caddo Parish sits on the border of Texas and Arkansas. Shreveport's greatest economic strengths are education, professional and technical services, and education, all considered knowledge-intensive industries. As the region's central city, it attracts economic activities that benefit from a central location and direct interactions, such as health care, media, professional services, finance, culture and entertainment, education, and in some cases, retail.[10]

Caddo Parish Public Schools is the largest employer, Willis-Knighton Health System is the second highest ranked employer with 6,732 employees, Ochsner LSU Health Shreveport Academic Medical Center is the third with 2,673, and LSU Health Service Centers is the fourth highest with 2,762 employees in the Shreveport-Bossier metropolitan area. Sam's Town Casino and Eldorado Resort Casino are the tenth and eleventh top employers; however, they are amusement, gambling, and recreation for locals and tourists. Caddo Parish has sixty-four schools with 38,199 students. Caddo Parish has forty elementary schools, sixteen middle schools, and fifteen high schools.

Shreveport City universities and colleges are Centenary College, Southern University-Shreveport, and LSU-Shreveport Medical School. Caddo Parish's neighboring parishes have universities and colleges in and near northwest Louisiana. Bossier Colleges consist of Bossier Parish Community College. In Grambling, Louisiana, there is Grambling State University. The universities in Monroe are the University of Louisiana at Monroe and Edward Via College of Osteopathic Medicine. Close to Monroe is Louisiana Tech University in Ruston, Louisiana. Northwestern State University is also in Natchitoches, Louisiana, and Northwest Louisiana Technical Community College is a public technical college in Minden, Louisiana.[11]

Shreveport is currently the third largest city in Louisiana, and Lafayette is the fifth largest city in Louisiana with almost 50,000 less in

10. North Louisiana Economic Partnership, "North Louisiana"; Shaw Environmental and Infrastructure, *Caddo Parish*, 3–15; Shreveport/Caddo Metropolitan Planning Commission, *Shreveport-Bossier*, 1.

11. North Louisiana Economic Partnership, "North Louisiana"; US News and World Report, "Caddo Parish."

population. However, Lafayette has ninety-five banks compared to sixty-nine bank branches in Shreveport.[12]

3.2.2 Analysis of Bossier Parish

Bossier Parish communities consist of Bossier City, Benton, Haughton, and Plain Dealing. Bossier Parish neighbors Caddo Parish and connects to the same air service, interstates, rails, multimodal transportation system of ports, and US highways as Caddo Parish. A large section of the Bossier area population commutes to Shreveport daily. Bossier Parish has a total area of 867 square miles (2,250 km²), of which 840 square miles (2,200 km²) is land and 27 square miles (70 km²) is water (3.1%). Several bridges crossing the Red River from the Shreveport area to Bossier City are critical to this community's livelihood. The closest bridges to the Central Business District (CBD) that connect Shreveport to Bossier City are the Texas Street Bridge and the I-20 Red River Bridge, then slightly south is the Westgate / Shreveport Barksdale Highway Bridge and slightly north is the Interstate 220 Bridge.[13]

From the QCEW from the Bureau of Labor Statistics (BLS), the number of retail businesses in Bossier Parish consisted of 577. The total number of restaurants is 199. Supermarkets and other grocery stores are at 19. The Bossier City labor force primarily consists of management, professional and related occupations, and sales and office occupations. The major employers of Bossier Parish are the Barksdale Air Force Base, Bossier Parish School Board, Horseshoe Bossier Casino, Diamond Jack Casino and Resort, State of Louisiana Civil Service, Margaritaville Resort Casino, and Boomtown Bossier City.[14] Bossier Parish has twenty-three elementary schools, thirteen middle schools, and seven high schools with 22,589 students.[15] Bossier colleges consist of Bossier Parish Community College. Bossier Parish's neighboring parishes have universities and colleges in and near northwest Louisiana. Shreveport City universities and colleges are Centenary College, Southern University-Shreveport, and LSU-Shreveport Medical School. In Grambling, Louisiana, there is Grambling State University. The universities in Monroe are the

12. Bank Map, "Lafayette, LA"; Shreveport Area, "Banking."

13. Bossier City Metropolitan Planning Commission, "Proceedings," 13.

14. Bossier Parish Police Jury, "About Bossier Parish"; TMG Consulting, "Commercial Market Assessment," 4.

15. US News and World Report, "Caddo Parish."

University of Louisiana at Monroe and the Edward Via College of Osteopathic Medicine. Close to Monroe is Louisiana Tech University in Ruston, Louisiana. Northwestern State University is also in Natchitoches, Louisiana, and Northwest Louisiana Technical Community College is a public technical college in Minden, Louisiana. As mentioned before, in the Shreveport area, which includes Bossier, there are approximately five hundred and twenty branches from forty-five credit unions and ninety banks, including various financial institutions. There are thirty-four total banks in the city of Bossier.[16]

3.3 RATIONALE FOR SELECTING QUALITATIVE METHOD

The researcher preferred using the qualitative research method to make meaningful and sound decisions to inform audiences regarding gathered data through research. In academia and other platforms, research can be indispensable or invaluable if one prefers to contribute to informed decision-making that will assist in making strategic goals and creating policy. Qualitative research is more about capturing people's emotions and options and not so much about number crunching. In the qualitative research method, the researcher will use the data collection methods of observation, interviews, and secondary data.

The researcher will use the systematic observation research method to look at the typical environment of the study area and subjects. Applying the observation provides details that participants may deem important or not disclosed during interviews.

Interviews provide information from participants through conversation-based inquiries where questions get asked and responses follow. Interviews tend to be structured to adhere to the researcher's purpose.

Secondary data or existing documents is a qualitative data collection method. It involves extracting significant and meaningful data from existing documents. The collector will be using a method called content analysis, or qualitative analysis method, for the analysis. Existing documents include books, government records, personal sources, journals, websites, newspapers, etc.[17]

16. North Louisiana Economic Partnership, "North Louisiana"; Bossier Parish Police Jury, "About Bossier Parish"; Bank Map, "Bossier City, LA."

17. Vaughan, "Qualitative Research"; Ostlund et al., "Combining Qualitative and Quantitative"; Tashakkori and Creswell, "Mixed Methods."

Document analysis is a part of qualitative research. Its implementation is a crucial part of this study. The document analysis will require electronic (Internet-transmitted and computer-based) and printed material. Document analysis as a research method is significant in qualitative case studies and/or intensive studies constructing plentiful descriptions of a single event, program, organization, or phenomenon. Documents provide ways of tracking development and change. Background information, historical insight, and data drawn from documents during interviews can bring follow-up or new interview questions.[18]

3.3.0.1 Rationale for Secondary Data—Quantitative Research Method Spatial Analysis: In poverty research, quantitative appraisals are one of the many specialized fields. The poverty phenomenon is complex and requires specialized, complex methods to research it. The quantitative approach is useful for collecting numerical data, which is analyzed using statistics more often and other mathematical practices.[19] The quantitative method will provide geographical visualizations, descriptive statistics, and the use of GIS (Geographic Information Systems) for spatial and statistical analysis. Two types of mixing suggestions get mentioned when it comes to poverty appraisals: simultaneous and sequential. The researcher will be using simultaneous mixing because many researchers have considered a combination of qualitative and quantitative methods to be extremely effective compared to other methods of poverty analysis.[20]

3.3.1 Qualitative Research Method: Advantages and Disadvantages

Qualitative research is good for gathering social science data/research and physical observation of the study area. That is why the researcher wanted to use this method. Qualitative methods pose complementary alternatives to quantitative methods or approaches. The qualitative method is a research method that gains comprehension of the human aspect of a phenomenon and the underlying beliefs, opinions, emotions, and motivations of a person in an exploratory manner. Furthermore, this tactic

18. Bowen, "Document Analysis."

19. Aliaga and Gunderson, *Interactive Statistics*, 75–263; Wyse, "What Is the Difference."

20. Hughes, "Mixed Methods Research"; Kanbur, "Q-Squared?"

is good for developing research questions with various hypotheses and ideas.[21]

In qualitative research, the structure can be based on available or incoming data and can be fluid. Qualitative research can adapt to the quality of data/information being collected rather than following a specific data collection process, information reporting, and patterns of question. The research can quickly switch gears and pursue other data in a different direction if the current data does not supply the results wanted. This system provides more key clues collection in this process regarding any subject, and the researcher will not be limited to a confined and frequently self-fulfilling point of view.

In the qualitative method, the researcher will focus more on observation as a systematic research method and use existing documents, which are called secondary data. The researcher looks at their subject's activity in their particular environment. Using observation supplies direct information regarding your research. The observation technique participants can bring forth information that participants may not look at as important during focus groups/interviews, or not think to reveal.

Using secondary data is extracting existing documents from relevant data. The process of analyzing previously collected data using qualitative methods is known as content analysis. The content analysis uses information extracted from existing documents, including journals, various published or unpublished data, emails, historical and statistical documents, magazines, newspapers, books, etc.

There are disadvantages to using qualitative research. One clear disadvantage is that there needs to be more statistical representation, meaning responses are not measured because they are perspective-based.

The influence of the researcher during the collection of the data can have a negative effect on the research. The observations and skills of the researcher in the qualitative method will determine the quality of the research collected. The information collected could be high quality or subpar. If the researcher has a biased perspective, then their point of view will be present in the influence of the data collected and the outcome. The researcher could make any affirmation and then use their partiality through qualitative research to prove their point. So, there must be

21. Mack et al., *Qualitative Research Methods*, 5–49.

controls in place to prevent such possible issues, biases, and integrity concerns.[22]

3.4 GEOGRAPHICAL INFORMATION SYSTEMS

Geographic Information System (GIS) is a framework for analyzing, managing, and gathering data. GIS integrates many types of data and can do so because it is a system that is rooted in the science of geography. A picture tells a thousand words, and a map tells a thousand pictures. GIS organizes and analyzes spatial location layers using 3D scenes and maps to relate the information to visualizations. GIS reveals deeper insights into data, such as relationships, situations, and patterns, helping users make intelligent decisions using these unique capabilities. Individuals can use GIS to illuminate issues driven by geography. GIS can forecast traffic and transportation patterns based on land use. GIS can set spatial analysis priorities by identifying problem areas in a geographical location. GIS assists with providing insight into data that spreadsheets might look over. The GIS maps can measure employment losses or growth in different industries and quantify local competitive advantage.[23] Governments and other organizations are beginning to use the GIS system to investigate and combat the effects of poverty. Creating ways to combat social problems, aid operations, maximize agriculture yields, distribute resources, and present the effects of natural disasters on poverty is major.

Furthermore, GIS can highlight geographical areas to show the population of races, education attainment, income levels, homelessness, and poverty, zooming in on census block groups and census tracts. Implementing policy informedly using the visual appeal of creating maps to show understandable data is very tangible. It also allows users to perform sensitivity analyses, where parameters can easily be changed and quickly get results.[24]

3.5 SPATIAL ANALYSIS

Spatial analytical tools identify the correlations among factors influencing rural poverty, the spatial relationship of poverty, and the possible

22. Vaughan, "Qualitative Research"; Gaille, "Qualitative Research."
23. ESRI, "What Is GIS."
24. Jerrett et al., "GIS Environmental Justice Analysis."

use of such numerical techniques as suggestions to improve the poverty alleviation program. In GIS, spatial statistical techniques can quantify notable spatial patterns—for example, concentrated poverty rates and spatial outliers. Spatial analysis can reveal stark and significant patterns of poverty. It can show distinctions between the south and the north demarcation of high versus low poverty concentrations. It can further show isolated pockets and low to high poverty within locations in which predominant rates of poverty are opposite. These insights are extremely useful. They explain in detail the essential process of creating such spatial patterns that result in concentrated poverty and wealth.

3.6 SPATIAL AUTOCORRELATION

Spatial autocorrelation refers to the degree to which attributes or values at some place on the earth's surface have similar attributes or values of nearby locations. Accounting for the spatial locations of each data observation in conjunction with the observation data value at each location is essential. Spatial autocorrelation, or spatial structure, is a complementary method for exploring the spatial values of the research data set. The researcher is considering using statistical analysis combining autocorrelation in targeting the geographical poverty areas in Caddo Parish, where the methods are explainable and transparent. The researcher will also combine methods with GIS to identify factors in Caddo Parish associated with poverty and how they are spatially related.[25]

3.7 Statistical Analysis

Statistical analysis is the science of exploring, collecting, and presenting large amounts of data to uncover and discover underlying trends and patterns. To become more scientific regarding options and decisions in research, government, and industry, statistics are applied daily for optimal results. The purpose of statistical analysis is to determine objectively the directions of the relationships between variables researched, whether positive or negative in the outcome, to know if the relationships are significant and to know the degree of the relationship. Observed with GIS,

25. Thonddara, "Using GIS," 157–59; Holt, "Topography of Poverty," 3–7.

the outcomes are significant in the study to support the validity of the conclusion.[26]

3.8 DIRECT OBSERVATION

There are commonly new dimensions of understanding that can add to a case study by direct observation. Direct observation is a source that has value when collecting data. Direct observation gives a researcher real-time event placement in which activities and events can be observed systematically.[27] The researcher can drive from a suburb or rural area to a CBD to see how long a route could take. The researcher can call or visit a public transportation venue to see if the researcher can get good service, obtain correct information, and see where the provided public transportation routes are traveled.

3.9 INTERVIEWS

The researcher will interview ten individuals who live in Caddo Parish and Bossier Parish who can provide insight into the impact of systemic racism in the area. The researcher has a key informant who will provide him with the names of these individuals. Snowball sampling will provide additional individuals for interviews for the research project. Snowball sampling is a non-probability sampling method often employed in field research whereby each person interviewed may be used or asked to suggest additional people for interviewing.

There are advantages to conducting interviews and disadvantages to conducting interviews. In most reference sources, the authors say "strengths versus weaknesses" instead of "advantages versus disadvantages."

The strengths that interviews provide are being detail oriented and sharing a rich new perspective or insight. An interview allows in-depth exploration; they also minimize errors of misrepresentation and misinterpretation due to the possibility of rephrasing, emphasizing, and repeating, due to their greater flexibility. Some interviews can be convenient if done over the phone or via Zoom. In-person interviews allow the

26. SAS, "Statistical Analysis."
27. Yin, *Design and Methods*, 3–106.

interviewer to observe nonverbal responses, probe for more questions, and ask for other sources.

Weaknesses of interviews can come from the actual interviewer, by becoming biased, subjective, and lacking interviewing skills. Therefore, the interviewer must work carefully to ensure that the reliability and validity of the interview data is fair. Interviews require financial resources and consume time, so highly skilled interviewers are needed. Interviews are flexible and sometimes can also be unreliable. If the interviews are in person, the interviewer has to hustle to meet the interviewee when time permits.[28]

3.10 DATA COLLECTION METHOD (SECONDARY DATA)

The researcher will be using observational methods and document analysis. Combining two or more data collection methods enhances the credibility of the study. The researcher will collect lots of literature as part of the study to incorporate the data into the research. The researcher will rely heavily on previous studies for sources of data for the description and interpretation of data. The analytic procedure entails selecting findings and appraising and synthesizing data contained in documents. Document analysis yields data excerpts, entire passages, or quotations which are then organized into categories, case examples, and major themes, specifically through content analysis. Documents that may be used for systematic evaluation as part of a study take a variety of forms. These documents include journals, background papers, agendas, attendance registers, minutes of meetings, manuals, books and brochures, journals, maps, charts, newspapers, press releases, program proposals, and summaries, organizational or institutional reports, survey data, and various public records.[29]

28. Hofisi et al., "Critiquing Interviewing"; Babbie, *Practice of Social Research*, 124–62.

29. Bowen, "Document Analysis."

CHAPTER 4

Results and Discussion

INTRODUCTION

THE OBJECTIVE OF THIS study is to determine if African Americans are being marginalized by certain factors in a systemic and unjust situation that keeps them in a vulnerable situation of poverty in Caddo Parish and Bossier Parish, Louisiana. The researcher compared African American / Black to White data to present the difference in each group. The researcher performed the data collection by secondary data, observation, and interviews. The major factors in this study are educational attainment (i.e., high school or higher, bachelor's or higher, and professional degrees), unemployment (hourly jobs versus salary jobs), income, homeownership, renter status, cost of living, transportation, and incarceration. Furthermore, the researcher wanted to understand the relationship between poverty and the harmful effects of urbanization and politics in the study area. The purpose of this chapter is to examine and analyze the use of the research methodology of qualitative research presented in earlier chapters. To get answers to the researcher's theory, the researcher asked the following research questions.

Research Question #1:   Is there a relationship between poverty due to the negative effects of urbanization and politics?

Research Question #2:   Is there a relationship between systemic racism, poverty, urbanization, and politics, and do these relationships affect lack of African American wealth in the Caddo Parish?

Research Question #3:   Is there a comparison between African American versus White poverty in Caddo Parish and African American versus White poverty in neighboring Bossier Parish?

Research Question #4:   Is there a relationship between population trends and job opportunities in Caddo Parish?

4.1 RESEARCH QUESTION ONE

Is there a relationship between poverty due to the negative effects of urbanization and politics?

First, understand that urbanization is caused when there are mass movements of populations from rural to urban settings in which this movement can trigger unplanned urban growth. The unplanned growth generates poor infrastructures such as housing and transportation and subpar water, sanitation, and health care services. Urbanization can lead to significant inequalities and health problems, marginalizing impoverished people. Greater poverty can be a result of intense urban growth or urbanization.[1]

Caddo Parish is unique when it comes to urbanization. Caddo Parish has 80.7% of its population migrated to Shreveport, the largest city. There has been a migration of the young population out of Shreveport for various reasons, but even with the population decline, Caddo's largest population is in Shreveport. African Americans comprise 57.09% of the population and Whites 37.2% in Shreveport. According to the US census, Caddo Parish poverty among African Americans is 34.01% and 12.19% among Whites. Most recent data shows Black poverty in Shreveport City is 35.19% for African Americans and 11.62% for Whites. With the majority of Caddo Parish's population living in Shreveport, the researcher will analyze the negative effects of urbanization occurring there. Bossier City, populated with 48.6% of Bossier Parish's population, is nearly half of Bossier Parish's population. In Bossier City, African Americans represent

1. Kuddus et al., "Urbanization," 1.

28.2% of the residents, and Whites represent 57.8%. In Bossier Parish, the White population outnumbers the Black population. However, Black poverty is 33.05%, much higher than White poverty at 11.06%. Black poverty in Bossier Parish has been at a higher percentage than Whites, in the double digits, for at least the past ten years. In 2011, Black poverty was over 29% higher than White poverty.[2]

Caddo Parish and Bossier Parish, which include the Shreveport–Bossier City metropolitan area, have issues of poverty, infrastructure, affordable housing, inadequate housing, higher paying jobs, health problems, and crime. The accumulation of these problems associated with urbanization leads the researcher to believe that urban growth in this area assisted in creating such disparities. Furthermore, these factors affect the African American community more than Whites. Knowing that Caddo Parish's and Bossier Parish's two largest cities are connected, they share some of the same infrastructure issues. The researcher will retouch on the findings that brought him to the conclusion that urbanization and politics have assisted in producing and are keeping Blacks in poverty in Caddo Parish and Bossier Parish.

The researcher established that urbanization could be a major factor in producing poverty. Also, the researcher has established that the Shreveport–Bossier City metropolitan area contains most of both parishes' populations. When there is a lack of jobs and resources in urban areas, crime will follow. The violent crime rate in the Shreveport–Bossier City metro area stands at 683 per 100,000—higher than in the vast majority of US metropolitan areas.[3] The groups affected the most, both in the parishes and in the metropolitan area, are the African American / Black residents, and the researcher will explain his reasoning.

This section covers infrastructure and transportation effects. Observing Shreveport from a researcher's lens suggests some infrastructure needs. Such infrastructure work needed in the area was recognized in the Caddo Parish 2030 Master Plan. One area of concern is street-network sprawl. Street-network sprawl is a way to measure urban sprawl worldwide through the connectedness of the streets. Less sprawl means more connected, more walkable streets. New York City's grid is an example of a well-connected streets system due to being more walkable and able to

2. US Census 2020, "Caddo Parish," 1; US Census 2021, "Caddo Parish," 1; World Population Review 2022, "Caddo Parish," 1; US Census 2020, "Bossier Parish," 1; US Census 2021, "Bossier Parish," 1; World Population Review 2022, "Bossier Parish," 1.

3. Stebbins and Comen, "Worst Cities to Live In."

be served by public transit. The Street Network Disconnectedness Index or SNDi measures street-network sprawl or disconnectedness. SNDi quantifies how connected the street network is. SNDi captures nodal degree, dendricity (the tree-likeness of the street network), circuity (the ratio of the distance by road to the straight-line distance of two locations on the street network), and sinuosity (the amount of curve of a street). A higher SDNi means fewer connected streets or more sprawl. Out of 10,137 cities measured, half of the cities fall between 1.08 to 3.25, and the average is 2.25. The permanency of street network connectivity affects the environmental footprint and the livability of cities in the future. The more connected the streets are, the more residents tend to walk more and drive less. Well-connected street networks are related to a better environment, outcomes for health, social integration, sustainable consumption, and equity. For development practices of street construction from 2001 to 2014 in Louisiana, Shreveport ranked 2nd out of the six most street-network disconnected cities and has held that same ranking since 1975. As of 2015, out of 315 US cities, Shreveport is ranked 205th most disconnected. In 2014, the most disconnected street network in the United was Roswell, Georgia, with an SDNi of 8.19 (highly disconnected); the most connected was San Angelo, Texas, with an SDNi of 0.49; and Shreveport scored 2.62 in the overall level of street-network sprawl. This score placed Shreveport in the 40th to 60th percentile of disconnectedness.[4]

---

4. SNDi Trends, "Street-Network Sprawl." Both figures from SNDi Trends reprinted with permission.

Figure 41: SNDi of Street Network Additions in Shreveport

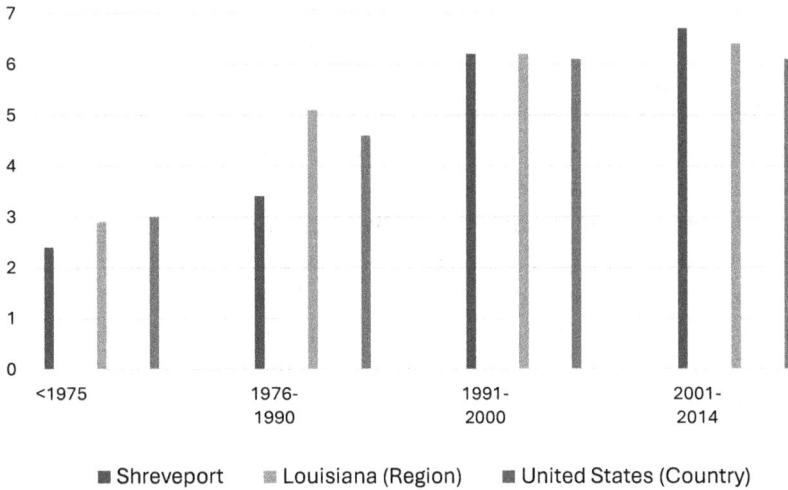

■ Shreveport   ▓ Louisiana (Region)   ■ United States (Country)

Shreveport and Louisiana follow the same trend in the disconnectivity of their street network constructions. The SNDi for both of these rose steadily

Shreveport and Louisiana have trended the same in the disconnectivity of their street network constructions. Both of these rose steadily in SNDi.

Shreveport and the United States do not trend the same in the disconnectivity of their street network constructions. The United States SNDi peaked in 1991–2000, and Shreveport steadily rose.

SNDi of Shreveport's street network over time

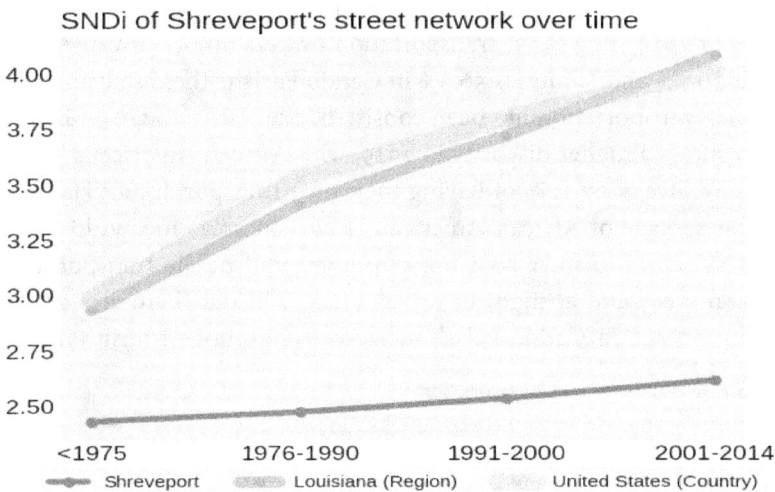

━●━ Shreveport   ▓ Louisiana (Region)   United States (Country)

Figure 42: Shreveport Street Network vs. Louisiana and the U.S. Over Time
SNDi Trends, (2015)

Shreveport and Louisiana have trended the same in disconnectivity of their aggregated street networks. Both of these rose steadily in SNDi. Shreveport and the United States do trend the same in the disconnectivity of their aggregated street network.[5]

With the sprawl, there is a disconnect in the street network that hurts the African American community in Caddo Parish and Bossier Parish. As mentioned before, there is a spatial mismatch between jobs and the labor force in the Shreveport-Bossier metropolitan area. Studies analyzed and presented data collected on jobs and people in metropolitan areas. Included in the data were job sprawl measures of employment decentralization for metropolitan areas. The findings revealed that Black residents living in metropolitan areas with higher levels of employment decentralization were at a greater spatial mismatch between themselves and job locations. The association of greater job sprawl as a higher spatial mismatch is not an issue for Whites but for Blacks. The results firmly imply that job sprawl magnifies particular dimensions of racial inequalities in the United States[6]

Sprawl or urban sprawl creates a situation where citizens need their own automobiles because of the scattered developments. These developments create a situation where citizens need automobiles to access the areas for jobs, adequate food, medical care, schools, and other public services. The citizens are affected by sprawl by way of urban decline, racial polarization, lack of affordable housing, and suburban/city disparities in public education.[7] The African American community in the Shreveport–Bossier City metropolitan area is experiencing these disparities. The US census of 2019 shows that transportation ownership of African Americans is 39.7% and Whites is 56.6% in Caddo Parish. The disadvantage of personal transportation has been consistent from 2010 to 2019.[8] Bossier Parish shows a higher disparity in 2019, with African Americans at 27% versus Whites at 67.10% of having their own transportation.[9] Having a high percentage of African Americans in urban areas in Caddo Parish with less access to their own transportation and public transportation (in rural areas and at night in urban areas) will put them at a greater risk of poverty. In Caddo Parish, citizens using public transit typically

5. SNDi Trends, "Street-Network Sprawl."
6. Stoll, "Spatial Mismatch Between Blacks and Jobs," 1–9.
7. Bullard et al., "Suburban Sprawl," 936–39.
8. US Census 2021, "Caddo Parish," 1.
9. US Census 2021, "Bossier Parish," 1.

experience greater travel times than the average commuters due to funding not allowing frequent service. There are few bike lanes in the Shreveport-Bossier metropolitan area to make biking a safe option. Sidewalk infrastructure conditions outside of the CBD/downtown are poor. The SporTran (public bus) service is a fixed route bus and paratransit for residents with disabilities, which is a demand response service. There used to be a hub-and-spoke system design centered downtown. There are limited routes that service crosstown access, which causes longer trips that call for riders to travel downtown, travel at the hub, then ride from the hub to their final destination.[10]

This section covers *observation of public transportation.* The researcher commuted on the SporTran public transportation bus inbound to the CBD across the street from the old South Park Mall location at 8932 Jewella Avenue, Shreveport, Louisiana, 71118. The stop is called the Jewella Avenue and Southside Inbound stop on the Southern Hills route. The researcher first took a ten-minute walk from 9029 Avalon Drive to the bus stop location. The researcher took the bus to the CBD, which is downtown Shreveport. The specific destination location was the Caddo Parish courthouse, which sits in the heart of downtown Shreveport at 501 Texas Street, Shreveport, Louisiana, 71101. From the old South Park location, the distance to the CBD is about 9 to 11 miles, depending on the route. The bus fare was free, and the driver was friendly. Per the response to Covid-19, the Shreveport–Bossier City metropolitan area assists riders with free fares effective as of January 2, 2022, for the next two years, applied by a federal grant. The researcher caught the 7:40 a.m. bus headed to the CBD, or downtown. The bus was a few minutes early and clean. There were eight riders, seven Black and one White, riding at this point, including myself. The bus took us to the Southwest Transfer Hub, approximately 4.2 miles away at the corner of West 70th Street and St. Vincent Avenue. Here riders could take multiple smaller transits to other parts of the city, which was a new procedure. There was only a short wait until the researcher rode a smaller transit near the CBD. There were only about five riders, including myself, and they were all Black. This transit was also clean, and the driver was friendly. The transit arrived at the Intermodal Terminal Hub on the corner of Murphy Street and Winston Street. This terminal included SporTran and Greyhound buses. The Intermodal Terminal Hub was 4.6 miles away from the Southwest Transfer Hub. There was at least a five-minute wait until a larger bus took us to the

10. Shreveport Metropolitan Planning Commission, "Population," 1.

CBD. There were around twenty-eight Black people and two White, totaling thirty people on this bus. The bus was clean. The bus arrived at the edge of the CBD in thirty-seven minutes total, and it took forty minutes total to get to Caddo Parish courthouse, which was the destination address. Then the bus traveled to the Bossier Transfer stop in Bossier City at the corner of Traffic Street and Broadway Street, located on the northeast edge of the Bossier City boardwalk. More than half of the riders got off here. The bus driver was nice, and she kindly asked where the researcher was going since it was the last stop. The researcher informed the driver he was riding back to the previous location. From here, the researcher rode the SporTran back to the old South Park Mall location, where he began.

The overall experience of the trip was good. The trip was quicker since no one had to pay to get on the bus. The bus driver kept a tally of the riders with a device. Looking for most routes on the SporTran website was easy. However, a rider must be familiar with technology, especially if they want to ride a route toward the suburbs. Extra steps are needed to see routes around nine to ten miles out of the CBD. The website would be complex for older people to understand. Listed below are the fares before the grant.

Table 4: Shreveport-Bossier City SporTran Public Bus Transportation Fare Cost

SporTran Fare Cost

Fare Type	Fare
Single Ride	$1.25
Discount Single Ride	
Child (under 37")	Free
Transfer Charge	$0.25
Special Event Shuttle (Round-Trip Ticket)	$2.50
Downtown Circulator Single Ride	$1.00
Downtown Circulator Discount Single Ride	$0.50
Downtown Circulator Monthly Pass*	$15.00
Day Pass	$3.00
Weekly Pass*	$15.00
Monthly Pass*	$40.00
Discount Monthly Pass*	$20.00
Paratransit (lift line) Single Ride	$2.50
Paratransit (lift line) 20-Ride Pass*	$40.00
City of Shreveport Employees (with ID)	FREE
*Only available to TouchPass card holder or TouchPass mobile app users	

Source: SporTran, (2022)

This section covers *observation of personal vehicle.* The researcher drove a personal vehicle from the same beginning address where he rode the SporTran public transportation to the CBD. The researcher left from 8932 Jewella Avenue, Shreveport, Louisiana, 71118, at 9:45 a.m. to 501 Texas Street, Shreveport, Louisiana, 71101. The researcher drove the 3132 Inner Loop Expressway to I-49, then I-20 to the CBD. This route was an eleven-mile trip that took around fifteen minutes. On the return trip, the researcher drove through a few neighborhoods leaving from the CBD. Leaving the CBD, quite a few buildings looked abandoned or not in use when heading south on Texas Street to Murphy Street, but it seems to be a bit cleaner and have some renovated buildings within the last few years. Heading down Murphy Street passing Pierre Avenue to Hearne Avenue, the researcher would see some identical rundown houses, uncut lawns, and no working vehicles in front of homes. Many Black communities have these same conditions in Shreveport, including the Lakeside, Allendale, Cedar Grove, Sunset Acre, Mooretown, and the Martin Luther King area neighborhoods.

The average US citizen spends around 13% of their household income on transportation, and lower-income people tend to spend a larger amount of their income on transportation. As these lower-income people move up in class, they pay a smaller portion of their income on transportation. People with the lowest income are burdened the most with paying transportation costs. In 2016, US citizens in the lowest earning 20% ($11,933) spent 29% of their income on transportation.[11] As stated, the US census of 2019 shows transportation ownership of African Americans (the majority population in Caddo Parish) is 39.7% and Whites is 56.6%. The disadvantage of personal transportation has been consistent from 2010 to 2019.[12] Bossier Parish shows a higher disparity in 2019, with African Americans at 27% versus Whites at 67.10% having their own transportation.[13] With the data of renters showing less transportation than homeowners, the renters in the suburbs and rural areas are at a higher disadvantage in getting to work, hospitals, medical facilities, and shopping. A high percentage of African Americans in rural areas and suburbs in Caddo Parish with less access to their own and public transportation will put them at a greater risk of poverty.

11. Institute for Transportation and Development Policy, "High Cost of Transportation."

12. US Census Bureau 2019, "Caddo Parish."

13. US Census Bureau 2019, "Bossier Parish."

With a lack of vehicles, long public transport times, few biking lanes, and street connectivity problems, African Americans are at a high disadvantage compared to Whites in obtaining and keeping a job and getting to school, adequate food, medical care, schools, and other public services.

This section covers *health care services and infrastructure.* Urbanization has affected access to medical care and hinders the population's health, especially African Americans. According to the United Health Foundation's State Health Rankings for 2004, Louisiana was ranked as the least healthy state in the nation for a combined measure of identified health outcomes and risk factors—a ranking Louisiana has held for fourteen of the last fifteen years.[14] Health rankings assist us with comprehending what factors influence how well and how long we live. The United States health outcome ranking data measures consistency of access to nutritious foods, high school graduation rates, and percent of children living in poverty, all of which impact the future health of communities (health factors). Health outcomes represent how healthy a specific county is currently. The four health factor areas in the model include health behaviors, clinical care, social and economic factors, and physical environment.[15] The figure below details health outcomes and health factors.

14. Louisiana Department of Health, "State Health Rankings"; Louisiana Office of Public Health, *2005 Parish Health Profiles,* 122.

15. Blomberg et al., *2022 State Report,* 2–6.

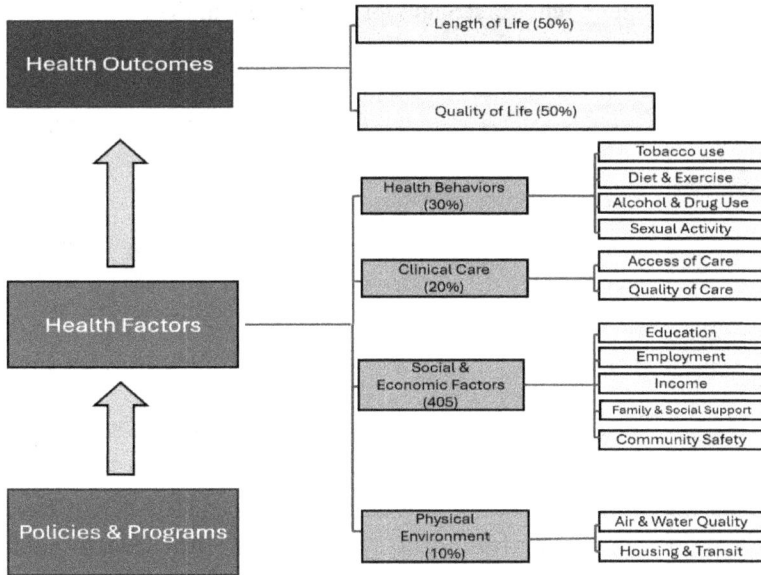

Figure 43: Health Outcomes and Health Factors
Source: Blomberg, Gennuso, Givens, Johnson, Muganda, and Olsen-Williams, (2022)

As of 2022, Louisiana is rated the fifth place for unhealthiest state in the United States In Louisiana, Caddo Parish ranked forty-eighth out of sixty-four parishes for health outcomes and twenty-second for health factors, and Bossier is ranked sixth in both categories. Health outcomes consist of length of life (potential life lost before age seventy-five) and quality of life (self-reported health status and percent of low birthrate newborns). Health factors have numerous categories, but when considering urbanization, the categories that matter are access to health care, quality of health care, income, housing and transit, and diet and exercise.

Health factors represent things that, if modified, can improve length and quality of life. They are predictors of how healthy our communities can be in the future. Health outcomes represent how healthy a county is right now. They reflect the physical and mental well-being of residents through measures representing the length and quality of life typically experienced in the community.[16]

16. Blomberg et al., *2022 State Report*, 2–6.

Table 5: Ten Worst States for Health Care in the U.S.

State	Overall Score
1. West Virginia	1
2. Mississippi	33.4
3. Alaska	33.7
4. Tennessee	38.3
5. Louisiana*	**44.7**
6. Oklahoma	45.6
7. New Mexico	47.2
8. Kentucky	48.9
9. Missouri	49.9
10. Arizona & Maine (Tie)	52.7

Source: Cohen, Bhatt, and Gawuga, (2022)

Lacking proper access to jobs and medical care due to not having ready transportation or having no transportation can lead to subpar health care or no health care. Also, proper transportation allows access to better food and nutrients and affordable housing as well as income. Frequent relocation, inadequate transportation, lack of phone access, having multiple children, living with disabilities, being pregnant, and working multiple jobs all can make it challenging to seek timely preventive medical care.

In Louisiana in 2002, the Black infant mortality rate was just over twice that of White infants.[17]

Between 2015 to 2017 (on average), Louisiana's infant mortality rate (per 1,000 live births) was highest for Black infants at 11.0, followed by Asian or Pacific Islanders at 5.3 and Whites at 5.2. During the first year of life between 2015 to 2017, Black infants were two times as likely to die. From 2014 to 2018, Caddo Parish's infant mortality rate was 10.4 deaths per 1,000 live births, greater than Louisiana's rate of 7.7. Bossier Parish's rate was 6.95 per 100 live births.[18] From 2015 to 2017, the Caddo Parish Black fetal mortality rate was 11.4, the White rate was 3.9, and all of Louisiana's rate overall was 5.8.

17. Louisiana Office of Public Health, *2005 Parish Health Profiles*, 122.

18. Louisiana Department of Health, "Health Data Explorer."

Caddo Parish
Fetal Mortality Rate 2015-2017
(Rates Per 1,000 Population)

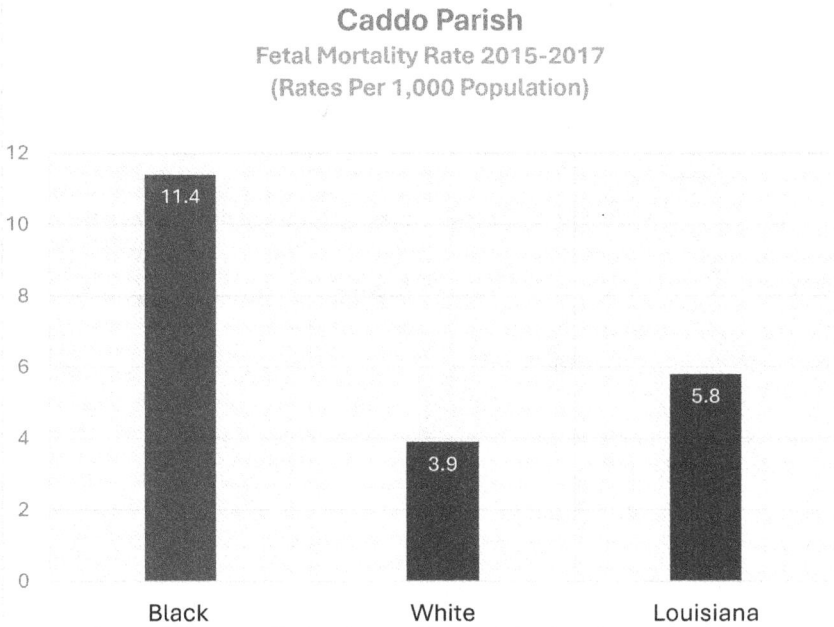

Figure 44: Caddo Parish Fetal Mortality Rate 2015–2017
Source: Louisiana Department of Health, (2020)

From 2015 to 2017, the Caddo Parish Black infant mortality rate was 14.8, that of Whites was 5.8, and all of Louisiana was 7.7. From 2014 to 2016, the Bossier Parish Black fetal mortality rate was 10.3, that of Whites was 4.7, and all of Louisiana was 5.8. From 2014 to 2016, the Bossier Parish Black infant mortality rate was 19.3, that of Whites was 4.1, and all of Louisiana was 7.5.[19]

In 2010, African American births in Caddo Parish boomed to 3,043, and White births were 751. The following year in 2011, African American births dropped to less than half that of the year before, to 1,487 Black births, and White birth numbers rose from 751 to 2,121, shown in the first figure of section 2.14.6. Black births haven't been over 2,000 since 2010, and White births have been consistently over 800 since 2010, reaching their highest of 2,121 in 2011.[20]

This section covers *housing and infrastructure*. Having adequate and affordable housing is an issue in Caddo Parish and Bossier Parish,

19. Louisiana Department of Health, "Caddo Parish"; Louisiana Department of Health, "Bossier Parish."

20. US Census 2020, "Caddo Parish," 1.

including in the majority-populated Shreveport–Bossier City metro area. Households with the lowest income earners have the least housing unit options to choose from and need more safe housing, which does not meet community needs. The options for those households earning below the 30% median income are limited to rental properties. Also, with limited housing stock, the lower earners tend to spend more on higher-priced rental housing. Nearly 60% of the renters in the city of Shreveport-Bossier cannot afford to live there. Some families must double up households together in one housing unit. There is a tremendous unmet demand or wait list for Section 8 and public housing for the Shreveport Housing Authority, with extraordinary demand for two- and three-bedroom housing.[21]

A significant number of households in the Shreveport area are categorized as extremely low-income (earning less than 30% of the median income). Analysis of the poverty data from Caddo Parish and Bossier Parish shows that African Americans in these parishes are the most poverty-stricken. White residents with higher incomes and less poverty have greater options for housing in the Shreveport area, plus the economy is segregated heavily, especially in home values. This information aligns with broader trends of racial inequity in the United States. The researcher can conclude that the negative effects of urbanization are hindering African Americans in Caddo Parish and Bossier Parish, especially in the Shreveport–Bossier City metropolitan area, by not being provided proper, affordable housing.[22]

The Shreveport-Bossier metropolitan area has a severe cost burden issue regarding the lack of affordable housing for extremely low-income households. In the Shreveport–Bossier City metropolitan area, those who are classified as low-income and cost-burdened (50.01%–80% of AMI) represented 55.8% (6,469) of the population of renter households. All cost-burdened renter households were at a total of 46% (26,894) of renter households.[23]

In a study that draws on data from the 2023 American Community Survey—dividing Louisiana into eleven regions, each defined by its own metropolitan statistical area, and calculating the area median income (AMI) for each—the Shreveport-Bossier region is noted as having 46% of renter households that are cost-burdened, a figure that rises to 82%

21. Bayliss, "Census 2020"; City of Shreveport, *2014–2018 Consolidated Plan*, 19–151; City of Shreveport, *2019–2023 Consolidated Plan*, 18–158.

22. O'Lear, "Racial Disparities."

23. White and White, *Rental Housing Affordability*.

among very low-income renters and nearly 69% among extremely low-income renters.[24]

Housing conditions are also an issue in the Shreveport–Bossier City metropolitan area. For a housing unit to be considered a problem unit, it has to have four reported housing problems. In Bossier City, someone reported that 30.79% of renter-occupied units had no housing problems, which means 69.21% of renter-occupied units had at least four reported issues with their housing. Owner-occupied units that reported no issues were at 48.55%, meaning that someone reported at least four issues in 51.45% of owner-occupied units. The conditions of housing units are highly associated with the income level of households that are residing in those housing units.[25]

In Shreveport, the cost-burdened households are the main housing problem. Other issues are standard housing (e.g., complete plumbing or kitchen facilities) and overcrowding. According to the 2015 CHAS data, there were 7,310 renters and 3,620 homeowners in the 0% to 100% AMI range spending more than 30% of their income on housing costs (AMI is the area median income). The data showed that in Shreveport, the lower the household income, the greater the factor of severe housing problems.[26] Data has shown that African Americans have the city's lowest income and highest poverty rates. Furthermore, 70% of all housing and 68% of rental housing built prior to 1980 in Shreveport had potential lead-based paint hazard issues. With some exceptions, the oldest neighborhoods in larger cities house the poorest people. In this case, the African American / Black community is Shreveport's most impoverished community. Bossier City had 36% or 9,383 out of 25,535 households that were cost-burdened, of which 12% were in the extreme cost-burdened category. When analyzed by race, African American / Black households disproportionately experienced a 14% cost burden.

The researcher suggests that the urban growth in Shreveport resulted in negative effects in urbanization and assisted with creating poverty with a high percentage of Black residents in Caddo Parish versus the White

24. Vines, "Affordable Rental Housing." Per the US Census 2024 for Shreveport, the total owner-occupied households housing cost (30% and above) was 44% (US Census Bureau 2024, "Shreveport Monthly Housing Cost"). Per the US Census 2023 5-Year Estimate for Bossier City, the total owner-occupied households housing cost (30% and above) was 36.4% (US Census Bureau 2023, "Bossier City Monthly Housing Cost").

25. City of Shreveport, *2019–2023 Consolidated Plan*, 18–158.

26. City of Shreveport, *2019–2023 Consolidated Plan*, 26.

residents. A heavy population of Bossier Parish residents in Bossier City, along with the negative effects of urbanization, has also created poverty with a high percentage of Black residents in Bossier Parish versus the White residents, even though the Black population is much smaller than the White population.

This section covers *politics, law, and poverty in the study area.* The US political system has not been favorable to Blacks in the US, including the study area. The political system in the US determines policy, sways voters, uses words to influence even with propaganda, determines where to distribute resources and utilize them, and dictates laws. In reference to laws, there are still Jim Crow laws present in the study area, and even with the elimination of some of the Jim Crow laws, there are Black inmates in prison due to those past laws. As the researcher presented earlier, the Thirteenth Amendment to the United States Constitution states that

> neither slavery nor involuntary servitude, except as a punishment for crime whereof the party shall have been duly convicted, shall exist within the United States, or any place subject to their jurisdiction.[27]

The key words in the Constitution clarified that there was to be no slavery nor involuntary servitude *except as a punishment for crime.* Richard Nixon's war on drugs and his war propaganda on Blacks boosted incarceration in US prisons and jails. The numbers grew from 300,000 to 2.3 million. At that time, people of color represented two-thirds of half of the people in federal prison jailed because of drug offenses disproportionate even though Whites use drugs at the same rate and are more likely to sell drugs, as the Washington Post reported.[28] President Ronald Reagan's campaign strategist, Lee Atwater, on a tape-recorded interview explained their Southern strategy on how to recruit other racists without sounding like a racist themselves (propaganda) but rather sounding more political, by substituting words in political speeches that insulted or worked against Black people for other terms. Bill Clinton's 1994 Crime Bill was responsible for sending many Black people to jail, especially Black men, which helped destroy Black communities.[29]

There is a disproportionate incarceration rate for African Americans / Blacks versus Whites in the state of Louisiana and in Caddo Parish

---

27. US Const. amend. XIII, §1.

28. Maxwell, "Southern Strategy."

29. Equal Justice Initiative, "Nixon Advisor"; Chung et al., "1994 Crime Bill."

specifically. One reason for this is the school-to-prison pipeline system in Louisiana. The Southern Poverty Law Center's School to Prison project revealed stark information that presented a significant percentage of children in Louisiana referred by the school system to the juvenile system. The Southern Poverty Law Center launched a first-class action administrative complaint against the Louisiana State Department of Education. The year-long investigation revealed that poor, emotionally disturbed African American students in the Caddo, East Baton Rouge, and Calcasieu Parish school districts were systematically having their rights violated. The number reached thousands each year. In 2006 a settlement agreement was reached with East Baton Rouge Parish, and in 2007 reached with Caddo Parish and Calcasieu Parish school systems. Also, the Southern Poverty Law Center filed a federal civil rights complaint with the US Department of Education for discriminatory policies of the Jefferson Parish Public School System in Louisiana that have pushed a disproportionate number of Black students and students with disabilities into alternative schools, where they often languish for months or even years before returning to school. These school districts played on these students' disabilities by routinely expelling or suspending these students for minor offenses that were related to the students' disabilities. In violation of state and federal regulations, Jefferson Parish further segregated these students in self-contained classrooms or trailers. All school districts involved did not arrange for the appropriate levels of related services (counseling, psychological services, and social work) and vocational training for emotionally disturbed children. The impacts on the students from such practices were substantial and pervasive. The tactics led to alarmingly high drop-out rates, abysmal graduation rates, and grade failures starting from their elementary school years.[30] Students have found themselves arrested for small incidents in Caddo Parish. Isaiah Heath was a star basketball player at Byrd High School in 2014 when he learned this lesson the hard way after a heated argument with his teacher. Several students witnessed the argument. "She said shut up, he said shut up back to her," Austin Gomez told KSLA News 12 in April 2014. The argument was enough to land Heath in jail at the Caddo Correctional Center, charged with assault on a schoolteacher and disturbing the peace. "I feel like it was really

30. Louisiana Public Defender Board, "School to Prison Pipeline"; Southern Poverty Law Center, "Discrimination Complaint"; KSLA News 12, "School-to-Prison Pipeline."

unnecessary to put him in jail for something so little," student Antoinette Van said in a 2014 interview.[31]

In Caddo Parish, thirteen specific offenses are in the district handbook that students can do to get themselves criminally charged if the evidence is present:[32]

- Using profanity toward school personnel
- Possession or using fireworks
- Participating in a fight
- Loitering on any school campus, bus, or school-sponsored events while suspended
- Cyberbullying
- Bullying, threatening, or hazing students
- Defacing, stealing, or destroying school property
- Sexual harassment
- Possessing weapons
- The battery of teachers or other school personnel
- Possessing or using any controlled substance or alcohol
- Initiating any false alarms and/or bomb threats
- Threatening teachers or other school personnel

Caddo Parish Juvenile Detention Center and Rutherford House (alternative school) keep track of arrest records for students under seventeen, but the Caddo Parish School Board does not keep track, as a spokesperson said in an interview. They reported 282 arrests for the 2014–2015 school year. In the 2015–2016 school year, they reported 253 arrests. Bossier Parish reported 192 arrests for the 2014–2015 school year and 162 for the 2015–2016 school year.[33]

The school-to-prison pipeline disproportionately leads Black youth to prisons, where they will again experience disadvantages. Between the years of 2003 through 2012, researchers inspected data prosecuted by the Caddo Parish district attorneys from more than three hundred felony trials. They found that some individual prosecutors struck Black prospective

31. KSLA News 12, "School-to-Prison Pipeline."
32. KSLA News 12, "School-to-Prison Pipeline."
33. KSLA News 12, "School-to-Prison Pipeline."

jurors at four and a half and five times the rate they struck those who are not Black. Prosecutors in Caddo Parish, on an overall basis, struck jurors of other races out at 15% and abruptly struck out Black jurors at 46%. With Caddo Parish being around 48% Black, the researchers found less than four African American members in a standard twelve-member jury trial. Per capita, Caddo Parish sentenced to death more people than any other county/parish in the United States. Today, majority-White juries in Caddo Parish are sentencing mostly Black defendants to death (83% in the study).[34] Also, the state of Louisiana is known for its lengthy history of selling captive labor or the labor of convicts to private companies. The data and the history of laws in the United States, Louisiana, Caddo Parish, and Bossier Parish disproportionately affect Black people more than Whites. The data appears in the figures in section 2.13.4.1. Through the political system, the judicial system is using laws to incarcerate disproportionate amounts of Black people to use as inmates as resources to produce more resources with cheaper labor.

Total incarcerated, prison and jail: 62,534
Prison population: 31,584
Prison incarceration rate per 100,000: 680 (#1 highest among all states)
Jail population (2013): 30,950
Jail incarceration rate per 100,000 (2013): 870 (#1 highest among all states)
Private prison population: 0
Probation population: 33,741
Parole population: 28,283
Life sentences (2020): 4,624
Life without parole (2020): 4,377
Juvenile life without parole (2020): 150
White imprisonment rate per 100,000: 381 (#11 highest among all states)
Black imprisonment rate per 100,000: 1,411 (#24 highest among all states)
Black to white ratio: 3.7

Figure 45: Louisiana Incarceration Demographics
Source: Stacker (2022)

To add insult to injury, studies such as the New York City hiring discrimination study presented data detailing that White male felons are more likely to receive callbacks for jobs over Black males with the same record and/or over Black males with no records at all.[35] Situations like this will help uplift Whites out of poverty as opposed to Blacks who will struggle to find employment, leading them to poverty and a life of crime.

34. Equal Justice Initiative, "Illegal Racial Discrimination."
35. Pager et al., "Sequencing Disadvantage."

This section covers how *politics with the IRS creates poverty*. The researcher presented information about the IRS using the tax system as a strategy to burden Black taxpayers and benefit White taxpayers. The researcher presented information to show how this system intends to preserve wealth inequality and racial disparities. The Jobs Act of 2017 and recent tax cuts help inflate these effects. This system works with pensions to alleviate costs associated with caring for parents as they enter senior status, such as tax-preferred 401(k) pensions. Not only do these pensions relieve children of costs associated with caring for aging parents, but they can also use the 529 college tax-deferred accounts to subsidize investment of the human capital of those same offspring. All the while, those able to purchase houses in high-class communities with good schools have been supported with home interest mortgage deductions purchased with tax-subsidized local property taxes. These benefits suggest inequalities between the 20% wealthy in the United States and the rest of the population. Tax policy affects the amount of wealth higher-income earners can stockpile yearly and add to their wealth, which causes overall wealth inequality. With private income such as dividends, earnings, and other incomes, the top 10% of households increased their income from 1963 to 2016 by 90%, for example. The families in the bottom 10% increased their income by less than 10% during the same period. According to the US Census Bureau data, Blacks are the only people encountering a median income decrease since 2000. The other races, including Hispanics, Asians, and Whites, experience income gains. The IRC creates a realized-based system for wealth and income disparities at a greater level. Tax incentives or expenditures are more available to high-income households than low-income household, and moderate-income households get significantly smaller benefits. The income gained from higher-income taxpayers enables them to make certain financial investments to increase their value significantly. The Tax Cuts and Jobs Act (TCJA) has assisted with continuing the increase of the racial wealth divide and inequality. Today, state codes still affect middle- and low-income households paying a sizeable share of their income taxes compared to wealthy households.

Combining all state and local income, property, sales, and excise taxes that Americans pay, the average effective state and local tax rate nationally is 11.4% for the poorest 20% of non-elderly residents, 9.9% for the middle 20%, and 7.4% for the top 1%.[36]

---

36. Strand and Mirkay, "Racialized Tax Inequity," 266–87; Institute on Taxation and Economic Policy, *Who Pays?*, 5–68.

States rely heavily on consumption taxes, especially sales tax. Consumption tax is a significant reason for inequality because it disproportionately affects low-income families. After all, they spend most of their income on consumables and cannot save or invest. Forty-five states in the US have regressive tax systems that exacerbate income inequality, with Louisiana being included.[37] Black people in Caddo Parish and Bossier Parish have many low-income and high-poverty residents, so this would affect them significantly compared to White residents.

This section covers *Social Security and disability and politics*. Blacks and other minorities have fewer retirement resources, such as assets and pensions, than Whites. Blacks lack income-producing assets and other income sources, unlike their White counterparts. Workers that earn lower wages have a difficult time creating sufficient savings. In 2016, White families had about six times more average liquid retirement savings than Black American families. In 2017, among Black Americans receiving Social Security, 35% of elderly married couples and 58% of unmarried elderly persons relied on Social Security for 90% or more of their income. Over a lifetime, the average Black man earns $1.8 million, while the average White man averages $2.7 million.[38]

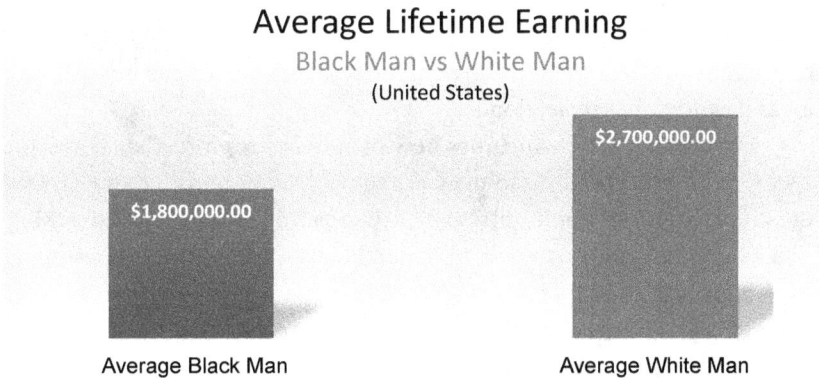

Average Lifetime Earning
Black Man vs White Man
(United States)

$2,700,000.00

$1,800,000.00

Average Black Man   Average White Man

Figure 46: Lifetime Earning Average Black man vs. White man in the U.S.
Source: NCPSSM, (2020)

African Americans / Blacks usually receive Social Security Disability Insurance (DI) benefits because they have a higher rate of disability. The higher benefits-received-to-taxes-paid ratio is received by workers

37. Institute on Taxation and Economic Policy, *Who Pays?*, 5–68.

38. National Committee to Preserve Social Security and Medicare, "Black Americans."

with a higher probability of becoming disabled. However, DI benefits are not enough to create wealth.

Politics in the United States, Louisiana, Caddo Parish, and Bossier Parish disproportionately affect African Americans versus Whites. Politics in Caddo Parish and Bossier Parish destroy Black families through national laws and state laws by disproportionately arresting Black people and giving them longer sentencing in jail, which creates poverty for inmates due to their inability to make income for their families. The IRS and Social Security drive the wealth gap between Blacks and Whites and cost Blacks more money, driving them into poverty.

4.2 RESEARCH QUESTION TWO

The second research question asks, Is there a relationship between systemic racism, poverty, urbanization, and politics, and do these relationships affect lack of African American wealth in the Caddo Parish?

Racism is the systemic oppression of one race over another; specifically, this network is a White race-operated system. Racism consists of nine areas of human activity. The researcher only used the areas of economics, education, labor, law, politics, and war in this research. Economics, education, labor, law, politics, and war are linked together as parts of the nine areas of human activity. The researcher presents how all nine areas link together in section 2.4.

Economics, which includes how people use resources such as land, water, plant life, and food to produce valuable commodities and distribute them among people, fits with urbanization, sprawl, and housing. The researcher has covered disproportionate distribution of resources to Whites versus Blacks where Blacks get fewer resources and benefits. Blacks in Louisiana experience disproportionate stationing in areas of toxic environments, including polluted land, water, and or air. Dr. Robert Bullard would call it the "wrong zip code" to receive protection.[39] Sometimes people live in the wrong community or subdivision to receive protection. In Caddo and Bossier Parish, Blacks are in areas with food and banking deserts but then are supplied with payday loan companies. In section 4.6, the figures provided show seventy-eight payday loan companies, twenty-two actual supermarket/grocery stores (versus Snap, noted in a separate image), and the number of bank branches in the area.

---

39. Bullard, "African Americans on the Frontline."

Education delivers or facilitates different learning of values, beliefs, habits, knowledge, and skills.[40] Under the system of racism, education miseducates African Americans / Blacks in the United States, including Blacks in Caddo Parish and Bossier Parish. The miseducation of Blacks in the study area has resulted in Black unemployment, underemployment, and lack of knowledge of politics and financial literacy, which keeps them in poverty. Disciplinary actions in schools get disproportionately placed upon students of color. Disciplinary actions such as in-school detention, suspension, and expulsion result in students missing classroom time and falling further behind in their studies. Institutional racism is strengthened by implicit racial bias and other biases that determine outcomes in the educational experiences of Black students. The gaps in academic performance of Black students compared to White peers can also explain the stress and other psychological effects of racial discrimination.[41] In Caddo Parish, there is a racial divide in the education system. Such gaps are shown in Caddo Parish and Bossier Parish through the figures in section 2.15.2. As presented before, AP courses and gifted programs are less likely options for Black students versus their White peers. Blacks are more likely to be expelled or suspended from school. In Caddo Parish, 43% of students in AP courses are Black, and 53% are White. Of students selected for gifted and talented composition, 20% are Black and 67% are White. Of students who receive out-of-school suspension, 80% are Black and 16% are White. Of the students who receive expulsion, 82% are Black and 15% are White.[42] Black students are also known to be denied certain schools because of their race in Caddo/Bossier Parishes, for example, in the Lemon v. Bossier Parish School Board case in Shreveport City Court. The racial divide in the Caddo Parish and Bossier Parish education system is shown in the number of Black students versus White to graduate high school and or receive higher degrees, which is a significant determinant of what type of employment a person can gain.

Labor can be considered the amount of social, physical, and mental strive used to produce goods and services in an economy.[43] To produce goods and services, individuals must accomplish these goals by way of employees, supervisors or managers, owners, and producers. The history of the United States is grounded in White racism. The nation was

40. Fuller, *United Independent Compensatory*, 1–5.
41. Johns, "Disrupting Implicit Racial Bias," 2–12.
42. Groeger et al., "Miseducation."
43. Amadeo, "Your Work Is Critical."

founded on the principles of Free Land (stolen land), Free Labor (cruelly extracted from enslaved African people), and Free Men (White men with property).[44] Some of the tactics have changed in racism. However, ultimately the motto, model, and goal have remained the same, with White being deemed supreme and other races being underneath Whites, emphasizing the Black race being at the bottom. The state of Louisiana is known for its lengthy history of selling captive labor or labor of convicts to private companies which produce goods and services. Even the Constitution outlawed this convict lease system in 1898. Louisiana State Penitentiary at Angola used prison labor without paying them well into the twentieth century. In Louisiana, the jobs pay from $0.86 an hour for picking cotton to offshore jobs that might pay up to $11.12 an hour, which are meager wages for the type of work performed.[45] The fact that this specific Black population was being disproportionately arrested, wrongly arrested, and given longer sentences to work as free laborers from Reconstruction to the twentieth century took away possibilities from these Black citizens and their families for gaining generational wealth, instead putting them in positions of generational poverty. Labor is also associated with employment, unemployment, and underemployment. Factors that can be included with not being gainfully employed are discrimination based on race, lack of education, and having a criminal record. In the United States, there has been a long history of employment discrimination to keep Blacks unemployed. Unemployment can result in negative behaviors. These behaviors are physical inactivity, unhealthy diet, alcohol use, and smoking among unemployed people. Those factors mentioned are vital to sustaining good health. Unemployed people usually lack a steady income stream, health care insurance, and access to health services, or they even delay their health care problems due to financial concerns. Premature deaths, a faster aging process, hopelessness, and intergenerational poverty result from financially insecure and unemployed people.[46] Unemployment can also lead to a life of crime. The figure in section 2.10.2 shows the Caddo Parish unemployment rate. Caddo Parish's unemployment average from 2010 to 2019 was Blacks at 9.51 versus Whites at 5.25, with Black unemployment nearly doubling that of Whites. In section 2.10.4, the figures show Bossier Parish's unemployment rate average from 2010 to 2019 was Blacks at 10.01 and

44. Bullard, *Confronting Environmental Racism*, 16.
45. Berlin, "Louisiana's Oil and Gas"; Arresting Inequality, "Jim Crow."
46. Pharr et al., "Impact of Unemployment."

Whites at 4.24, with the Black unemployment rate more than double that of Whites. In 2019 the United States unemployment rate was 3.5, with Blacks in Caddo Parish and Bossier Parish nearly tripling the rate of unemployment in the United States[47] As discussed before, the data from 2017 shows that Caddo Parish has 3,761 White employer firms and 142 African American / Black employer firms. The White firms have a total of 42,745 employees with an annual payroll of $1,654,794, and the African American firms have a total of 2,317 employees and an annual payroll of $38,757. Neighboring Bossier Parish, as of 2017, has 1,460 White employer firms and 46 African American / Black employer firms. The White firms total 21,860 employees with an annual payroll of $768,426, and the African American firms total 1,643 employees and an annual payroll of $24,235. African Americans have fewer chances of hiring their people than Whites in Caddo Parish and Bossier Parish. The number of African American–owned businesses does not reflect the population versus the Whites in Caddo Parish. Education is a factor when getting hired for a higher paying job, but companies in the United States have a long history of not hiring Blacks that are just as qualified and/or more qualified than Whites. A recent notable example was when the United States Department of Labor and FedEx reached a $3 million settlement in 2012 for discrimination. FedEx faced allegations of discriminating against 21,635 job seekers in fifteen states at twenty-four FedEx facilities. Discriminatory hiring practices had to change within FedEx as part of the settlement. Another example was when the Bank of America Corporation was investigated for their hiring practices, which resulted in the corporation being ordered to pay 1,147 Black job applicants $2.18 million back in 2013.[48] Racial biases still exist in favor of Whites versus Blacks when it comes to gaining employment.

"Law is a rule of civil conduct prescribed by the supreme power in a state, commanding what is right and forbidding what is wrong."[49] Some US government laws have been made and used to oppress Black people and keep them in poverty since the existence of America, both written and unwritten. Laws maintain control in all areas of human activity. These laws are to keep Racism White Supremacy intact.[50] As discussed, White people used laws to put insurance policies on enslaved

47. US Census 2020, "Caddo Parish," 1; US Census 2020, "Bossier Parish," 1.
48. Insureon Staff, "Employment Discrimination."
49. Bigelow, "Definition of Law," 1.
50. Fuller, *United Independent Compensatory*, 150.

Black people during American slavery that assisted Whites in creating generational wealth. Research indicated that at least sixty other companies were involved in the business at the time, including New York Life, AIG, Aetna, and Manhattan Life. As stated in the labor section above, Louisiana has used laws to give Blacks lengthy prison sentences and sold captive labor or labor of convicts to private companies which produce goods and services. Jim Crows laws oppressed Black people, and some of these laws still exist in Louisiana today. There are inmates in prison that are still under the old Jim Crow laws that were changed. Black inmates serving lengthy sentences cannot escape poverty and gain wealth. Politics is also a way to manipulate and use laws against Blacks.

Politics is considered the way we interact with people and is largely defined as the set of activities that are associated with making decisions in groups, or other forms of power relations between individuals, such as the distribution of resources. Law is supposed to produce justice; however, the law produces and maintains injustice under racism.[51] In the United States, the law has been used to produce and maintain White supremacy at any given moment. Politics can play a role in using humans as resources because if someone has power or control over a person, then that person in power can use a person through politics or force.[52] There have always been political agendas in the United States to use laws and policies to oppress Blacks. For example, the US Constitution at one time legalized slavery (slave laws), then there were the Black Codes, the Jim Crow laws, President Nixon's Comprehensive Drug Abuse Prevention and Control Act of 1970 (or the war on drugs), President Clinton's Crime Bill, and IRS policies. The researcher has covered these laws and policies in the literature. These laws and policies imprison Blacks unjustly and/or keep them in poverty.

War is a state of usually open and declared hostile armed conflict between states or nations.[53] The results and/or actions of war can be slavery and/or oppression. Racism White Supremacy is war on Black people. The researcher concludes that Blacks are being oppressed in the focus areas presented and in all areas of human activities by Racism White Supremacy. War reparations are payments by one state or country to another at the end of a conflict, intended to compensate for the damage

51. Fuller, *United Independent Compensatory*, 150.
52. Groeger et al., "Miseducation."
53. Long, "What Is War?"

and injury inflicted during the war.[54] The losers of the war or conflict would pay compensation for economic loss. The term has become more inclusive, where payments get made to smaller groups or individuals. Currently, we are witnessing the term *reparations* include one group who tries to remedy a wrong done to another group. Typically, this is done by paying money or giving the injured party something else of monetary value. However, reparations have also been used throughout history to punish a group or country for its role in a war or atrocity.[55] The United States paid reparations to Japanese Americans in 1990, the Ottawas of Michigan in 1986, the Chippewas of Wisconsin in 1985, the Seminoles of Florida and the Sioux of South Dakota in 1985, Klamaths of Oregon in 1980, and Alaska Natives for land settlement in 1971. Payments of reparations are made when a war is over. No reparations have been paid to African Americans from 1865 to the present for American slavery and the Jim Crow era.[56] The researcher is not presenting this information about war reparations because he thinks African Americans are owed reparations from slavery and the Jim Crow era. The researcher argues that White supremacists are still at war with African Americans, resulting in no reparations to this group. Even with reparations payments to African Americans with just money or land, the system of racism will still exist. Reparations for Black natives and or the descendants of enslaved Africans brought here through the transatlantic slave trade would have to include equity and equality in every human area of activity to begin to repair the African American community.

A reparations bill was introduced by US Representative Sheila Jackson Lee, of the eighteenth congressional district in Texas, on January 3, 2019, to the House of Representatives. The bill presents verbatim.

> This bill establishes the Commission to Study and Develop Reparation Proposals for African Americans. The commission shall examine slavery and discrimination in the colonies and the United States from 1619 to the present and recommend appropriate remedies. Among other requirements, the commission shall identify (1) the role of the federal and state governments in supporting the institution of slavery, (2) forms of discrimination in the public and private sectors against freed slaves and their

---

54. Blank, "War Reparations for Ukraine."
55. Schottman, "History of Reparations."
56. Davis, "Timeline of Reparations."

descendants, and (3) lingering negative effects of slavery on living African Americans and society.[57]

The lingering effects of slavery have been tremendous against African
Americans.

One common war tactic that White supremacists have done is to
turn other races against African Americans, including other African
Americans and/or African diaspora (other Black nationalities). Non-
White people cannot be White supremacists because they are not White
and are subjected to racism themselves at any time. These people (or race
soldiers) can carry out orders of White supremacy and obtain given special privileges from White supremacists. Differentiating other races from
Blacks can be easily done by seeing skin color and other distinct features.
However, it is sometimes difficult to determine if another Black person is
a race soldier for Racism White Supremacy because of their non-White
appearance. This divide and conquer tactic is considered part of the psychological warfare the researcher discussed in section 2.4.2.6.2. It is a
divide and conquer tactic that White supremacists have used to establish
racism. Physical racist warfare is easier to see, such as when Dylan Storm
Roof shot and killed nine people in a Charleston, South Carolina, church
on June 17, 2015. Dylan Roof admitted killing those Blacks because of
the color of their skin and further proclaimed that he didn't regret it.[58] A
scenario that is difficult to recognize is a young, elementary-aged Black
student purposely targeted for their failure in school by a suspected
White racist female or male teacher. Researchers work to figure out why
young Black students are failing, dropping out, being suspended more
frequently, placed into special education more often, and/or not allowed
into advanced placement classes in schools. This tactic of war against
Black people is critical in maintaining the system, which assists in keeping Blacks in poverty within the focus areas.

4.3 RESEARCH QUESTION THREE

Is there a comparison between African American versus White poverty
in Caddo Parish and African American versus White poverty in neighboring Bossier Parish?

---

57. Commission to Study and Develop Reparation Proposals for African Americans Act of 2021–2022, H.R. 40, 117th Cong. (2021).

58. Zapotosky, "Charleston Church Shooter."

The researcher analyzed the data regarding poverty in Caddo Parish and Bossier Parish and compared it to the Black population versus the White population. The researcher advised his audience that he would present information regarding the last thirty years of his study areas' poverty issues. The researcher presented information in the literature that detailed how Blacks have been in poverty since the transatlantic slave trade and up to the past thirty years. However, the US Census Bureau gives the details of yearly data for the past eleven years.

As stated before, Louisiana has one of the widest gaps between its richest and poorest residents, according to the Center on Budget and Policy Priorities (based in Washington, DC) analysis released in December 2016.[59] Second in the nation in child poverty is the state of Louisiana.

How Louisiana Compares to the Country

Poverty Rate: **3rd Highest**

Child Poverty Rate: **3rd Highest**

Income Inequality: **4th Highest**

Median Household Income: **7th Lowest**

**Figure 47: 2015 Louisiana vs. Country (U.S.) in Poverty and Income
Source: Albares, (2016)**

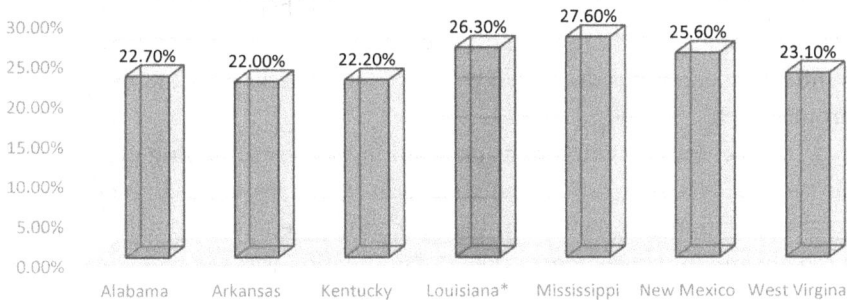

**Figure 48: 2020 States with Highest Child Poverty in the U.S.
Source: Stebbins, (2022)**

59. Crisp, "Biggest Gaps."

Comparing the two parishes' Black versus White poverty shows that Black poverty in both parishes is significantly higher than that of Whites. Caddo Parish Black poverty has averaged 34% and Whites averaged 11.9% from 2010 to 2020. Black poverty in Caddo Parish is significantly higher than that of the Whites. Black poverty from 2010 to 2020 has nearly tripled the average of the White population. In Bossier Parish, Black poverty has averaged 30.4% and Whites have averaged 11.4% from 2010 to 2020. In both parishes, Black poverty is significantly higher than Whites. Black poverty in Caddo Parish has an average of 34%, and Black poverty in neighboring Bossier Parish with 30.4%, from 2010 to 2020. White poverty in Caddo Parish has averaged 11.9%, and White poverty in neighboring Bossier Parish has averaged 11.4% from 2010 to 2020— almost identical.[60]

4.4 RESEARCH QUESTION FOUR

Is there a relationship between population trends and job opportunities in Caddo Parish?

The researcher wanted to see if there is a relationship between job opportunities and population trends in Caddo Parish. The researcher examined the population and job data from the past thirty years in Caddo Parish and the Shreveport metro area. The researcher presented census data (section 2.5.3, second figure) which provided population numbers from 1990 to 2020 in Caddo Parish. In 1990, Caddo Parish's population was 248,253 with Whites comprising 59% and Blacks 40% of the population. By 2020, Blacks were 50.3% and Whites 43.6% of the total. After reviewing the census data, the researcher found that the population decreased from 248,253 to 237,848, a 4.2% decrease from 1990 to 2020. The White population has decreased by 15.4%, and Blacks have increased by around 7.3%.

Bossier Parish's thirty-year population has been trending upwards. Bossier Parish's 1990 total population was 86,088. In the year 2000, the total population was 98,310. In the year 2010, the total population was 117,522; and in the year 2020, the total population was 128,746. Reviewing Bossier Parish's population-based on White alone non-Hispanic, in 1990, Whites were 76.4% and African Americans 20.2%. In the following

---

60. US Census Bureau 2020, "Caddo Parish"; US Census Bureau 2020, "Bossier Parish"; World Population Review 2021, "Caddo Parish"; World Population Review 2021, "Bossier Parish."

2000 census, the White population was 72.9% and African Americans 21.3%. In 2010, the White population was 69.2% and African Americans 23.1%. In the recent 2020 count, the population of Whites was 66.3% and African Americans were 23.3%. The White population is a large majority in Bossier Parish.[61] However, the White alone non-Hispanic population base decreased by 10.1% from 1990 to 2020. The total population has increased by 33%. Due to recent activities of job loss, increase in crime in Shreveport, and building of affordable housing, the researcher suggests more Whites have moved to Bossier Parish along with the 3.3% Black resident increase from 2010 to 2020. As mentioned before, Bossier Parish grew more in the early 2000s because of a seventy-million-dollar bond to build three schools in 2004. Furthermore, production of the schools led to the construction of the Louisiana boardwalk (featuring Bass Pro Shops, several restaurants, outlet shopping, a bowling complex, and a fourteen-screen movie theater), Haynesville Shale, several casinos, Cyber Innovation Center, Millennium Studios, StageWorks, and natural gas play perhaps has made the Bossier area more attractive. Even though Bossier Parish has seen some population gain since the 1990s, Caddo Parish still has more population.[62]

The affordable housing trend in Bossier Parish has assisted with an average net in-migration of three hundred residents yearly, migrating across the Red River from the Caddo submarket during the 2000s.[63] Texas is the closest state with a better economy than Louisiana and other neighboring states. A 2015 ACS (updated 2019) shows that 31,044 Louisianians have moved to Texas.[64]

The researcher gathered information and presented a timeline below from the past forty years of major employers' trends in Caddo Parish and the Shreveport-Bossier metropolitan area.

61. US Census of Housing 1990, "Population and Housing," 220; US Census Bureau 2020, "Caddo Parish"; US Census Bureau 2020, "Bossier Parish"; US Census of Population and Housing 2010, "Louisiana," 6.

62. Shaw Environmental and Infrastructure, *Caddo Parish*, 12–21.

63. US Department of Housing and Urban Development, *Comprehensive Housing Market Analysis* (2012), 3–17.

64. Larino, "Top 10 States."

4.4.1 Historical Timeline of Employment Trends Shreveport-Bossier Metropolitan Statistical Area

1980s (Losses/Gains)

- In the 1980s, a depression in Louisiana results from a global crash in the oil industry. The drop in tax revenues was due to a drop in oil prices.

- These drops cause job losses because of suspensions in the government-funded activity that created jobs.

- Both Caddo Parish and Bossier Parish are affected. Caddo Parish is affected the most by its visible population decline.

- In 1981, a General Motors plant opens.

1985–1989 (Losses)

- During the 1985 to 1989 period, the Shreveport–Bossier City metropolitan area (Caddo Parish, Bossier Parish, and Desoto Parish) endures a prolonged and extensive period of job losses.

- There are multiple reasons for the decline. One reason is due to a declining exploration industry.

- AT&T downsizes starting in 1985. AT&T lays off nearly 900 employees.

- The downsizing assists in causing a lengthy recession in the metro area. AT&T downsizes again; its Shreveport phone equipment manufacturing facility downsizes from 7,450 employees to close to 1,100 employees.

1994 (Gains)

- In 1994, the addition of riverboat casinos with large hotel construction adds an average of 4,600 jobs to the Shreveport–Bossier City metropolitan statistical area (MSA).

2000 (Losses)

- AT&T plant closes for good.

2001–2003 (Losses)

- Between the years 2001 to 2003, the Shreveport–Bossier City MSA experiences a loss of 4,300 jobs over the period—the worst decrease of jobs in Louisiana in both length and percentage terms.
- There are layoffs at Beaird, Frymasters, Exide Technologies, and some large manufacturing facilities. Also, the casinos have a decline in business due to the recession.
- The Beaird company alone goes from employing 700 people to 30 people.

2004–2008 (Gains)

- Frymaster, GM (General Motors), and Beaird halt job losses by growing for five consecutive years.
- GM goes from 2,400 employees to 3,600 employees.
- The Beaird company is bought out by Eakin Company and goes from 30 employees to 570.
- Fry Master's employment level goes over 600 people.
- Haynesville Shale exploration adds funds.
- Barksdale Airforce Base in Bossier City adds 700 positions.

2009–2010 (Losses)

- GM drops 2,800 jobs.
- Verizon closes a call center that employs 300 people, and Capital One closes its call center that employs 150 people.
- The total Black incarceration population in Caddo Parish increases by 21.95% from 2000 to 2010.
- According to the 2010 US census, Shreveport loses an estimated 8,848 residents, a 4.4% decline.

2012 (Losses)

- GM closes, and 800 high paying jobs are lost.
- Haynesville Shale activity drops 84%.
- Barksdale Airforce Base drops from its troops from 8,655 to 6,609.

2014 (Losses)

- Shreveport–Bossier City MSA gaming sector, which includes a casino and the racetrack, has job losses of 1,378—primarily due to competitions from Native American casinos in Oklahoma.
- The area's gross revenues from gaming fall by $67.2 million.
- Data collected by 24/7 Wall St. from June 2014 to June 2019 puts Shreveport–Bossier City on the list of cities losing the most jobs with a −3.6% employment change (183,363 to 176,850).

2016 (Losses, Gain)

- ProActive Technologies at Barksdale Airforce Base lays off 51 employees.
- ExpressJet announces in November 2016 the closing of its Shreveport Regional Airport maintenance facility, laying off 286 jobs by June 2017. The closure is due to the consolidation of ExpressJet's heavy aircraft maintenance work.
- ARKLATEX Energy Services lays off 78 employees.
- An estimated 2,359 population decline occurs in Shreveport from July 2016 to July 2017, a 1.21% decline from 194,394 to 192,036. The reason for the population decline is the result of the loss of higher paying jobs.
- GLOVIS America locates a logistics processing center in Shreveport with 150 new jobs and generating $1 million in capital investment.

2017 (Losses)

- Blue Cliff College lays off 40 employees in February 2017.
- Lifecare Specialty Hospital of North Louisiana closes in Ruston in June 2017, laying off 167 employees.
- ExpressJet Airlines closes its maintenance facility at Shreveport Regional Airport, laying off the remaining 53 workers still on staff.

2018 (Losses)

- FTS International, an oil and natural gas well stimulation services provider, closes its Shreveport operations due to declining market demand, displacing 89 employees.

- Monster Moto, a motorbike manufacturer, closes its Ruston assembly plant, laying off 30 workers in May 2018.

2019 (Losses)

- WestRock, a corrugated packaging manufacturer, closes its Monroe operations in June 2019, displacing 83 employees.

- CenturyLink closes its Shreveport call center in October 2019, its focus on operational efficiency and business transformation. The Shreveport call center employed 145 people. Individuals are given the option to relocate to the CenturyLink headquarters in Monroe, use a company-provided daily shuttle, work from home, or leave with a severance package. According to the Warn Notice filed with the Louisiana Workforce Commission, 54 employees are laid off.

2020 (Losses)

- Due to the Covid-19 pandemic, a multitude of local companies lay off employees, hopefully only temporarily. Those are not listed here. The 2020 closings listed below are those companies that have announced permanent closings/reductions.

- Dolet Hills Lignite, a lignite-fired coal plant in De Soto Parish, announces in March 2020 that it will be closing its operations resulting in the displacement of 100 employees.

- Graphic Packaging International permanently shuts down the operation of one of its paper machines in its West Monroe location, resulting in the permanent layoff of 56 employees.

- Libbey, Inc., a glass tableware manufacturer, announces in July 2020 its plans to close its glass manufacturing facility in Shreveport. The closure will displace approximately 400 employees. The company cites its decision to close the facility as part of its effort to reduce costs and match manufacturing capacity with new lower levels of projected demand.[65]

In the 1980s, a depression in Louisiana resulted from a global crash in the oil industry. General Motors and AT&T/BellSouth closed in the 2000s in Shreveport, which led to the loss of around 7,000 jobs. General Motors was closed in August 2012. According to an analysis done by 24/7 Wall St., between 2010 and 2018, the Shreveport–Bossier City area had the highest net migration decline among the metro areas in Louisiana.[66]

According to the 2010 US census, Shreveport lost an estimated 8,848 residents, a 4.4% decline. An estimated 2,359 population decline occurred in Shreveport from July 2016 to July 2017, a 1.21% decline from 194,394 to 192,036. The reason for the population decline is the result of the loss of higher paying jobs. Data collected by 24/7 Wall St. from June 2014 to June 2019 put Shreveport–Bossier City on the list of cities losing the most jobs, with a 3.6% employment change (183,363 to 176,850).[67] The data suggest that the major employers left the Shreveport–Bossier City metro area. A large percentage of White residents and a smaller percentage of Blacks left.

4.5 INTERVIEWS

The researcher interviewed nine former General Motors (GM) employees from the Shreveport location. There was a schedule of ten interviews, but one declined. Their positions at the plant ranged from regional civil rights delegate, union steward, EAP representative, UAW organizer, quality inspector, general technician, team leader, material department worker, coordinator, line worker, well checker, skilled trade carpenter, paint department worker, women's committee chairperson, and skill tradesman/electrician. Some employees held different positions during their tenure at GM. Interviewee #2 has been employed with GM for forty

65. Shaw Environmental and Infrastructure, *Caddo Parish*, 3–15; Scott, "Northwest Louisiana"; Bayliss, "Census 2020"; Prison Policy Initiative, "Louisiana Profile"; UPI, "AT&T to Lay Off"; Wendling, "US Election 2016"; North Louisiana Economic Partnership, "Caddo Parish Competitive Advantages."

66. Listing Bidder, "Real Estate Commission"; Wendling, "US Election 2016"; The Center Square, "Shreveport–Bossier City."

67. Bayliss, "Census 2020."

years. Interviewee #2 started at GM in 1982 with the second wave of hires and transferred when the Shreveport plant began to lay off employees. To the best of their recollection, the interviewees provided me with an average of over four thousand workers employed at GM while they were there. The racial demographic the interviewees gave for employees were 31% Black, 62% White, 4% Hispanic, and 4% other. To the best of their recollection, the interviewees provided me with racial demographics of the percentage of managers that worked at GM during their employment years. The racial demographics of managers were 16% Black, 80% White, 2% Hispanic, and 2% other. After GM closed its plant, employees relocated. The interviewees stated the estimations of the population and demographics of GM employees and management were presented on a seniority board, in team meetings, department meetings, safety meetings, union meetings, and employee boards. Management shared information with the workers regarding GM employee breakdowns as well. Many employees retired or found other means of work just to stay close to their families. An estimated 70% of the employees transferred, 28% retired, and 2% quit. The employees were given an option of forty GM locations to transfer to. Most employees chose to go to Arlington, Texas, right outside of Dallas, Texas, which is a 208-mile drive from Shreveport and takes around three hours and forty-five minutes of travel time. Others went to plants like Wentzville, Missouri, because this plant was seniority friendly, meaning an employee could get more flexibility with job bidding—after all, plant rules favored the seniors. A very small number of employees transferred to other plants close to their families. Every interviewee mentioned experiencing racism, seeing it happen, and hearing stories within the GM plant.

Below are examples of racist incidents mentioned by the interviewees at GM.

1. "When I started in 1983, many workers felt comfortable wearing their KKK T-shirts to work" (Interviewee #1).

2. "Yeah, it was a noose. When they were finding nooses hung in the plant at different places. And near the trucks" (Interviewee #2).

3. "I personally had a White lady call me a Black nigger bitch. Of course, I punched her in her mouth and head (not proud of that). I did not get disciplined for fighting (neither did she) simply because they did not want to deal with the core of the issue-racism in the plant" (Interviewee #1).

4. "Went to supervisor/manager class and got highest scores but did not get the job. Had a White superintendent tell me that as long as he was in a management position that I would never get a management position; regardless of the score" (Interview #7).

5. "When they asked a question, one of the White guys said that he did have a problem with a Black guy being a superintendent because he said that was a job for a White man to have" (Interviewee #3).

6. "They prevented upward mobility. I remember a White girl who had a degree in engineering and a Black guy did too. Management put the Black guy on the line and the White Lady in management. The White lady was much younger" (Interviewee #4).

7. "Overtime was supposed to be offered according to a scale of who is low on overtime hours. Many times, grievances were filed because White men were allowed to work Saturday and Sunday despite not being eligible. This was a common practice that was watched on the regular. We would let them work and just file and get paid" (Interviewee #8).

8. "When I passed the test for skilled trades, they still did not want me to get the job position. That position was given, even though they said you had to pass tests, on buddy-buddy system. Some people that I think flunked tests were given the position because of who they were" (Interviewee #5).

9. "I can tell you what I faced. Some Whites were in cahoots with White supervisors. They would go back and tell certain things and then you would start being watched. Click up" (Interviewee #9).

10. "Those in power want to stay in power and nonprogressive. When bidding on a job and qualified with top seniority, they would come up with a disqualifier for that person. The union did not help sometimes because they had someone else in mind also. The buddy system" (Interviewee #1).

11. "The usual racism like on most jobs. The UAW helped curtail a lot of things" (Interviewee #6).

12. "White females would go after certain Blacks if situations wasn't going right for them" (Interviewee #9).

13. "Management trying to pin people against each other. They do that all day long. They do that in Texas" (Interviewee #2).

Most former employees stated they were thankful and grateful for having a well-paying job with benefits that they could retire from. The workers stated they also had good workdays when everything went well. However, Black workers were uncomfortable knowing that their White coworkers, especially the ones who treated Blacks cruelly and less than Whites, mingled with White management outside of work, including hunting and fishing with one another. Every interviewee experienced and or heard about racism in the GM plant. The nooses hanging in the GM plant, White coworkers wearing Ku Klux Klan T-shirts, and being called "nigger" and having management tell them they would not have a chance of receiving a promotion and/or a better position because they were Black signified the systemic racism and the intimidation that coincides with racism existed in the culture at the GM plant in Shreveport. Furthermore, working at the GM plant, workers enduring short-term and long-term injuries due to repetitive motions required in some positions. Blacks being passed up for qualifiable positions and Blacks receiving harsh treatment by White management and White fellow employees made some workdays worse than others.

Three Takeaways

1. When Blacks were hired with certain qualifications or gained qualifications after employment to become managers, they were frequently turned down for management jobs (shown with the racial demographics of managers from interviews).

2. Blacks encountered overt racism from fellow White employees and White management.

3. The Blacks were thankful to receive benefits and good pay, so they stayed working for General Motors.

4.6 GIS MAPS AND COMMUNITY MAPS

The researcher analyzed the study area using census data, GIS, Google Earth, and Google Maps to provide visual information for this study. The first six images provide the spatial distribution of Caddo Parish and Bossier Parish African Americans / Blacks versus Whites in variables of poverty, unemployment, high school education, bachelor's degree, homeownership, and renters. The GIS maps are self-explanatory, showing the percentages of Black and White distributions in census tracts according to the variables. The following two figures present local neighborhoods, hospitals, and urgent care facilities. The hospitals are close to the inner city, not far from the CBD and suburban south. There are no hospitals and urgent cares on the west side of Shreveport, and there are a significant number of African Americans in the northwest, including the Martin Luther King Jr. area, and the west, which includes the Pines Road area Lakeside community and Greenwood, Louisiana. Greenwood population demographics are 38% Black and 57% White residents.[68] The next figure shows the SNAP grocery overlay; however, this snapshot is very misleading because it gives the impression that all the yellow dots represent regular groceries stores and/or a place where residents can shop for a variety of fresh groceries. In this map, some yellow dots are convenience stores, gas stations, and liquor stores with little to no fruits and vegetables, but some of the stores include the word "groceries" in their names. Using the next two figures in sequence, showing supermarkets and grocery stores in the study area, we can see an example of this. King's Grocery on Dr. Martin Luther King Drive has some cooked food such as spaghetti, fried foods, meatloaf, a few cooked vegetables and liquor, canned goods, candy, sodas, other snacks, and petroleum gas. There is no fresh produce, such as various fruits, vegetables, and other healthy foods. One block away, there is Hy-Lo Grocery and Liquor, which is the same concept as King's Grocery but with an added refrigerated meat and cheese selection and no petroleum gas. Directly across the street, there is a Dollar General store. Exactly one mile west is Quick Pack Groceries which has the same selection food-wise as King's Grocery and Hy-Lo Grocery. The image showing both supermarkets *and* grocery stores gives a better snapshot of *actual* supermarkets and grocery stores in Shreveport. However, the figure showing locations along the Martin Luther King Dr. that have the *supermarket* label shows King's Grocery as an *actual* grocery store. Best case scenario, a resident looking for fresh produce in this area might find a small basket of fruit in one of these convenient stores near the cash register and must simply hope the fruit is fresh. The US Department of Agriculture (USDA) defines food deserts as low-income census tracts with low access to healthy food, meaning residences more than one mile away from a grocery store or supermarket in urban areas (or ten or twenty miles in rural areas). Observing the Google map, there is not a grocery

68. World Population Review 2022, "Caddo Parish," 1.

store / supermarket in the entire Martin Luther King Jr. area until you get to Shoppers Value Foods located at 1867 Nelson Street 1 #1, Shreveport, LA, 71107. Traveling south of these store locations, a residence will not encounter an actual grocery store for five miles until they get to Cotten's Grocery & Market (3656 Lakeshore Drive, Shreveport, LA, 71109) and Piggly Wiggly across the intersection (located at 3723 Lakeshore Drive, Shreveport, LA, 71109). This would make the Martin Luther King Jr. area a food desert. The researcher sees this pattern in the Hollywood Heights area, Moortown, and parts of the Sunset Acres, Morningside, Garden Valley, and Northern Cedar Grove area, all predominantly Black neighborhoods.

Following the supermarket maps, the next two figures provide locations of bank branches and then payday loan lenders in the Shreveport–Bossier City metropolitan area. As explained in section 2.12, a community or neighborhood without financial services or banking institutions is deemed a banking desert. When banking deserts occur, the replacements are with payday loan companies which charge high-interest rates and more frequently generate a cycle of high-interest loans that are a struggle for borrowers of the loans to pay off. These borrowers continue to borrow even more funds to cope with overlapping debt and continue a cycle of poverty.[69] Banking deserts or areas without banks or financial institute branches exacerbate maintaining banking relationships, cost, and/or inconvenience of cashing checks, establishing deposit accounts, and obtaining loans. The first of the two maps shows banking deserts areas such as the Martin Luther King Jr. area, Allendale-Lakeside, Hollywood Heights, Mooretown, Sunset Acre, Garden Valley, and Morningside, all predominately African American / Black communities.[70] The next details the seventy-eight payday loan lenders in the Shreveport–Bossier City metropolitan area, which outnumber banks in the African American communities.

The remaining images in this section provided present details from the CBD/downtown and community neighborhood conditions. The researcher also consulted street view images of the areas to assess area conditions. Analysis shows a lack of biking lanes in the largest city in

69. Smith, "Bank Deserts"; MacNeil, "Cedar Grove."

70. The Shreveport/Bossier bank branches map is shared here with permission and updated 2025 information from the National Community Reinvestment Coalition (NCRC). The researcher first accessed the image through Abello, "Greater Shreveport," in 2020.

Caddo Parish. Even outside of the CBD, there are no biking lanes. There are abandoned, unmaintained, slightly maintained, spray-painted, and graffitied buildings in downtown Shreveport. Further review showed eyesore neighborhoods less than 1 mile to 1.6 miles away from downtown Shreveport, with abandoned buildings, rundown homes both occupied and unoccupied (which include signs of bad roofs, makeshift fences, boarded windows, etc.), slightly maintained to unkept sidewalks, lawns not manicured, broken down vehicles in the drive or lawns, and weeds and vines growing up on street poles. The researcher grew up in the Allendale and Lakeside community.

The researcher also consulted street view images of a street where he previously lived, and further images three blocks from another address where the researcher lived. Figures have been included here of parts of Sunset Acre, Cedar Grove, and the beginning of the Lynbrook community, where the researcher saw no bike lanes, no sidewalks, and other not-so-pleasant conditions until a person travels to the Lynbrook community. The Greenbrook subdivision was also reviewed, a 97% White community in the Cedar Grove area.

A figure has been included of Linwood Junior High School, with the demographics of 94.7% African American / Black, 0.3% White, 3.9% Hispanic/Latino, 0.9% two or more races, and 0.1% Asian or Asian / Pacific Islander.[71] The Lynbrook community neighborhood is predominantly Black at 87% and Whites at 9%. The Greenbrook subdivision is predominately White at 97%.[72] There is a small neighborhood in the Janet Lane area that is 43.5% Black and 50.5% White.[73] Cedar Grove area, Sunset Acre, Garden Valley, Morning Side, Lynbrook communities, and Greenbrook subdivision share part of the same 71106 zip code, but there is a difference once you cross the railroad tracks traveling south of Linwood Avenue passing West 84th Street to Janet Lane and the Greenbrook subdivision. The houses are older but well-maintained—manicured lawns with landscaping, no weeds or vines up the light poles, no broken down cars in driveways or lawns, and no makeshift fences. At 409 Janet Lane, there is Brown E. Moore Head Start Center School which is 1.3 miles away or a three-minute drive from Linwood Junior High School. Brown

71. US News and World Report, "Linwood Public Charter School."

72. City Data, "Lynbrook Neighborhood"; Spokeo, "N Greenbrook Loop."

73. NeighborWho, "Janet LN, Glen Cove."

E. Moore Head Start Center School's demographics are 45% African American / Black, 47% White, 2% Latino, and 1% Asian.[74]

When comparing the demographics of the residences, the demographics of the schools in this zip code, and the demographics in the subdivisions of the predominantly Black section of the 71106 zip code, the Black sections are less maintained while the predominantly White sections are well maintained. Below are some maps of the study area.[75]

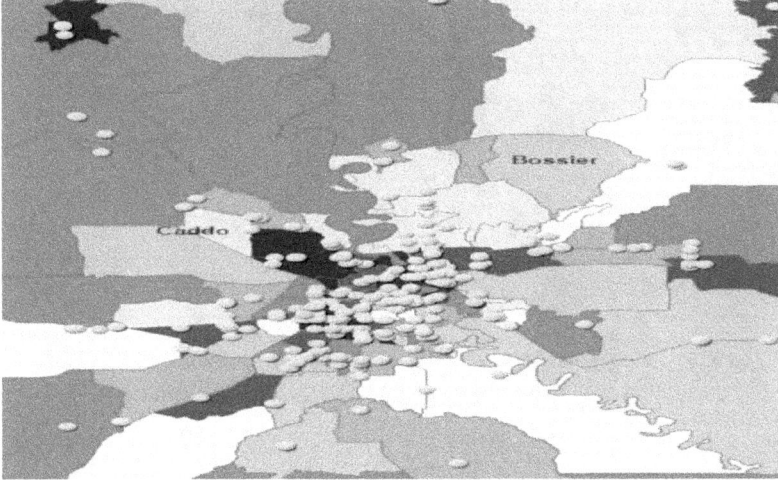

Figure 49: FEMA Map Snap grocery overlay with % below poverty
Source: FEMA, (2022)

74. Donors Choose, "Brown E. Moore."

75. Spatial distribution maps that follow were generated through ArcGIS, using data from US Census Bureau 2020, "Caddo Parrish," and US Census Bureau 2020, "Bossier Parrish."

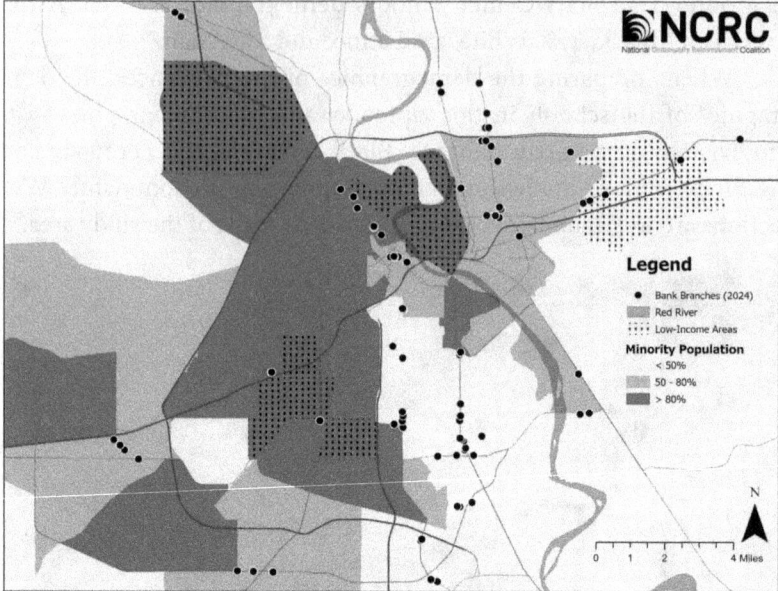

Figure 50: Shreveport/Bossier Bank branches, low-income areas, and minority
population 2025 NCRC (National Community Reinvestment Coalition)

Sunset Acres
Linwood Junior High School
401 W. 70th Street

Figure 51: Linwood Junior High Sunset Acres
(No bike lanes, scattered to no sidewalks)
Source: Google Earth, (2022)

Cedar Grove Community
7455 Linwood Ave

Figure 52: Cedar Grove (No bike lanes and no sidewalks)
Source: Google Earth, (2022)

Sunset Acre Community
Cedar Grove Community
Lynbrook Community

Figure 53: Sunset Acres to Lynbrook
(No bike lanes, sidewalks at Lynbrook Community)
Source: Google Earth, (2022)

Lynbrook Community
400 Block of Janet Ln

Figure 54: Janet Ln Lynbrook Community (Well-kept community)
Source: Google Earth, (2022)

CHAPTER 5

Summary, Conclusion, and Recommendations

SUMMARY

Urbanization and sprawl in Caddo Parish and Bossier Parish, Louisiana, contribute more to African American population poverty versus the White population in this area. The major factors that immensely impact African American poverty in the Caddo Parish and Bossier Parish area are educational attainment (i.e., bachelor's, master's, doctorate, and professional degrees), unemployment/underemployment (hourly jobs versus salary jobs), homeownership, bank deserts, food deserts, payday loan companies, Jim Crow laws, incarceration, transportation, IRS inequalities, health care inequalities, bad politics, and miseducation.

This chapter summarizes findings and data on poverty, birth rates, mortality rates, population trends, incarceration rates, homeownership, renters, cost-burdened homes, transportation, occupation and wages, income, incarceration, education attainment, and the historical timeline of employment trends in the study area.

The previous chapters highlight the history of systemic racism, findings, data, interviews, graphs, and analysis of how the factors contribute to high African American poverty in the study area versus the White population. This chapter summarizes findings on incorporating equity, equality, and social and racial justice to minimize African American poverty in Caddo Parish and Bossier Parish. The chapter also includes concluding thoughts and policy implications. Furthermore, the chapter highlights limitations, delimitations, and future research recommendations.

5.1 CONCLUSION

This research builds on prior studies regarding the understanding and application of poverty reduction theories and methods. Poverty categories include housing poverty, transportation poverty, food insecurity poverty, and energy poverty.

The measurement process has to include a multicomponent method, which has to consider the quality of housing, the standard of living, electricity, access to clean water, sanitation, and education that each contribute to the foundations of providing individuals and families the ability to lead an adequate lifestyle.[1] One of the nation's leaders in child poverty is the state of Louisiana. The state of Louisiana has the second largest proportion of children living in poverty (26.9%) in the United States, following the state of Mississippi (27.7%). Many poor children live in single-parent households in Louisiana, and with the growing number of single women birth rates, the amount will grow.[2]

This section covers *how to address the issue of urbanization and poverty*. In many instances, there has been a negative effect of urbanization that has ushered in new sources of poverty. Negative effects of urbanization can be a lack of resources, poverty, unemployment, and overcrowding. Furthermore, the migration from rural areas to metropolitan areas causes congestion that impedes growth and bolsters the negative issues from geographically concentrated poverty, such as crime and violence in Shreveport. As the crime rate in urban areas increases, it creates a barrier to urban development. A larger share of the poor appears indeed to be living in urban areas nowadays, coined the "urbanization of poverty," as you see in the Shreveport–Bossier City metropolitan area. So, to remedy Black poverty due to the urbanization in the study area, there has to be more investment into Black business owners (with a focus on Foundational Black Americans, or FBA) that can hire dozens to the thousands of Black employees, more job opportunities with higher wages, a good

1. Habitat for Humanity, "Poverty and Housing."

2. Benson, "Poverty Rate of Children"; Council for a Better Louisiana, "Poverty Summary."

education system with Black student support, a better public health care system, and ready as well as affordable transportation.

Other strategies to remedy this issue should include funding for expensive children's sports, such as baseball, volleyball, tennis, and swimming, as well as adult sports and recreation. The researcher suggests generating market potential by developing shopping complexes, malls, food, and cultural activities. The study area needs more affordable and adequate housing to accommodate the Shreveport–Bossier City metropolitan area population. The Shreveport–Bossier City metropolitan area should become more highly tech-savvy with sophisticated communication, infrastructure, social amenities, and medical facilities.

Caddo Parish and Bossier Parish should have better urban planning, institutional reforms, and financing. The local and state government should show more initiative in managing urban lifestyles. Land use planning and government transfers should consider the significant influx of workers migrating into urban areas. An environmentally friendly and sustainable way of living should be in place in the study area. Conserving natural ecosystem techniques needs more development. Campaigns and counseling for active health clinics and family planning need to be provided by stakeholders in the parishes. Tourism promotion and sustainable use of natural resources should be a foundation for job creation, public governance, and social management.[3]

This section covers *how to address sprawl (urban sprawl and job sprawl) and its effect on poverty.* Sprawl is random, unplanned growth characterized by inadequate access to essential land uses such as housing, jobs, and public services like schools, hospitals, and mass transit. The citizens are affected by sprawl by way of urban decline, racial polarization, lack of affordable housing, and suburban/city disparities in public education. Sprawl-driven development has "literally sucked the population of jobs, investment capital, and tax base from the urban core."[4] Equality in neighborhoods, communities, and/or residential areas does not exist. Apartheid-type development policies, housing, and employment have caused decreased residential choices, reduced neighborhood options, mobility limitations, and declining job opportunities for African Americans / Blacks.[5] The African American / Black community

---

3. Bhasin, "10 Causes of Urbanization"; Christiaensen et al., "Urbanization and Poverty Reduction," 13–17.

4. Bullard et al., "Suburban Sprawl," 936.

5. Bullard et al., "Suburban Sprawl," 936.

in the Shreveport–Bossier City metropolitan area is experiencing these disparities caused by sprawl, racism, and discrimination.

This section covers *smart growth*. We can avoid sprawl or urban sprawl by providing a way of urban planning and transportation theory in which we can concentrate growth in compact centers that are walkable, which is considered Smart growth.[6] Smart growth is a distinctive approach to planning communities and places that promotes public health while preserving and enhancing natural and cultural resources, housing, and employment, and expands the range of transportation with its sustainable development goals. Smart growth also advocates for various housing choices by having mixed-use development, neighborhood schools, walkable communities, and transit-oriented and bicycle-friendly land use in a compact area. Smart development can reduce sprawl. There are benefits and advantages to smart development because it contributes to job creation and housing affordability and provides health for communities. African Americans and other minority communities would be recipients of the benefits from smart development.[7]

Job sprawl is the spatial mismatch between populations and jobs. The Black population is associated with a higher spatial mismatch in metropolitan areas, but it is not the same for Whites. Southern metropolitan areas rank low on spatial mismatch and job sprawl for Blacks. Job sprawl in metropolitan areas is a paramount factor affecting spatial mismatch for Blacks and Latinos overall.

As mentioned before, in the Shreveport-Bossier metropolitan area, there is a spatial mismatch between jobs and the labor force, including in two of the top employers in the area: the LSU Health Services Center and the Willis-Knighton Health System. However, these systems are not the only employers in town. The researcher argues that this is an important factor in high unemployment and poverty in Caddo Parish and the Shreveport–Bossier City metropolitan area for Blacks. To improve the Black population's unemployment and poverty scenario, the researcher suggests linking job growth with existing residence patterns and creating policies to promote balance in metropolitan development to help narrow the spatial mismatch between Blacks and jobs.[8]

This section covers *green design*. Green design should be an option for all people and not just for folks that can afford to live in such places,

6. Smart Growth America, "What Is Smart Growth?"
7. Smart Growth America, "What Is Smart Growth?"
8. Stoll, "Black Employment Disadvantage."

which is a part of green design within a smart growth development. Urban decline, polluted water, worsening air, disappearing wildlife habitat and farmland, racial polarization, increased health and safety risk, city and suburban disparities in public education and lack of affordable housing, and erosion of community are the costs that US citizens are paying for sprawl.[9]

> Smart growth with Green design can assist African Americans and other minorities that live and work within constructions and buildings while safeguarding the air and water in our communities.[10]

Green design is environmentally friendly and should include biodegradable products, use of recyclable products, and green architecture. Eco-design is an example of sustainability, as it minimizes environmental impact by utilizing biodegradable products and recyclables, thereby extending a product's lifecycle. Many consumer goods incorporate eco-design, such as biodegradable furniture and recycled tableware. Other products include bamboo sunglasses, toothbrushes, edible coffee cups, and ecological gold jewelry. Clothes and shoes made with plastic recovered from the ocean exist too. Sustainable development is the development that meets the needs of the present without compromising the ability of future generations to meet their own needs.[11]

Green architecture, which is part of green design, is an approach to building for the purpose of protecting human health and the environment by minimizing the harmful effects of construction projects. The green architect or designer's goal is to safeguard the earth, water, and air by optioning eco-friendly construction practices and building materials.[12]

Green architecture and design may include the following:

- Adaptive reuse of older buildings

- Efficient use of space

- Alternative renewable energy power sources, such as solar power or wind power

- Landscaping with native vegetation and planned to maximize passive solar energy

9. Bullard et al., "Suburban Sprawl," 936–47.
10. Freilich and Popowitz, "Umbrella of Sustainability," 4.
11. Iberdrola Corporativa, *Innovación*, 1.
12. Craven, "Green Architecture."

- Use of recycled architectural salvage
- Locally obtained wood and stone, eliminating long-haul transportation
- Optimal location on the land, maximizing sunlight, winds, and natural sheltering
- Non-synthetic, non-toxic materials used inside and out
- Ventilation systems designed for efficient heating and cooling
- Energy-efficient lighting and appliances (e.g., Energy Star products)
- Water-saving plumbing fixtures
- Minimal harm to the natural habitat
- Rainwater harvesting and gray water reuse
- Responsibly harvested woods[13]

This section covers *sustainable community development*. A sustainable community makes use of resources in the present while simultaneously guaranteeing that adequate resources are available for future generations to come. A sustainable community's goal is for its residents to have a good quality of life while at the same time preserving nature's ability to function over time by preventing pollution, minimizing waste, developing local resources to revitalize the economy locally, and promoting efficiency. A sustainable community should mirror a living system in which the human race, nature, and economic elements draw strength from one another and are interdependent. There should be shared information among community members, and decision-making would come from a rich communal life.

Environmental technology, improved and redesigned infrastructure, knowledge-based services, improved natural resources and management, and tourism are all great areas for supportive government policies, expanded training, and private sector investments for the Caddo Parish, Bossier Parish, and specifically the Shreveport-Bossier metropolitan area. These may include the following:

13. Craven, "Green Architecture."

- Energy-efficient and people-friendly designs
- Upgrading the efficiency of energy use in buildings, products, and transportation systems
- Developing, manufacturing, and marketing products, services, and technologies that reduce environmental burdens
- Expanded delivery and use of information technologies
- Recycling and remanufacturing of solid and hazardous waste into marketable products
- Adopting and implementing sustainable forestry, fisheries, soil, and watershed management practices
- Adding value to fish, agricultural, and forest products
- Sustainable tourism activities centered around areas of environmental, cultural, and historical significance.[14]

Researchers argue that the strategy for fair wealth distribution (i.e., for conflict resolution) will help grow the economy so that the study area will have more redistribution. Likewise, to improve environmental (i.e., conflict resolution) quality in the study area, researchers suggest expanding the economy, thereby having sufficient funds to buy environmental protection. This strategy will ensure fair distribution to the poor community to protect and restore their environment.

Reputable planners' inclusion is critical in the process. Urban planners will have essential knowledge of how economies, ecologies, and cities interact, and they should put forth farsighted, specific designs that promote sustainable cities and communities. Planners will have the challenge of dealing with the conflict between competing interests by discovering and implementing complementary users. With concise planning, planners are likely to have the best results for conflict resolution.[15]

5.2 PUBLIC POLICY IMPLICATION

Urban planners must work diligently to bring forth change to overcome and subdue obstacles to create smart growth and cleaner and greener communities while simultaneously promoting equality and eliminating

14. Simon Fraser University, "What Is Sustainable."
15. Campbell, *Green Cities*, 214–40.

inequities. The researcher looks to reduce poverty by comprehending the factors that cause this phenomenon and implementing innovative strategies that reduce it. This research will shed light on laws and policies that should be reexamined and amended at the state and local levels.

To boost the economy as well as help remedy Black poverty in Caddo Parish and other parts of northwest Louisiana, this study suggests policy and law change recommendations to increase homeownership, end discriminatory loan practices, revitalize downtown Shreveport, create job opportunities, improve the local school system, and increase funding and Foundational Black Enrollment at our HBCUs in the northwest region.

A. Since Caddo Parish has a large Black renter population, we could expand the policy so Blacks can have access to small-dollar mortgage loans. New policies assist Black households in gaining access to sustainable and affordable homeownership. Also, this will help existing homeowners with repair and renovation financing.

B. Through the use of tax incentive programs and trust funds, there could be a policy for additional programs to address neighborhood-level issues which include new local products, place-based initiatives, and policies that reduce racial homeownership gaps.

Example

For example, tax incentive programs can be part of the first-time home buyers program offered in each state. The researcher received a first-time homeowners Federal Housing Administration (FHA) loan. The FHA loans are a popular choice for first-time homebuyers because they offer low down payments and more lenient credit requirements. These loans are intended to make homeownership more attainable for individuals who may not qualify for traditional mortgages. The FHA was through Wells Fargo as a tax incentive program. In addition to tax credits, these programs often offer zero-interest loans and grant money for a down payment. Louisiana offers this to first-time homebuyers, low to moderate–income buyers, and veterans purchasing a home in designated areas. It is called the Mortgage Credit Certificate program (MCC), and the buyers who use the program can obtain a federal tax credit of up to 40% of their annual mortgage interest payments for the life of their loan.[16]

16. McCargo et al., *Building Black Homeownership*, 2–11; City of Shreveport, *2019–2023 Consolidated Plan*, 3–41; Bundrick, "First-Time Home Buyer"; Louisiana Housing Corporation, "Mortgage Credit Certificate Program."

Some states allow buyers to use mortgage tax certificates. Tax certificates offer home buyers the chance to deduct a significant amount of the mortgage interest buyers pay on their annual federal tax return. Furthermore, buyers might even be able to combine that tax break with closing cost assistance and a down payment. Some participants are Loan Depot, Home Bridge, and Fairway. In Caddo Parish, there is a homestead exemption. It is a tax exemption on the first seventy-five thousand dollars of the value of a person's home. This exemption applies to all homeowners. The home's value is exempt up to seventy-five thousand dollars from parish property taxes and state taxes.[17]

C. Building costs are increasing, and a greater portion of construction occurs at the higher end of the market. Reform of land-use regulations and zoning are options.[18]

Example

Local jurisdictions can help increase the units of housing in parishes or counties, towns, and cities by modifying zoning policies, which will also help with residential growth, higher density residential uses, and local jurisdictions. Other reform uses can be considered revising occupancy codes that restrict the number of unrelated people permitted to live together in a unit. Shared housing allows lower-income households to split the costs of utilities and rent. Shared housing can reduce individual housing costs.

D. To increase homeownership supply and affordability, we need a policy for more factory-built housing production, such as manufactured and modular housing. Research shows that these homes appreciate as well. New credit scoring also needs to address the racial biases embedded in the existing system. African American credit scores have been an issue in their community. Due to historical structural barriers to accessing banking and credit products, mortgage credit has become more difficult to obtain for Black households.

Example

There are racial biases embedded in the existing system, and new credit scoring also needs to be addressed. African American / Black

17. Caddo Parish, LA, "Parish of Caddo."
18. McCargo et al., *Building Black Homeownership*, 2–11.

loan borrowers are more likely to be given higher-cost mortgages than Whites in similar households amid housing market booms, as recent studies have shown Compared to financial records similar to those of White households, African Americans are charged higher rates by traditional lenders and financial technology.

E. Make outreach and counseling to renters and "mortgage-ready" millennials available. These programs include implementing and designing saving programs and down payment programs. Enhancing awareness of the available county, city, state, and federal programs would help African Americans in Caddo Parish. This strategy will focus on engaging local stakeholders.[19]

Example

About 33% of millennials are ready for mortgages according a recent study by Freddie Mac based on debt-to-income ratios and credit scores. Where the house prices for the market are considered, above 90% of millennials can afford homes in the metropolitan area where they reside. However, 20% of Black millennials are mortgage ready. In metropolitan areas, more than 1.7 million Blacks have ownership potential. We have to reach out to them. This high-potential group is the target of accelerated outreach. Counseling to renters is providing access to young Black renters by teaching them homeownership tools in which we deliver incentives of significant down payment assistance, and first-time homebuyer tax credits can provide young African American households a better chance to build future wealth through home purchasing. Furthermore, we need other counseling resources such as reserve and saving strategies, credit building, how to maintain a home, and a guide through the home-buying process.

Who are the stakeholders in Caddo Parish that need to be engaged? Local stakeholders should include housing counselors, financial institutions, schools, real estate agents, and faith-based organizations.

F. Enforcing existing fair housing and fair lending would help. Fair housing and fair lending goals must be included in policies and initiative programs, and implemented at the national, state, and local

19. McCargo et al., *Building Black Homeownership*, 2–11; Bayer et al., "Vulnerability of Minority Homeowners"; City of Shreveport, *2019–2023 Consolidated Plan*, 3–41.

levels. Supporting fair housing also includes equipping local fair housing organizations with the resources to work with stakeholders to enforce and ensure equitable housing markets.[20]

Example

Promote an equitable and accessible housing finance system by using technology to expand responsible credit in all communities and incorporate alternative data in credit history, such as rental payments and phone bills. Modernize the FHA insurance program (e.g., technology, operations) and expand FHA lending to Black communities and responsibly expand small-dollar mortgages for purchase and renovation.

G. We need new policies to produce fair and nondiscriminatory outcomes with our technological and data science methods uses in housing and finance. Discriminatory technology can have serious fair housing implications.[21]

Example

By speaking of a discriminatory technology, we must mean a way of getting something done which produces a discriminatory effect. In this effect, there must be first discrimination in the moral sense of drawing distinctions in this particular case which is between persons or races. Pervasive discriminatory practices in technology hurt folk who do not speak or look like the people creating the technology.[22] So, if someone wants to discriminate against Black folk trying to get approved for loans and buying homes, White folk can use program technology to do so.

H. Support a public facility project in the CDBG-targeted areas of Shreveport or an underdeveloped area.[23]

---

20. McCargo et al., *Building Black Homeownership*, 2–11.

21. McCargo et al., *Building Black Homeownership*, 2–11.

22. Wittkower, "Discrimination."

23. City of Shreveport, *2019–2023 Consolidated Plan Shreveport*, 3–41. The Community Development Block Grant (CDBG) is a federal program administered by the US Department of Housing and Urban Development (HUD). It provides annual funding to states, cities, and counties to help build and maintain viable urban communities. The program focuses on meeting housing, infrastructure, and economic development needs, particularly for low- and moderate-income residents.

Example

The City of Shreveport Department of Community Development Annual Action Plan contains a range of objectives, goals, and calculated outcomes formulated to address needs identified for affordable housing, non-housing community development, and homelessness. The specific objectives included are to support permanent supportive housing units available to homeless populations, increase the viability for potential homeownership opportunities, increase the number of newly constructed homes available, improve the condition of housing for low-moderate income homeowners, support public facility projects in CDBG-targeted neighborhoods or an under-developed area, expand job creation opportunities by supporting businesses and individuals engaged in economic development activities, revitalize housing conditions in low-income neighborhoods, and strengthen the capacity of nonprofits and faith-based housing developers to build affordable housing.

I. Alleviate the dangerous eyesores in the neighborhood, and make the vacant properties more attractive, safe, and secure.[24]

Example

Caddo Parish / Shreveport areas that are eyesore neighborhoods consist of neighborhoods/communities with rundown homes and buildings; abandoned homes; buildings, properties, and yards not manicured; and polluted areas. These eyesores lower the property value, are a health and safety risk, and are hard to sell homes and establish businesses in.

J. Policies to expand job creation opportunities by supporting businesses and individuals engaged in economic development activities will promote an increase in homeownership because African Americans could make higher incomes to afford homeownership. We should create increased access financing for small businesses and Small Business Technical Assistance programs.

Example

Expansion of job creation is to get Caddo Parish to bring back major corporations such as General Motors, General Electric, and Boots

24. City of Shreveport, *2019–2023 Consolidated Plan Shreveport*, 3–41.

Pharmaceuticals or any pharmaceutical company. Also, Caddo Parish can solicit other companies, such as Amazon and any other up-and-coming companies. Caddo Parish can also expand on existing companies such as Libby Glass Company. Caddo Parish and Bossier Parish should also solicit African American / Black–owned (specifically FBA) corporations such as Dai Technologies, Derek Automotive, MIMS Motor Corporation, Aurora Solar, WeSolar, and Uncharted Power.

K. Help restore the quality of life and housing conditions in low-income neighborhoods. Increase the livability of the citizens by becoming a healthy and active community.[25]

L. Discriminatory technology can have serious effects on fair housing methods. There has been much growth in the technology and data science methods of the housing and financing arena. There has been an effort to improve the use of technology to improve systems, create better efficiencies, gauge consumer behavior, and expand product delivery—such as data used in algorithm-based systems, artificial intelligence, and the development of automated methods. Both technical and data science methods have ways that produce adverse outcomes in housing and finance. We must ensure these improvements are not being used for discrimination in the housing and finance process to discriminate against minorities. We must ensure that new technology, data science methods, and developments do not continue to perpetuate inequitable outcomes.[26]

   Policies produce fair and nondiscriminatory outcomes with our technological and data science methods in housing and finance.

M. The DSDC (Downtown Shreveport Development Corporation) wants to help with the revitalization of downtown Shreveport. One of the ways they can help is through the low-interest loan program. This financial incentive design provides rehabilitation funds for small businesses, property owners, and interested in renovating downtown's older buildings.[27]

---

25. City of Shreveport, *2019–2023 Consolidated Plan Shreveport*, 3–41.

26. Wittkower, "Discrimination."

27. Downtown Shreveport, "Information on Incentives." See the section titled "DSDC Low Interest Loan Program."

Increased access to financing is needed for small businesses, especially for African American/Black-owned businesses and African American/Black-owned corporations. Expanding Small Business Technical Assistance programs is recommended.

N. Effective tutoring models through national service programs, volunteers, fellowships, and high-quality virtual tutoring are needed. Every low-performing student needs high-quality tutoring. Funding should come from federal funds and existing state and local funds.

O. Since childhood hunger is still a major issue, free breakfast and lunch should be offered to all students regardless of income. Free healthy food will help all students' nutritional health and save some embarrassment to the lower-income students.

P. Technical training and workplace experience should be provided, combined with college preparatory academics. Students should be able to earn college credits and or professional certifications to prepare them for college and their careers. There should provision for training and support, higher wages paid to teachers, and recruitment of higher quality teachers.

Q. A healthy and safe school environment needs to be ensured by providing enough security, school social workers, school psychologists, and school counselors.[28]

Examples

Reforming No Child Left Behind

The plan relieves states from the most onerous requirements in NCLB for states moving forward on critical reforms for students and educators. Obama released a blueprint for reauthorizing the Elementary and Secondary Education Act (ESEA), the legislation NCLB had reauthorized in March 2010 and called on Congress repeatedly to fulfill its obligation to repair the law and offer needed relief to state and local leaders, teachers, parents, and students.

---

28. Partelow et al., "Education Policy Ideas," 1–8; Wyatt, "Black Males in Special Education," 5–12.

R. Adopting World-Class Standards and Aligned, High-Quality Assessments

This plan involves adopting high academic standards that prepare all students for success in college and careers. This plan also involves implementing college and career-ready standards and aligned assessments for their students.

Having a good K-12 education experience is a crucial element to having a successful adulthood. The researcher thinks African Americans in Caddo Parish can benefit from improved education policies. Below are suggestions to improve education services in Caddo Parish.

S. Connecting America's Classrooms

In June 2013, President Obama unveiled a bold, new initiative called ConnectED to connect 99% of America's students to the Internet through high-speed wireless and broadband Internet.[29]

Another factor that can reduce poverty is comprehending the single greatest driver of student achievement: household income.[30] Nearly all high-achieving public school districts are part of a thriving community of economically secure middle-class families. These middle-class families also have the sufficient political power to demand great schools, resources, the time to participate in those schools, and the tax money to fund them steadily. In other words, a thriving middle class produces excellent public schools and pays people enough to secure dignified middle-class lives to have high-quality public schools without poverty.[31]

Reparations should be awarded to the descendants of enslaved Black people brought to America through the transatlantic slave trade, as well as Indigenous Black people who were enslaved and those who were free who contributed to building America's infrastructure. The unpaid labor of formerly enslaved Foundational Black Americans (FBAs)[32] played a

---

29. White House, *Giving Every Child*, 4–57.

30. Hanauer, "Better Schools."

31. Hanauer, "Better Schools."

32. The term *Foundational Black American* is used to refer to Black Americans who are direct descendants (lineage-based) of enslaved people within the United States' system of chattel slavery. FBA also includes Black indigenous people in the US, who were also enslaved. To be clear, at least one parent must come from a nonimmigrant background in the US. This lineage is regarded as representing a distinctive connection to the historical development and establishment of the US. A person whose paternal

pivotal role in shaping the economic, political, and cultural foundations of the United States. Additionally, Indigenous Black Americans who were in this country before the slave trade that had land taken during American slavery should be recognized as well. FBA reparations should come in the form of monetary compensation, land or housing compensation, as well as transportation assistance (in the spirit of "forty acres and a mule," Sherman's Special Field Orders No. 15), free college education at our historically Black colleges and universities (HBCUs) for FBAs with a specified GPA (2.8 and above, for no less than 500 years), two free years of trade schools for those who don't want attend college (for 500 years), accurate world history implemented in education, better school funding in predominantly African American schools K–12, funding for academics and athletics at our HBCUs, job opportunities specifically for the African American community (with a guaranteed hiring percentage of HBCU graduates), funding and unique criteria for African Americans to purchase affordable homes in non–environmentally hazardous areas, and investing and funding for Black-owned businesses. Furthermore, HBCUs should be a one-stop shop for our students, faculty, and staff—meaning, they should all have proper medical facilities, a financial institution (bank), a grocery store, and indoor and outdoor agricultural and/or horticultural facilities. This should be included in reparations or included in a state and/or federal funding plan.

Free college education would attract more African Americans to attend college so they could have a better chance at gaining higher paying jobs, which would get them out of poverty and unemployment. In section 4.2, "Research Question Two," the researcher also mentions the reparations bill introduced by US Representative Sheila Jackson Lee, Texas's eighteenth congressional district, on January 3, 2019, to the House of Representatives.

This section covers *the Green New Deal*. The Green New Deal is a plan created by two congressional Democrats to overcome climate change. Representatives Ocasio-Cortez of New York and Markey of Massachusetts propose this plan to slowly move the United States from using

and maternal ancestry traces back to slavery in the Caribbean is not considered a Foundational Black American. The 1870 census offered the first comprehensive record of the Black population in the US. If a person can trace their ancestry to individuals listed in the 1870 census, they are likely descendants of FBAs who were formerly enslaved. The 1900 census also serves as a valuable verification tool, as it provides even more detailed information—such as race, citizenship status, birthplace, and the birthplaces of parents—especially during a period marked by a significant influx of immigrants to the US. Foundational Black Americans, "FBA History."

fossil fuels to start using cleaner energy sources.[33] Caddo Parish has particularly strong concentrations of employment in mining (oil and gas). However, this plan would not be enforced by law. Steering the US from using fossil fuels and reducing global warming greenhouse gas emissions has not been popular. One major initiative of the plan is to guarantee high paying careers in the clean energy industries.[34]

Natural gas technician, green construction scheduler, environmental field technician, hazardous waste technician, and safety coordinator are five environmental green jobs that are open to workers who do not have a college degree.

A. Natural Gas Technician

Technical institutes usually offer one-year certificate programs that provide technical training in installing field equipment, conducting scientific tests, and monitoring drilling activities.

B. Construction Scheduler

Community colleges offer certificate programs that teach people how to use contractor software, contract law and blueprints, and technical specifications. People should have some background in a construction-related field.

C. Environmental Field Technician

Technical institutes offer nondegree training on how to collect samples of water, soil, and air; erect equipment to monitor pollution levels; and prepare reports that explain test results. Some entry-level jobs in this field only require a high school diploma or GED.[35]

D. Hazardous Waste Technician

Many organizations, companies, and agencies offer training programs approved by the US Environmental Protection Agency. Many workers complete training programs that employers sponsor and meet Occupational Safety and Health Administration standards. Nuclear decontamination requires a license obtained by completing forty hours of training in compliance with the Nuclear Regulatory Commission.

33. Friedman, "What Is the Green New Deal?"
34. Friedman, "What Is the Green New Deal?"
35. King, "Environmental Jobs."

E. Safety Coordinator

Community and technical colleges offer one-year certificate programs in occupational safety. Some companies accept entry-level
job seekers who do not have formal education in the field. They
simply receive on-the-job training to ensure that employees comply
with workplace safety standards.

Also, for people living in poverty, the objective of the Green New Deal is
to have clean water, clean air, and healthier foods and to save the United
States from damages caused by climate changes such as stronger and
more damaging storms.[36]

5.3 RESEARCH IN A BROAD CONTEXT

This study is essential to understanding a broader context, which includes
structural inequality in jobs, wages, and sustainable careers for Blacks to
raise their families due to systemic barriers such as historical redlining in
Louisiana, job discrimination, and unlawful practices in the education
system. This research incorporates President Joe Biden's Justice 40 Initiative, the Inflation Reduction Act (IRA), and the Bipartisan Infrastructure
Law (BIL) to improve the quality of life for Black residents in Caddo Parish and Bossier Parish.

5.3.1 Caddo Parish Labor Area Percentages

Caddo Parish employment percentages in retail trade is 12.9% and in
government / public administration is 7.2%. People receiving retirement
income is 25%, and people receiving Social Security is 33%.[37] Shreveport
employment percentages in retail trade is 7.2% and in government / public services is 4.9%.[38] For people in Caddo Parish who commute to work,
78% drove alone, 10.5% carpooled, 0.8% took public transportation (no
Taxi), 1.2% walked, 2.7% were "other," and 6.6% worked from home.

---

36. King, "Environmental Jobs"; Friedman, "What Is the Green New Deal?"
37. US Census 2021, "Caddo Parish," 1.
38. Louisiana Workforce Information Review, *Department of Labor*, 1.

5.3.2 Relocations of Louisiana Locals

A study from the 2015 ACS (updated 2019) showed which states people from Louisiana are moving to when they leave Louisiana. The top ten states listed with the number of Louisiana migrants are below.

(1) Texas: 31,044; (2) Mississippi: 8,678; (3) Florida: 6,560;

(4) California: 6,324; (5) Virginia: 3,993; (6) Arkansas: 3,601;

(7) Georgia: 3,277; (8) Colorado: 3,007; (9) Tennessee: 2,784;

(10) North Carolina: 2,632.[39]

Texas is the closest state with a better economy than Louisiana and other neighboring states. Many of the researcher's friends and family have moved to Texas, with most living in Dallas, Houston, Austin, and San Antonio. The researcher moved from Caddo Parish and did not consider living elsewhere in northwest Louisiana. The researcher moved to southern Louisiana and Houston, Texas, because of limited employment opportunities in Caddo Parish and southern Louisiana.

In terms of domestic migration, Louisiana is one of the least diverse states. In Louisiana, four out of five residents were born locally in the state, which shows there is little migration to the state.[40]

5.3.3 Shreveport Redlining

The Shreveport redlining map was created in the 1930s. The map assisted local banks and lenders in ensuring that particular neighborhoods continued to be White and increasing in value. At the same time, other oppressed and minority residents had to retain deteriorating homes. To specify each area, the Shreveport Area Description Real Estate Report described the redlining map classifications of each neighborhood. Explicit racism turned into structural racism incorporated by the process of redlining. The results of the redlining maps still exist today, shown geographically and in wealth gaps. Black residents are nearly five times more likely to own a home in a formerly redlined area. Redlining has resulted in not only a decrease in home equity but also overall economic inequality of Black families. The effects of this type of structural racism

39. Larino, "Top 10 States."
40. Aisch et al., "Where We Came From."

are still felt in Caddo and Bossier Parish today.[41] The Shreveport redline map is below:[42]

Shreveport areas by grade are labeled as green (20%) for Grade A, "Best"; blue (9%) for Grade B, "Still Desirable"; yellow (29%) for Grade C, "Definitely Declining"; and red (28%) for Grade D, "Hazardous." The Real Estate Redline descriptive map describes the green sections A1 and A2, which have a 100% White population in the higher bracket of business professionals, as moderately wealthy to wealthy residents. Blue sections B1 to B4, which have a 100% White population, are described as medium to higher class salaried workers such as mechanics, tradesmen, business executives, and merchants (B4 located in Bossier City).

Yellow section C1 is 80% Black, 15% foreign White, and 5% native-born White. Section C3 is 50% White and 50% Black. The White population consists of a "good" (as described in the map key) class of salaried workers, and Blacks are domestic workers employed adjacent to White areas. Sections C2, C4, and C5 are a 100% White population, with C2 having better class workers and C4 and C5 with middle-class salaried workers. Section C6 is 70% Black and 30% White, composed of laborers, mechanics, and tradesmen. Section C7 is 90% White and 10% Black, composed of middle-class salaried workers. Sections C8, C9, and C10 are 100% White in population. Section C8 is in Bossier City, made up of lower-bracket salary workers. Sections C9 and C10 are middle-class salaried workers with some business and professional workers.[43] Red section D1 is 60% White and 40% Black, a low-income class of laborers and mechanics. Section D2 is 80% Black, 10% native-born White, and 10% foreign-born White. Section D3 White residents are moving away as fast as they can dispose of their properties due to the detrimental influences of the Black population and the encroachment of commercial districts. These areas are composed of Black laborers and low-income workers. Section D5, historically known as "Hicks Quarters," was originally the Black residential area of the former "Hicks Plantation." Approximately 95% of the properties in this area are occupied by Black homeowners.[44]

---

41. United Way of Northwest Louisiana, "Housing and Redlining."

42. Area maps and descriptions are in the public domain through Digital Scholarship Lab, "Mapping Inequality," accessed through United Way of Northwest Louisiana, "Housing and Redlining."

43. United Way of Northwest Louisiana, "Housing and Redlining."

44. United Way of Northwest Louisiana, "Housing and Redlining."

Shreveport, LA

Areas by Grade

Area		Grade
23%		A "Best"
11%		B "Still Desirable"
34%		C "Definitely Declining'
33%		D "Hazardous"

Demographics

98,167	Total Population (1940)
61.8%	Native-born white
36.6%	African American
1.5%	Foreign-born white

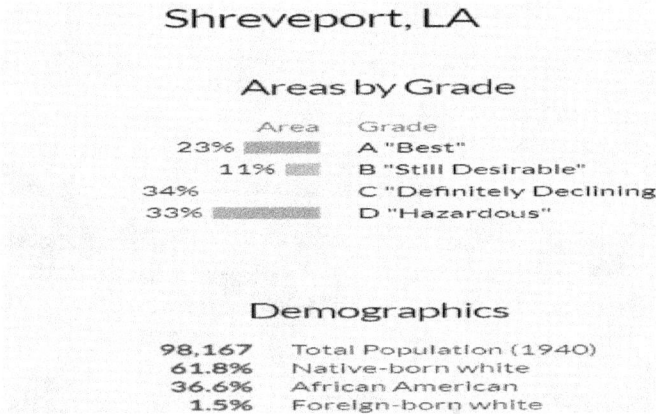

Figure 55: 1940 Descriptions of Areas by Grade and Demographics Shreveport, LA
Source: United Way NWLA, (2021)

D5 Hicks Quarters

This section was originally the negro quarters of what was the "Hicks Plantation" and is known as "Hicks Quarters" and about 95% of the negro properties are occupied by home owners and this accounts for this area right in the center of a much better grade of properties. Negro population consists of laborers and domestics and white population consists of middle-class salaried people.

Figure 56: Description of Grade D Hazardous Area D5
Source: United Way NWLA, (2021)

D3

White residents of this section moving away
as fast as they can dispose of their properties
due to detrimental influences of negro
population and encroachment of commercial
district.

D8

Negro population consists of laborers and
domestic workers employed in the adjoining
better class areas.

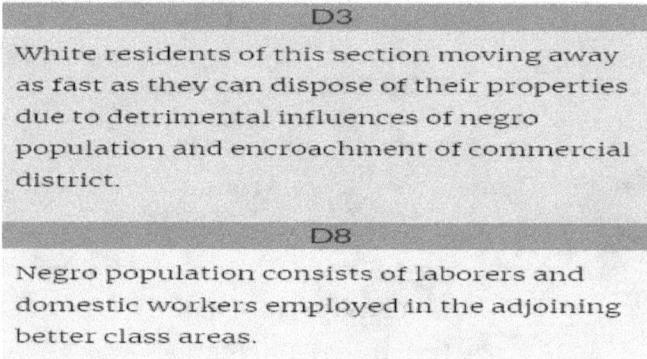

**Figure 57: Description of Grade D Hazardous Area D3 and D8
Source: United Way NWLA, (2021)**

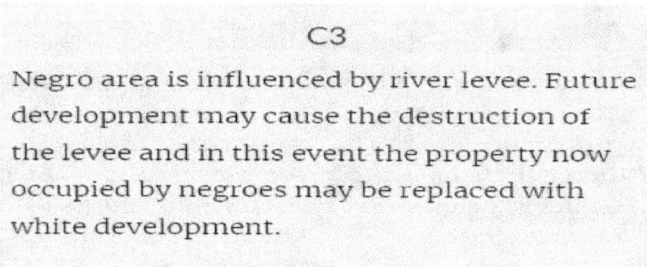

C3

Negro area is influenced by river levee. Future
development may cause the destruction of
the levee and in this event the property now
occupied by negroes may be replaced with
white development.

**Figure 58: Description of Grade C Definitely Declining Area C3
Source: United Way NWLA, (2021)**

5.3.4 HBCUs and Other Universities and Colleges in Northwest Louisiana

There are two Historically Black Colleges and Universities (HBCUs) in northwest Louisiana: Southern University of Shreveport in Shreveport and Grambling State University in Grambling. HBCUs are 80% African American, with over three hundred thousand students in the United States. For more than one hundred and fifty years, HBCUs have provided a nurturing environment and stability for students in danger of not completing college or most at risk of not entering college. For students and faculty, HBCUs provide diverse learning environments making sure every student has the opportunity to succeed. HBCUs provide chances for first-generation and low-income college students, with more than 70% qualifying for federal Pell Grants and 80% receiving federal loans.[45]

This section covers the *Southern University of Shreveport*. Southern University of Shreveport, or SUSLA junior college, is an HBCU in Shreveport located in the Martin Luther King area. SUSLA opened for instruction on September 19, 1967. SUSLA offers a selection of associate degrees, certificates, and technical diplomas. The student population enrolled at SUSLA is 89.9% Black / African American, 5.54% White, 1.79% Hispanic or Latino, 1.19% two or more races, 0.299% Asian, 0.166% Native Hawaiian or other Pacific Islander, and 0.133% Native American or Alaska Native. There were a total of 225 degrees awarded in undergraduate and graduate programs in 2020. African Americans were the most common ethnicity population/race with twelve times more degrees, 212 degrees. White students were the next closest group, obtaining 17 degrees. Also, in 2020, women were awarded 73.3% of the degrees, and men 26.7% of the degrees.

Total enrolment is 3,013 students: 1,325 full time (44%) and 1,688 part time (56%). Full-time undergraduate students at SUSLA are 61.9% Black / African females, 28.1% Black males, and 3.62% White females. There are no graduate students.

The nursing program is very popular at SUSLA. The most common job that degreed SUSLA graduates have is nursing—one of the five most specialized majors at SUSLA. The top specialized major is in registered nursing (1,383,731 people).

The next most specialized groups are accountants and auditors (1,063,938), other managers (782,751), software developers (546,831), and finance managers (470,619). The most specialized majors are in health (132 degrees awarded), liberal arts and humanities (45 degrees), business (41 degrees), protective services (21 degrees), and computer and information sciences and supportive services (10 degrees).

The highest paying jobs for SUSLA degree holders are as surgeons, physicians, skincare specialists, radio disc jockeys, broadcast announcers, and magnetic resonance imaging technologists. Men outnumber women 17-to-1 as Emergency Medical Technicians (EMT paramedic) and females outnumber men 9.75-to-4 as registered nurses.[46]

45. Lomax, "HBCUs."
46. Data USA, "Southern University at Shreveport."

This section covers *Grambling State University*. Grambling State University, or GSU, is also an HBCU higher learning education institution located 64.6 miles from Shreveport in Grambling, Louisiana. African American is the most common race to receive degrees, with 663 degrees in 2020. There were 768 degrees awarded across all of the undergraduates and graduates in 2020. There were 5,438 students enrolled, of which 4,269 (78.5%) were full time and 1,169 (21.5%) were part time. The student demographics are 90.5% Black / African American, 1.97% two or more races, 0.754% White, 0.147% Native American or Alaska Native, 0.129% Asian, and 0% Native Hawaiian or other Pacific Islander. The largest number of full-time undergraduate students are Black / African American females at 57.3%, followed by African American males at 32.5%. The largest graduate group is Black / African American females at 57.9%, followed by African American males at 28.1%.

Among GSU's five most specialized majors, the most common career path is social work, with 165,935 people employed in various other related fields. Next is other managers (143,670 people); police officers (137,612); elementary and middle school teachers (133,672); and judges, lawyers, magistrates, and other judicial workers (130,235).

GSU's most specialized majors are in protected services (199 degrees); parks, recreation, and leisure (74 degrees); public administration and social services (75 degrees); engineering technologies (46 degrees); and history (14 degrees).[47]

Physicians, cardiovascular technologists and technicians, surgeons, computer hardware engineers, and clinical and counseling psychologists are the highest paying jobs for those with degrees in those most specialized majors.[48]

This section covers *Centenary College of Louisiana*. Centenary College of Louisiana, located in Shreveport, has 563 enrolled students, of which 548 (97.3%) are full time, and 17 (2.7%) are part time. For undergraduate and graduate students, 63.6% are White, 17.2% are Black / African American, 9.59% are Hispanic or Latino, 3.55% are two or more races, and 1.07% are Asian. Students enrolled in full-time graduate programs are 100% White males. In 2020, 84 degree holders were White, and 18 were Black / African American.[49] There was no breakdown in degrees in racial demographics.

47. Data USA, "Grambling State University."
48. Data USA, "Grambling State University."
49. Data USA, "Centenary College of Louisiana."

This section covers *Louisiana Tech University*. Louisiana Tech University, or LA Tech, is a higher institution of learning located 67.4 miles outside of Shreveport in Ruston, Louisiana, in Lincoln Parish. In 2020, there were 11,126 students enrolled at LA Tech. Full-time students numbered 8,570 (77%), and there were 2,556 (23%) part time. Undergraduate and graduate students are 71.3% White and 11.1% Black / African American, 3.9% Hispanic or Latino, 2.98% two or more races, 1.38% Asian, 0.422% Native American or Alaska Native, and 0.0629% Native Hawaiian or other Pacific Islander.[50] There was no breakdown in degrees in racial demographics.

This section covers *Louisiana State University-Shreveport*. Louisiana State University-Shreveport, or LSUS, is located in Shreveport. The most common bachelor's degree is in general business administration and management. In 2020, the total student enrollment was 9,955. LSUS has a full-time enrollment of 3,507 (35.2%) students and a part-time enrollment of 6,448 (64.8%) students. Undergraduate and graduate students enrollment is comprised of 46.8% White, 19.9% Black / African American, 6.63% Hispanic or Latino, 3.72% two or more races, 2.7% Asian, 0.382% Native American or Alaska Native, and 0.211% Native Hawaiian or other Pacific Islander. The most common graduate students enrolled are White females (25.6%), White males (18.6%), and Black / African American females (15.2%).[51] There was no breakdown in degrees in racial demographics.

This section covers *Bossier Parish Community College*. Bossier Parish Community College, or BPCC, is a higher education institution 13 miles outside of Shreveport, located in Bossier City. In 2020, the most common degree recipients were Whites with 1,182 degrees and Black / African Americans with 568 degrees. BPCC has a total student enrollment of 6,090. Full-time student enrollment is 2,892 (47.5%), and part-time enrollment is 3,198 (5.25%) students.

The BPCC enrolled student population for undergraduate and graduate is 45.8% White, 38.4% Black / African American, 5.17% Hispanic or Latino, 4.42% two or more races, 2.64% Native Hawaiian or other Pacific Islander, 0.837% Asian, and 0.624% Native American or Alaska Native.

The most common students enrolled in full-time undergraduate programs are White females (30.1%), Black / African females (27.6%),

50. Data USA, "Louisiana Tech University."
51. Data USA, "Louisiana State University-Shreveport."

and White males (17%). There are no graduate programs. There was no breakdown in degrees in racial demographics.[52]

This section covers *Northwestern State University*. Northwestern State University is a higher education institution located in Natchitoches, 75.2 miles from Shreveport. The most popular degrees in 2020 were in registered nursing with 258 degrees, general studies with 126 degrees, and general business administration and management with 123 degrees. There were 6,396 (55.9%) full-time students and 5,051 (44.1%) part-time students. Student demographics for both undergraduate and graduate are 57.2% White, 26.9% Black / African American, 6.13% Hispanic or Latino, 4.53% two or more races, 1.31% Native American or Alaska Native, 1.11% Asian, and 0.0961% Native Hawaiian or other Pacific Islander. The most common undergraduate program students are White females (36.1%), Black / African American females (22.3%), and White males (14.9%). The most common graduate students are White females at 40.8%, White males at 18.9%, and Black / African American females at 18%.[53]

5.3.5 Louisiana Black Farmers

There were nearly a million Black farmers in 1920, and today there are just 45,000. In 1920, the number of Black farmers in the United States peaked at 949,889. Today, American farmers total 3.4 million, and only 45,508, or 1.3%, are Black, according to recent data from the US Department of Agriculture released in April 2019. They own a small portion of US farmland at 0.52%. To compare, 95% of America's farmers are White.[54] White farmers tend to make $190,000 annually, and Black farmers make less than $40,000 annually, and this is probably due to the average acreage of the White farmers being much larger. Black farmers experience denied loans for their businesses. John Boyd Jr., a Black farmer in Baskerville, Virginia, filed six complaints against a loan officer for discriminatory practices and treatment. After the USDA Civil Rights Office of Virginia investigated the officer, Boyd filed and won the first ever discrimination lawsuit against the USDA. The lawsuit encouraged other Black farmers to do the same since they were experiencing the same mistreatment. Boyd

52. Data USA, "Bossier Parish Community College."
53. Data USA, "Northwestern State University."
54. Sewell, "Black Farmers."

founded the National Black Farmers Association in 1995 after meeting with other Black farmers. John Boyd Jr. and four hundred other Black farmers sued the USDA in 1997. The lawsuit, Pigford v. Glickman, alleged that from 1981 to 1997, complaints from Black farmers of their loans and other support being denied were ignored because of rampant discrimination by USDA officials. The government settled in 1999 and awarded over sixteen thousand Black farmers $50,000 each, equaling $1 billion. Still, more Black farmers were unaware of the lawsuit and were left out. Boyd became an advocate for over eighty thousand late claimants. In December 2010, President Obama signed a bill authorizing $1.25 billion in compensation for the late settling of the Pigford II lawsuit. Some of those farmers were from Louisiana, such as Jerry Lee Amerson from Shreveport, who was discriminated against by the UDSA.

Boyd's National Black Farmers Associations (NBFA) met in Shreveport for its Twenty-Eighth Annual Conference in November 2018. The free annual two-day conference is a chance for Black farmers to form a network support system and outline the USDA resources that are available for their use.[55]

Louisiana farmers are upset about the last several decades of shrinking land they are able to lease because of their claims of racist politics. Farmers say they continue to lose land leases with White property owners who prefer to work with new, often White farmers who have better equipment and resources. Also, when Black farmers go to the USDA and apply for a million-dollar loan, they receive only two hundred thousand. They start losing land, and yields go down. Multiple Louisiana Black farmers said they could barely get resources.[56]

5.3.6 Black Heir Property in the US and Northwest Louisiana

In the United States, the leading cause of Black "involuntary land loss" has been the loss of heirs' property. From the years 1910 to 1997, 90% of the loss of Black-owned farmland nationwide has been due to Black involuntary land loss, according to the USDA. There are many complications with heirs' property. When a landowner or property owner dies and does not have estate planning in place or a will for the transfer of ownership of land to another party before death, heirs' property is created.

55. Childers, "Millions Owed"; Sewell, "Black Farmers."
56. Chatlani, "Black Louisiana Farmers."

In the case of first-generation Black landowners / property owners, it is common for them not to have access to the legal system. The land/property gets informally passed to the heirs of the owner who died. As each generation changes hands many times, the original owner's name is listed on the deed, proving ownership becomes increasingly challenging. Heirs wanting to farm the land run into complications, such as being unable to participate in USDA programs because one must provide proof of ownership to obtain a farm number. Farm numbers make owners eligible for USDA programs, including lending, participation in county committees, and disaster relief programs. Recently the 2018 Farm Bill was passed because of the long hard fight of the Federation of Southern Cooperatives (born out of the Civil Rights era to save Black-owned farms and land) for heirs to obtain a farm number and qualify for USDA programs.[57]

There are more complications when there is more than one heir and they have different interests in the property. All the heirs own a proportional stake in the land/property, so all heirs must agree on decisions regarding the property, and with each death, the number of heirs increases. In some cases, some heirs want to sell their stake of interests, so they bring a lawsuit to force the sale to resolve their heirship. Furthermore, there are instances where one heir has sold their stake without the other heirs knowing these developers exploit families. Developers use this lack of cooperation and clarity to their advantage to purchase one heir's stake and force land sales in court.[58]

Northwest Louisiana is no stranger to the heirs' property debacles. In a particular instance, a man named of Fred Wardlaw, who had heirs' property from his grandparents, was being forced into a sheriffs' sale / land auction. The mortgage was paid off, there were no taxes owed, and no other heirs or family members wanted to sell the property. The court was involved. A system of centuries-old laws took land from families, especially Black families. Wardlaw is a descendant and one of the heirs of a formerly enslaved man named Jacob Loud, who acquired one hundred and sixty acres of land in the mid-1850s. According to legal papers in 1999, a White man named W. G. Dowden, who was not a member of the family nor related to the family, brought a partition action in the court. The issue arose on June 30, 1980, when Mr. Wardlaw's great uncle John

---

57. Fahy, "Black-Owned Farmland."
58. Fahy, "Black-Owned Farmland."

sold his one-twenty-fifth share of ownership to two White men, who then sold it to W. G. Dowden, who later sold it to Timberland Services in 1992.

Uncle John's stake was 4%. Once brought into court, the judge had multiple options to resolve the matter. One option was to have parties agree on what 4% to give to Timberland Services. Instead, the judge's verdict was to have every party sell the land and split the proceeds among everyone who jointly owned the land. The sheriff put the notice in the local paper, and the auction to sell the land went up. So, a party can have one heir sell one-twenty-fifth of their stake and lose 100% of the land/property.[59] This process has happened to many Black heirs' family members in the US, not just in northwest Louisiana. To add insult to injury, a lawyer named Thomas Mitchell discovered that this law was not in a single property law casebook or treatise. From 1910 to 2000 this practice was performed against Black families. Black families were frozen out by the banks and government programs until being foreclosed on or just run off by violence. If a local or a developer sees this, it is easy pickings because it is a courthouse auction listed in the local paper, so not many people know. Then no one is allowed to inspect the land ahead of time. Lastly, anyone who wants to purchase has to do so with 100% cash, making it difficult for the losing families to come up with the cash to repurchase the property.

Thomas Mitchell, who later became a law professor, stated,

> A lot of people conceded that it was unjust—but they said the law exists the way it exists because African Americans—heirs' property owners—fundamentally lack economic and political power, and the law is going to serve the interests of those who are more powerful, including those who want to take the land from these African Americans.[60]

Mr. Mitchell fought to change the heirs' property unjust law system. In 2011, Mitchell began to succeed, and the legal language his team wrote up to fix the heirs' property system was changed in Nevada, and then Georgia changed a law in 2012. Seventeen states adopted Mitchell's law. Eight of the seventeen southern states adopted the laws, but Louisiana did not. Eventually, Louisiana only changed that if an heir owns less than 20% of the property, the court cannot force the sale of all the

---

59. NPR, "Jacob Loud's Land."
60. NPR, "Jacob Loud's Land."

property. The Timberland company eventually purchased all of the Wardlaw's property.[61]

5.3.7 Black Homeownership Gap and Devaluation in Shreveport

Black homeownership in Shreveport is widening between Blacks versus Whites. According to the National Community Reinvestment Coalition (NCRC) Home Mortgage Report, private mortgage lending companies are struggling to meet Black households' needs, contributing to the significant homeownership gap. The NCRC report also indicates that the laws intended to increase access to credit, and the private mortgage market, have not helped achieve the Black community's homeownership rates. Many people of color live in credit deserts, including African Americans in Shreveport, who are affected by compounding the issue of the homeownership gap. It is challenging to obtain homes with little access to mainstream credit, which results in absence of or low credit scores. Shreveport's Black homeownership gap is 22.1%, seventy-sixth lowest among all metro areas.[62]

Owner-occupied homes equal home appreciation, contributing to higher home values, and owners create wealth. The Shreveport–Bossier City metropolitan area Black communities experience devaluation of owner-occupied housing. Acquiring homes is more accessible due to devaluation, but once purchased, the buyer is at a clear disadvantage if the home does not appreciate. The owner who usually can benefit from selling at a higher value, refinancing, or borrowing against the home can't do so when the home is experiencing devaluation. Devaluation also affects rental property owners and how much they can charge renters. In comparing home values in majority neighborhoods with those where less than 1% of the residents are Black, there is a −9.6% difference in the Shreveport–Bossier City area and an absolute price difference of −$15,308.[63]

61. NPR, "Jacob Loud's Land."
62. Stacker, "Black Homeownership Gap."
63. Perry et al., "Black Neighborhoods."

5.3.8 Justice 40 Initiative

Under the Justice 40 Initiative, the US federal government's goal is to contribute 40% of the overall benefits of certain federal investments circulated to disadvantaged communities that are underserved, marginalized, and overburdened by pollution. President Biden signed Executive Order 14008 quickly after taking office. Certain federal investments fall under categories such as remediation and reduction of legacy pollution, clean energy and energy efficiency, clean transit, climate change, affordable housing, sustainable housing, critical clean water and wastewater infrastructure development, and training and workforce development. All categories can benefit Caddo and Bossier Parish and also all of Louisiana. Every program covered under Justice 40 is mandated to engage in stakeholder consultation. Furthermore, community stakeholders are required to be involved in deciding program benefits, and those programs covered must have a data report on how the benefits get to disadvantaged communities. The program should include the disadvantaged communities in Caddo and Bossier Parish, which require addressing decades of underinvestment and environmental justice needs. Justice 40 benefits can address Caddo and Bossier Parish's critical needs of affordable and sustainable housing, infrastructure, sprawl, and training and workforce development. To advance environmental justice, federal agencies are making investments in President Biden's Bipartisan Infrastructure Law, Inflation Reduction Act, and American Rescue Plan.[64]

5.3.9 The Inflation Reduction Act

The Inflation Reduction Act is a promise that President Biden delivered on building an economy that works for working-class families, which include communities that have been underserved and underinvested for years. This act includes major investments in environmental justice and establishing certain new environmental justice grant programs. The Inflation Reduction Act is to beat back special interest backed by President Biden and congressional democrats to advance environmental justice while building a cleaner future, lowering energy costs, and growing from the bottom up and middle out.[65] The Inflation Reduction Act will benefit Caddo Parish and Bossier Parish's disadvantaged community's cost

64. White House, "Justice 40 Initiative."
65. White House, "Inflation Reduction Act."

of living disparities. The economic growth will help generate jobs for producing goods and services in the study area.

5.3.10 Bipartisan Infrastructure

President Biden signed the Infrastructure Investment and Jobs Act (IIJA, also known as the Bipartisan Infrastructure Law) into law, which will assist with federal investment in infrastructure. The act will include resilience, mass transit, roads, bridges, water infrastructure, and broadband. The law provides $550 billion over fiscal years 2022 through 2026. These funds could bring better infrastructure, lower emissions from trucks, remedy the street disconnectivity issues, and bring more jobs (green jobs) to the Caddo and Bossier Parish area. The Bipartisan Infrastructure will also address legacy pollution matter, extreme weather resiliency concerns, water infrastructure and elimination of lead service piping, and climate change in the study area.[66]

5.3.11 Green Banks

Green banks, or green investment banks, are financial firms whose mission is to transition to clean and sustainable energy technologies by using innovative financing techniques and other tools to combat climate change.[67] The job of the green banks is to invest in renewable energy sources, smart power networks, and electric automobiles. Green banks stop financing fossil fuels and scale up low-carbon technology to attract eco-conscious investors and government agencies. These types of funding help green banks go after greater national and global climate goals.

Green banks' goals are to combat the effects of climate change. The effect of climate change and polluting industries have been detrimental to the Black community and has affected them disproportionately in Louisiana and nationwide. Green banks can benefit Black people because

> African Americans need clean air, clean water, healthy food, high-quality jobs, clean energy, green and affordable transportation, and access to safe, natural environments. Green Banks contributing to The Green New Deal Resolution is a positive step that presents climate solutions to move the United States in

66. Infrastructure Investment and Jobs Act of 2021, Pub. L. No. 117-58, 135 Stat. 429 (2021).

67. Gary, "Green Banking."

the right direction toward a just, clean energy economy for all—
solutions that eliminate greenhouse gases, create millions of
high-wage American jobs (especially African Americans), build
green and accessible public transportation, reduce poverty and
inequality, promote equal protection of workers, frontline communities and vulnerable populations, and provide safeguards
against climate and related environmental health threats.[68]

These positive outcomes from the transitions would have huge and
positive impacts on African Americans. Green banking will attract eco-
conscious investors to Caddo and Bossier Parishes. Green banks invest
in renewable energy systems, smart power networks, and electric automobiles.[69] These investments also equal more jobs and notably can bring
electric automobile manufacturing jobs to replace the loss of General
Motors jobs. Investment in sustainable low-carbon businesses will attract
middle-class society to the study area.

5.3.12 Gaming in the Shreveport–Bossier City Metropolitan Area

In a 2019 interview with Professor David Hoass of Centenary College,
he provided important information regarding the gaming industry
in Shreveport–Bossier City. He explained that the gaming industry in
Shreveport–Bossier City had been stable with the opening of Margaritaville's arrival. However, the market has not expanded, and that ultimately
affects jobs. When casinos came twenty-five years ago, there was a real
boom in unskilled labor. People began working for casinos that did not
have advanced degrees and who previously worked more physical labor
jobs. During the interview, he continued to explain that he did not think
things had gotten worse for unskilled laborers in the metropolitan area.
However, he didn't think there were ongoing impacts in an instance
where things continued to improve every year. Professor Hoass explained
that the local government gets its fair share of money produced from the
casinos, and when the casinos started paying better, other jobs had to
increase their pay. Bossier City's casino revenues financed Bossier City's
CenturyLink building (a multi-event center). Furthermore, it was supposed to be a boon for education, but he had not seen a lot of dollars go
toward the education movement, and if it had, then it had to be a very

---

68. Bullard, "African Americans on the Frontline."
69. Gary, "Green Banking."

subtle movement. He could not see bad money use but hadn't seen what gaming has done for the area.[70]

According to the Louisiana Casino Association, state gaming taxes that generated from riverboat casinos fund essential state services, including teacher salaries, elementary and secondary schools, police and fire protection, and highway construction. The Louisiana State Police receives 40% of its annual budget from riverboat gaming taxes. Louisiana would have higher taxes if the riverboat gaming tax revenue did not help fund many essential government services. Most of the gaming taxes collected by Louisiana get deposited into the state general fund, then monies are dispersed at the preference of the Louisiana Legislature each year. Once any business, including casinos in Louisiana, gives taxes over, they have no control over fund spending.[71]

There was a dissertation study in 1997 that performed linear multiple regression models with a single quantitative dependent variable used to evaluate the empirical relationship between independent variables and teachers' salaries. Data were collected for a five-year period before and after Louisiana began the lottery. One model attempts to evaluate the impact of the lottery on elementary and secondary teachers' salaries. A second model attempted to measure any differences in university salaries before and since the adoption of the lottery. The impact of the lottery on teachers' salaries is analyzed using 1986–1995 data collected from sixty-six school systems within the state. A second data set collected from sixteen public universities in Louisiana analyzed the lottery's impact on the salaries of university teachers during the same periods. The two periods studied are 1986–1990 and 1991–1995. A sample of 2,160 observations was collected for the elementary and secondary teachers. The university teachers' model includes 6,338 observations.[72] The study revealed that the Louisiana lottery revenues did not affect teachers' salaries among elementary and secondary teachers. In contrast, empirical findings rejected the second hypothesis. The lottery did affect the university teachers, but slightly. There was no significant difference in university teachers' salaries before and after Louisiana adopted the lottery. The dollar impact of this variable on university teachers' salaries is $2.49 per year or about $0.20 a month. Inferences should reflect whether the variable's contribution is relevant. Lottery revenues do not appear to be relevant to university

70. Ferrell, "Gambling in Shreveport-Bossier."
71. Louisiana Casino Association, "Louisiana Economic Impact."
72. Melancon, "Louisiana Lottery," 59.

salaries. The rejection of the null may be attributable to model mis-specification. Education and experience positively correlate with salaries in both models. An added dimension to university teachers' salaries was the rank of the teacher. Education and experience positively correlate with salaries in both models.[73]

The last twenty-five years have seen increased competition, which meant there was a limit to growth. With the Native American tribe casinos in Oklahoma and casinos in Mississippi, the gaming industry in the Shreveport–Bossier City area has seen much decline in business. There has been a loss of 1,378 jobs to the area's gaming industry, with no foreseeable gains of any more jobs. In the Louisiana Outlook for 2020 and 2021, LSU economist Loren Scott wrote that there is "no hope that there will be an arresting of the downward employment trend in this industry."[74] Job loss is not the only concern. Harrah's Louisiana Downs and the six casinos' gross revenue fell $67.2 million at the time, or a 9.1% decline. In 2022 the local market declined about 13% compared to 2021.[75]

5.3.13 Civil Rights Era to Benefit Blacks in Shreveport and the Rest of Louisiana

It took more than one hundred years and unjust laws after the American Civil War to make rights real for Blacks in the United States. Civil rights activists in the 1950s, 1960s, and through the 1970s inherited fearlessness, courage, and resilience and passed it on during the years. The civil rights activist trail went through Louisiana, and these activists heroically strategized, marched, boycotted, sat down, stood up, preached, and sang for change. They dedicated their lives to making real change possible and making rights real for themselves and future generations in Louisiana and the rest of the United States. To make these changes possible, it took the nation's first sit-ins in New Orleans on Canal Street, the bus boycott in Baton Rouge, and Bogalusa's 105-mile march to the state capital in Louisiana to spearhead the modern Civil Rights Movement. In the 1950s and 1960s, Black commercials thrived in Louisiana, like on Texas Avenue in Shreveport, and were rich in culture and opportunity—being home to many Black businesses in the 1950s and 1960s, including several

73. Melancon, "Louisiana Lottery," 138–41.

74. Ferrell, "Gambling in Shreveport-Bossier."

75. Ferrell, "Gambling in Shreveport-Bossier"; Lofton, "Shreveport-Bossier Gaming."

restaurants, bakeries, haberdashers, drug stores, the Star Theatre, and the Shreveport Star. In 1979 Texas Avenue was placed on the National Register of Historic Places. In Shreveport, restaurants weren't just places to dine, churches didn't just serve as places of worship and fellowship, and beauty salons weren't just for servicing one's look. Rather, these establishments acted as organizing places for civil rights meetings. Civil rights activists held their primary meetings at Little Union Baptist Church (the church the researcher attended) and the Old Galilee Baptist Church in Shreveport. Little Union Baptist Church was a central ground for civil rights activists in the 1960s. Under the leadership of Reverend Claude Clifford McLain, who served for thirty-two years, he made his church a site for mass civil rights meetings to boycott hiring practices by downtown stores. The famous Dr. Martin Luther King Jr. made his last public appearance at Little Union Baptist Church, delivering his speech from the pulpit at a voter registration rally.[76] Dr. King also spoke in Galilee Baptist Church in Shreveport in 1958, discussed in the film documentary *Beyond Galilee* by the North Louisiana Civil Rights Coalition and coproducer T. D. Antoine, written by coproducer Joey Kent.[77] Anne Brewster and Mamie Love Wallace were civil rights leaders, along with owners and beauticians of the Modern Beauty Shop, who hosted voter registration workshops and political forums. The University of Louisiana at Lafayette in Lafayette—formerly known as Southwestern Louisiana Industrial Institute, then the University of Southwest Louisiana[78] (USL, where the researcher graduated as an undergraduate)—was previously an all-White school and state-supported college in the South. The university peacefully desegregated after winning a lawsuit allowing Black students to attend in 1954 and then play sports. Four older students spearheaded this movement.[79] These types of movements helped put in place the Civil Rights Act of 1964. The movements led to the legal end to the Jim Crow era (even though some remnants still exists in Louisiana), and it allowed African Americans equal access to restaurants, jobs, public facilities, and transportation. The Civil Rights Act of 1968, along with the Voting Right Act of 1965, expanded the protections of housing and voting.[80]

76. Louisiana Civil Rights Trail, "Story of Pride."

77. Pointer, "Premiere of Documentary."

78. The university went through two name changes.

79. Louisiana Civil Rights Trail, "Story of Pride."

80. See Library of Congress, "Civil Rights Act of 1964."

5.3.14 North Louisiana Racism vs. South Louisiana Racism

The Republican Party controlled the Louisiana congress five years after the American Civil War, aiming to push strong civil rights legislation to secure Blacks' political rights. After the abolishment of American slavery, the Fourteenth Amendment was to guarantee Blacks the same rights of citizenship and equal protection under the law. The federal government assisted Blacks by establishing nearly four thousand schools for Blacks in the South. Furthermore, over one thousand five hundred Black Americans ran for state and national office representatives.[81]

Many White Louisianians worked to reverse the progress of Blacks made during Reconstruction in the late 1800s. The Jim Crow era gradually institutionalized before 1880 during Reconstruction. The Louisiana legislature began implanting the Black Codes Law in 1865 to form the foundation for racial segregation. Black Codes regulated and restricted the movement of enslaved people. They restored the southern social order of Whites and Blacks before the American Civil War, where Whites occupied a higher status than Blacks. Black Codes were in every parish of Louisiana but aggressively enforced in the northern and eastern parishes of Louisiana. Black Code Laws put limits on Blacks, such as the type of businesses Blacks could own, times they could travel downtown, and requiring that no more than three Blacks could gather in one place, and it gave regular White citizens authority over Blacks when police were not on duty.

The freedom was mainly due to the large racial demographics in southern Louisiana and particularly New Orleans. New Orleans had three identifiable racial groups: Whites, free people of color, and enslaved people of African descent. Free people of color in New Orleans were usually of mixed-race heritage. They commonly enjoyed measures of freedom in their social interactions and businesses not found in the rest of Louisiana.[82]

Louisiana sent several Black politicians to the House of Representatives at the start of Reconstruction. P. B. S. Pinchback was a Black governor who served from 1872 to 1973. However, upon the federal troop removal from Louisiana, all Black politicians were defeated, and federal intervention on behalf of Blacks also seemed to disappear. Black men were strong supporters of the Republican Party, so the Democratic

81. Brown, "Jim Crow and Segregation."
82. Brown, "Jim Crow and Segregation."

Party formed a plan to completely remove the Republican Party from the South by 1890. Despite the rights Blacks gained by the Fourteenth and Fifteenth Amendments, the Democratic Party put in requirements and clauses that prevented Black people from registering to vote. Black citizens were systemically excluded from the political process, paving the way for widespread social segregation. Louisiana passed one of the first laws preventing rights to Black men from voting registration rights. Then Louisiana segregated schools, restaurants, nightclubs, public facilities for adults, cemeteries, amusement parks, playgrounds, trains, jails, hospitals, armed forces, jury duty, churches, and institutions (some institutions excluded Blacks altogether). White people received priority over Black people in every instance.

In northern Louisiana, lynchings dramatically increased after the 1900s, especially in Caddo, Quachita, and Morehouse Parishes. More than half of the lynchings in Louisiana happened north of Alexandria between 1900 and 1930. Most statistical details were a bit skewed due to the fact that northern parish police officials did not consider lynchings a homicide. These lynchings helped to enforce Jim Crow.

The Civil Rights Movement led to the Jim Crow era's demise even though some Jim Crow laws were in effect in northwest Louisiana. Along with World War II, the Civil Rights Movement ushered in key successes over racial segregation that continued in Louisiana and other southern states in the 1950s and 1960s. The Civil Rights Act outlawed discrimination based on race and segregation in restaurants, hotels, schools, and universities. Louisiana didn't fully integrate public schools until the 1970s. The Jim Crow era effect has had a staying power that has left Blacks in extreme poverty in Louisiana, especially in North Louisiana.[83]

5.3.15 Cost of Living in Shreveport, Bossier, and Baton Rouge (2.5.4)

Refer back to the last figure of section 2.5.4, "Cost of Living Cities of Study Area Parishes."

5.3.16 Poverty Gaps in Caddo and Bossier Parish

Looking at Caddo poverty from 2010 to 2020 (the first figure in section 2.3), one can see that the poverty gap increased between Blacks versus Whites over this period. In 2010, the poverty percentage gap was 19.3%,

---

83. Brown, "Jim Crow and Segregation."

with Black poverty being 29.40% and White poverty at 10.10%. The lowest percentage of poverty gap from 2010 to 2020 was 16.9% in 2011, and the largest gap was in 2017, with a 27% poverty gap between Blacks and Whites.

Looking at Bossier Parish poverty from 2010 to 2020 (the second figure in section 2.3), one can see that the poverty gap increased between Blacks versus Whites over this period. In 2010, the poverty percentage gap was 19%, with Black poverty being 28.1% and White poverty at 9.10%. The lowest poverty gap from 2010 to 2020 was 5.4% in 2019, and the largest gap in 2011 was a 29.6% gap between Blacks and Whites. After 2019 the poverty gap spiked again in 2020 to 21.99%.[84]

5.4 LIMITATIONS

Limitations in this research will be the limited research and studies performed on African American / Black poverty in Caddo Parish and Bossier Parish, Louisiana. With the General Motors layoffs, transfers, and retirements beginning over twenty years ago, it's difficult to track down ex-employees. The researcher currently resides in Houston, Texas. The study area is in northern Louisiana, and there is some distance between the two areas geographically. Part of the study will call for the researcher to travel, when possible, to the study area for data, interviews, and personal observations.

5.5 DELIMITATIONS

Delimitations that exist will be to use similar study areas to compare Caddo Parish. Caddo Parish is unique regarding its population, geographic make-up, the African American population, education system, city infrastructure, and history. Furthermore, specific plans and policies suggest that the area should be specific and unique to the make-up of the Shreveport–Bossier City metro area.

---

84. US Census 2021, "Caddo Parish," 1; US Census 2021, "Bossier Parish," 1; World Population Review 2022, "Caddo Parish," 1; World Population Review 2022, "Bossier Parish," 1.

5.6 FUTURE RESEARCH

The need to solve Black poverty in the United States, Louisiana, Caddo Parish, and Bossier Parish is a work in progress. The uphill battle will require a group effort of young and elder to establish a network with specific agendas to solve this phenomenon. The researcher's future studies will include research on new, greener, and environmentally friendly industries such as production systems. The systems include turning solid waste into recycled and reusable clean water using solar, water, and wind energy. This study aims to bring such technology to the education systems in the study area and solicit such businesses to come to the study areas for jobs, in addition to using such knowledge to create a smarter, greener, and more sustainable Shreveport–Bossier City metro area.

Shreveport–Bossier City metropolitan area is in competition with other counties, parishes, cities, and states for young, well-educated twenty-first-century knowledge, job seekers, and employees who are more attracted to better surroundings, such as better employment opportunities, paying jobs, cultural attractions, urban amenities, walkable environments and access to outdoor recreation, attractive natural environments, and entertainment. The Shreveport–Bossier City metro area must make competitive changes to attract these younger job seekers.

The researcher will also connect with the informant used in the General Motors interview study to interview fifteen to twenty more people to perform a one- to one-and-a-half-hour intensive interview with the interviewees. With longer intensive interviews, the researcher will press the interviewees to express themselves more, how and why they view the subject discussed, their behaviors, reactions, and strategies for dealing with situations discussed in the study. To resolve the study, the researcher will work diligently through factors in the study area, including wealth, employment, health care, education, laws, housing, transportation, and poverty, in order to produce justice, equality, and equity in northwest Louisiana and the United States.

Bibliography

Abello, Oscar P. "Greater Shreveport Fighting Predatory Lending by Tackling Banking Deserts." Next City, 2018. https://nextcity.org/daily/entry/shreveport-predatory-lending-banking-deserts.

Adiele, Pius. *The Popes, the Catholic Church, and the Transatlantic Enslavement of Black Africans 1418–1839*. Hildesheim: Georg Olms Verlag, 2017.

Aisch, Gregor, et al. "Where We Came From and Where We Went, State by State." *New York Times*, last updated Aug. 19, 2014. https://www.nytimes.com/interactive/2014/08/13/upshot/where-people-in-each-state-were-born.html.

Albares, Nick. "Poverty Gap Widens Between Louisiana and U.S." Invest in Louisiana, 2016. https://www.labudget.org/2016/09/poverty-and-inequality-in-louisiana/.

Aliaga, Martha, and Brenda Gunderson. *Interactive Statistics*. 2nd ed. Upper Saddle River, NJ: Pearson Education, 2002.

Allen, Renee. "Over 1k Requests for New Trials by Inmates Serving Sentences in Louisiana Based on Jim Crow Jury Verdicts." KTAL News, Apr. 20, 2021. https://www.arklatexhomepage.com/news/state-news/louisiana/over-1k-requests-for-new-trials-by-inmates-serving-sentences-in-louisiana-based-on-jim-crow-jury-verdicts/.

Amadeo, Kimberly. "Why Your Work Is Critical to the Economy." The Balance, Dotdash Meredith, 2020. https://www.thebalance.com/labor-definition-types-and-how-it-affects-the-economy-3305859.

Amanfo, Addai B. "Interesting African Quotes and Proverbs About Education." Studentshubgh, 2019. https://www.studentshubgh.com/interesting-african-quotes-and-proverbs-about-education/.

American Apartment Owners Association. "Louisiana Landlord Tenant Law." https://american-apartment-owners-association.org/landlord-tenant-laws/louisiana/?sr sltid=AfmBOop8V2Luit79ImxQDdYkJszbw4w9z7hA6oNQUcAwyOjBjUZud-1N.

Arresting Inequality. "Jim Crow in New Orleans." Department of History University of Georgia, 2015. https://arrestinginequality.org/jim-crow.

Babbie, Earl. *The Practice of Social Research*. 13th ed. Belmont, CA: Wadsworth, 1998.

Bank Map. "Find a Bank in Bossier City, LA." Accessed 2021. http://www.bank-map.com/banks-in-Bossier+City_LA.

———. "Find a Bank in Lafayette, LA." Accessed 2021. http://www.bank-map.com/banks-in-Lafayette_LA.

Barker, Ernest. *The Politics of Aristotle*. London: Oxford University Press, 1958.

Barnum, Matt. "Race, Not Just Poverty, Shapes Who Graduates in America—and Other Education Lessons from a Big New Study." Chalkbeat, Mar. 23, 2018. https://www.chalkbeat.org/2018/3/23/21104601/race-not-just-poverty-shapes-who-graduates-in-america-and-other-education-lessons-from-a-big-new-stu.

Bayer, Patrick, et al. "The Vulnerability of Minority Homeowners in the Housing Boom and Bust." *American Economic Journal* 9 (2017) 344–45.

Bayliss, Deborah. "Census 2020: Shreveport–Bossier City Officials Aim to Count Every Resident." *Shreveport Times*, Dec. 18, 2019. https://www.shreveporttimes.com/story/news/local/2019/12/18/shreveport-bossier-city-census-2020/2678378001/.

———. "Nearly 60 Percent of Shreveport Renters Cannot Afford to Live Here." *Shreveport Times*, Jan. 30, 2020. https://www.shreveporttimes.com/story/news/2020/01/30/shreveport-rent-prices-too-high-60-percent-affordable-housing/4553042002/.

Benmergui, Leandro. "Housing Development: Housing Policy, Slums, and Squatter Settlements in Rio De Janeiro, Brazil and Buenos Aires, Argentina, 1948–1973." PhD diss., University of Maryland, 2012.

Benn, Domonique, et al. "Crews to Begin Removal of Caddo Confederate Monument in 2022." KSLA, Mar. 31, 2022. https://www.ksla.com/2022/03/31/crews-begin-removal-caddo-confederate-monument-2022/.

Benson, Craig. "Poverty Rate of Children Higher than National Rate, Lower for Older Populations." United States Census Bureau, Oct. 4, 2022. https://www.census.gov/library/stories/2022/10/poverty-rate-varies-by-age-groups.html.

Berger, Eugene, et al., eds. *World History: Cultures, States, and Societies to 1500.* Dahlonega, GA: University of North Georgia Press, 2016.

Berlin, Carly. "How Louisiana's Oil and Gas Industry Uses Prison Labor." Scalawag, Mar. 24, 2020. https://scalawagmagazine.org/2020/03/powerlines-prison-labor-oil/.

Best Places. "Cost of Living in the State of Louisiana." Accessed 2021. https://www.bestplaces.net/cost_of_living/state/louisiana.

Bhasin, Hitesh. "10 Causes of Urbanization—Positive and Negative Effects of Urbanization." Marketing91, Dec. 19, 2020. https://www.marketing91.com/causes-of-urbanization-positive-effects-negative-effects/.

Bigelow, Melville M. "Definition of Law." *Columbia Law Review* 5 (1905) 1–19. https://doi.org/10.2307/1109712.

BlackPast. "Racial Violence in the United States Since 1660." https://www.blackpast.org/special-features/racial-violence-united-states-1660/.

Blank, Laurie. "War Reparations for Ukraine: Key Issues." Just Security, May 2, 2022. https://www.justsecurity.org/81341/war-reparations-for-ukraine-key-issues/.

Blomberg, Elizabeth, et al. *2022 State Report: Louisiana; County Health Rankings and Roadmaps.* Madison, WI: University of Wisconsin Population Health Institute, 2022. https://www.countyhealthrankings.org/health-data/louisiana/data-and-resources.

Bossier City Metropolitan Planning Commission. "Proceedings of the City Council of Bossier City State of Louisiana." Mar. 19, 2013. http://www.forward-now.com/wp-content/uploads/2013/04/MinSpecialMeetingMarch192013.pdf.

Bossier Parish Police Jury. "About Bossier Parish." Accessed 2021. https://bossierparishla.gov/experience-bossier-parish/about-bossier-parish.

Boushey, Heather, and Adam Hersh. "The American Middle Class, Income Inequality, and the Strength of Our Economy." Center for American Progress, May 17, 2012. https://www.americanprogress.org/article/the-american-middle-class-income-inequality-and-the-strength-of-our-economy/.

Bowen, Glenn. "Document Analysis as a Qualitative Research Method." *Qualitative Research Journal* 9.2 (2009) 27–40. https://www.researchgate.net/publication/240807798_Document_Analysis_as_a_Qualitative_Research_Method.

Bradley, Michael, and John H. Clarke. *The Iceman Inheritance: Prehistoric Sources of Western Man's Racism, Sexism, and Aggression*. New York: Kayode, 1991.

Bromwich, Jonah. "Louisiana Sheriff's Remarks Evoke Slavery, Critic Say." *New York Times*, Oct. 12, 2017. https://www.nytimes.com/2017/10/12/us/prison-reform-steve-prator.

Browder, Anthony. *Nile Valley Contributions to Civilization*. Washington, DC: Institute of Karmic Guidance, 1992.

Brown, Nikki. "Jim Crow and Segregation." 64 Parishes, last updated Dec. 13, 2024. https://64parishes.org/entry/jim-crowsegregation.

Bryan, Erika. "Frances Cress Welsing (1935–2016)." BlackPast, Mar. 19, 2016. https://www.blackpast.org/african-american-history/welsing-frances-cress-1935-2016/.

Bullard, Robert D. "African Americans on the Frontline Fighting for Environmental Justice." 2019. https://drrobertbullard.com/african-americans-on-the-frontline-fighting-for-environmental-justice/.

———. *Confronting Environmental Racism: Voices from the Grassroots*. Boston, MA: South End, 1993.

———. "Environmental Justice in the 21st Century." Environmental Justice Resource Center, Clark Atlanta University, 2005. https://www.uwosh.edu/sirt/wp-content/uploads/sites/86/2017/08/Bullard_Environmental-Justice-in-the-21st-Century.pdf.

———. *Invisible Houston: The Black Experience in Boom and Bust*. College Station, TX: Texas A&M University Press, 1987.

———. "The Legacy of American Apartheid and Environmental Racism." *Journal of Civil Rights and Economic Development* 9.2 (1994) 445–74.

Bullard, Robert D., and Bob Evans. *Just Sustainabilities: Development in an Unequal World*. Edited by Julian Agyeman. Cambridge, MA: MIT Press, 2003.

Bullard, Robert D., et al. "The Costs and Consequences of Suburban Sprawl: The Case of Metro Atlanta." *Georgia State University Law Review* 17 (2001) 935–39, 945–47, 961–65.

———. *Environmental Health and Racial Equity in the United States: Building Environmentally Just, Sustainable, and Livable Communities*. Washington, DC: American Health Association, 2011.

———. *Highway Robbery: Transportation Racism and New Routes to Equity*. Cambridge, MA: South End, 2004.

Bundrick, Hal M. "8 First-Time Home Buyer Loans and Programs." Nerdwallet, 2020. https://www.nerdwallet.com/article/mortgages/programs-help-first-time-homebuyers.

Burby, Henry. "Italian Immigration in NYC." ePortfolio, Macaulay Honors College, Mar. 7, 2016. https://eportfolios.macaulay.cuny.edu/murphy16/2016/03/09/italian-immigration-in-nyc/.

Burnett, Paul. "Ancient Egypt, Science and Greek Literature." UC Berkeley Library, Feb. 11, 2015. https://update.lib.berkeley.edu/2015/02/11/ancient-egypt-science-and-greek-literature/.

Burris, Alexandria. "Transportation Study up for Review." *Shreveport Times*, last updated Jan. 2, 2016. https://www.shreveporttimes.com/story/news/local/2016/01/01/transportation-study-up-review/77756034/.

Caddo Parish, LA. "Parish of Caddo." 2020. http://www.caddo.org/Faq.aspx?QID=150.

Caddo Parish Public Schools. "About Caddo Parish Public Schools." Accessed 2020. https://www.caddoschools.org/page/about-caddo.

Campbell, Scott. *Green Cities, Growing Cities, Just Cities? Urban Planning and the Contradictions of Sustainable Development.* Ann Arbor, MI: Wiley, 2016.

The Center Square. "Shreveport–Bossier City Has Largest Net Population Outflow Among Louisiana Cities." June 23, 2020. https://www.thecentersquare.com/louisiana/shreveport-bossier-city-has-largest-net-population-outflow-among-louisiana-cities/article_78c8e62e-a5ef-11ea-9ad0-47637734b9a7.html.

Chae, Lee. "War and Peace: Towards a Theory of Just Peace." PhD diss., University of California, 2016. https://escholarship.org/uc/item/5hd971nm.

Chatlani, Shalina. "Black Louisiana Farmers' Land Leases Are Vanishing. Some Say Racist Policies Are to Blame." WWNO, Oct. 19, 2021. https://www.wwno.org/news/2021-10-19/black-louisiana-farmers-land-leases-are-vanishing-some-say-racist-policies-are-to-blame.

Childers, Fred. "Millions Owed to Black Farmers." KSLA, Sept. 7, 2010. https://www.ksla.com/story/13115267/millions-owed-to-black-farmers/.

Chimbiri, Kandace. *The Story of Early Ancient Egypt: Prehistoric and Old Kingdom Egypt (20,000–2,181 B.C.)* London: Golden Destiny, 2011.

Chipeta, Catherine. "Best Data Collection Methods for Quantitative Research." Conjointly, June 15, 2020. https://conjointly.com/blog/data-collection-quantitative-research/.

Christiaensen, Luc, et al. "Urbanization and Poverty Reduction: The Role of Rural Diversification and Secondary Towns." Policy Research Working Paper 6422, World Bank, 2013. http://hdl.handle.net/10986/15562.

Chung, Ed, et al. "The 1994 Crime Bill Continues to Undercut Justice Reform—Here's How to Stop It." Center for American Progress, Mar. 26, 2019. https://www.americanprogress.org/article/1994-crime-bill-continues-undercut-justice-reform-heres-stop/.

City Data. "Lynbrook Neighborhood in Shreveport, Louisiana (LA), 71106 Subdivision Profile." Accessed 2022. https://www.city-data.com/neighborhood/Lynbrook-Shreveport-LA.html.

City of Shreveport. "Shreveport, Louisiana—Official Website Complaint File." 2021. https://www.shreveportla.gov/1532/File-a-Complaint.

City of Shreveport. *Analysis of Impediments to Fair Housing.* Department of Community Development, 2008. https://www.shreveportla.gov/DocumentCenter/View/54/Analysis-of-Impediments-to-Fair-Housing?bidId=.

———. *2014–2018 Consolidated Plan.* Department of Community Development, 2013. https://www.shreveportla.gov/DocumentCenter/View/1722/2014---2018-Consolidated-Plan-and-2014-Annual-Action-Plan?bidId=.

———. *2019–2023 Consolidated Plan and 2019 Annual Action Plan.* Department of Community Development, 2019. https://www.shreveportla.gov/

DocumentCenter/View/15484/Shreveport-2019-2023-ConPlan-Template-05-24-2019-For-Publication.

Clark, Versa. "Shreveport, We're Better than This." *Shreveport Times*, Oct. 25, 2019. https://www.shreveporttimes.com/story/opinion/columnists/2019/10/25/shreveport-slowest-growing-city-opinion-column/4090986002/.

Clarke, John H. "Race: An Evolving Issue in Western Social Thought." *Présence Africaine* 3 (1970) 155–62. https://doi.org/10.3917/presa.075.0155.

Clemens, Austin, and John Sabelhaus. "Can Policymakers Reverse the Unequal Decline in Middle-Age U.S. Homeownership Rates?" Washington Center for Equitable Growth, Oct. 13, 2020. https://equitablegrowth.org/can-policymakers-reverse-the-unequal-decline-in-middle-age-u-s-homeownershiprates/.

Cohen, Rima, et al. "The Best and Worst States for Health Care." MoneyGeek, 2022. https://www.moneygeek.com/insurance/health/analysis/2022-top-states-health-care/.

Coleman, Booker T. "Humanity Is Born in Africa: Africans Travel the World; A Study Guide." Course Hero, 2013. https://www.coursehero.com/file/7191582/AfricansBorn-StudyGuide/.

Coleman-Moore, Kesha. "Creating the Black American Dream: Race, Class and Community." PhD diss., University of Pennsylvania, 2002. https://www.proquest.com/docview/305504061.

Cortright, Joseph. "Theories of Urban Success. Impresa Consulting and CEOs for Cities." Forward Cities, 2008. https://forwardcities.org/old/wp-content/uploads/2018/04/City-Success_Theories-of-Urban-Prosperity.pdf.

Council for a Better Louisiana. "Poverty Summary." CABL Futures Institute, 1999. https://cabl.org/poverty-summary/ (page discontinued).

County Office. "Louisiana Department of Labor in Shreveport, Louisiana." Louisiana Department of Labor. https://www.countyoffice.org/louisiana-department-of-labor-shreveport-la-5a1/.

Cox, Chelsey. "Texas Teen Banned by High School from Attending Graduation After Refusing to Cut Dreadlocks." *USA Today*, Jan. 24, 2020. https://www.usatoday.com/story/news/nation/2020/01/24/black-texas-teen-barred-high-school-after-graduation-not-cutting-dreadlocks/4562210002/.

Craven, Jackie. "A Primer on Green Architecture and Green Design." ThoughtCo, June 21, 2019. https://www.thoughtco.com/what-is-green-architecture-and-green-design-177955.

Creamer, John. "Poverty Rates for Blacks and Hispanics Reached Historic Lows in 2019." US Census Bureau, Sept. 15, 2020. https://www.census.gov/library/stories/2020/09/poverty-rates-for-blacks-and-hispanics-reached-historic-lows-in-2019.html.

Crisp, Elizabeth. "Louisiana Has One of Biggest Gaps Between Its Richest, Poorest Residents, a New Report Says." Advocate, Dec. 15, 2016. https://www.theadvocate.com/baton_rouge/news/politics/article_860b6480-c24d-11e6-98a8-17fcde65b6f8.html.

Curry, Leonard P. "Urbanization and Urbanism in the Old South: A Comparative View." *Journal of Southern History* 40 (1974) 43–60. https://www.jstor.org/stable/2206056?seq=1.

Dahl, Drew, and Michelle Franke. "Banking Deserts Become a Concern as Branches Dry Up." Federal Reserve Bank of Saint Louis, July 25, 2022. https://www.

stlouisfed.org/publications/regional-economist/second-quarter-2017/banking-deserts-become-a-concern-as-branches-dry-up.

Dalakar, Joseph. "The 10-20-30 Provision: Defining Persistent Poverty Counties." R45100. Washington, DC: Congressional Research Service, 2019. https://www.congress.gov/crs-product/R45100.

Data USA. "Bossier Parish Community College." 2021. https://datausa.io/profile/university/bossier-parish-community-college.

———. "Centenary College of Louisiana." 2021. https://datausa.io/profile/university/centenary-college-of-louisiana.

———. "Grambling State University." 2021. https://datausa.io/profile/university/grambling-state university.

———. "Louisiana State University-Shreveport." 2021. https://datausa.io/profile/university/louisiana-state-university-shreveport.

———. "Louisiana Tech University." 2021. https://datausa.io/profile/university/louisiana-tech-university.

———. "Northwestern State University of Louisiana." 2023. https://datausa.io/profile/university/northwestern-state-university-of-louisiana.

———. "Southern University at Shreveport." 2021. https://datausa.io/profile/university/southern-university-at-shreveport.

Davis, Allen J. "An Historical Timeline of Reparations Payments Made from 1783 Through 2022 by the United States Government, States, Cities, Religious Institutions, Universities, Corporations, and Communities." University of Massachusetts Amherst, last updated June 2, 2025. https://guides.library.umass.edu/reparations#s-lg-page-section-7637938.

Death Penalty Information Center. "Report: Black People 7.5 Times More Likely to Be Wrongfully Convicted of Murder than Whites, Risk Even Greater If Victim Was White." October 2022. https://deathpenaltyinfo.org/report-black-people-7-5-times-more-likely-to-be-wrongfully-convicted-of-murder-than-whites-risk-even-greater-if-victim-was-white.

DeJong, Ninke. "Unit 7: Urbanization and Cities." May 29, 2014. YouTube video, 08:11. https://www.youtube.com/watch?v=RrEUwOyGuZI.

Department of Numbers. "Bossier Parish Louisiana Residential Rent and Rental Statistics." Accessed 2021. https://www.deptofnumbers.com/rent/louisiana/bossier-parish/.

———. "Caddo Parish Louisiana Residential Rent and Rental Statistics." Accessed 2021. https://www.deptofnumbers.com/rent/louisiana/caddo-parish/.

———. "East Baton Rouge Parish Louisiana Residential Rent and Rental Statistics." Accessed 2021. https://www.deptofnumbers.com/rent/louisiana/east-baton-rouge-parish/.

DeVault, Majorie. "Here Are the Advantages and Disadvantages of Quantitative Research." The Balance, Dotdash Meredith, 2020. https://www.thebalancesmb.com/quantitative-research-advantages-and-disadvantages-2296728.

Diab, Ehab. "Urban Public Transportation Systems: Understanding the Impacts of Service Improvement Strategies on Service Reliability and Passenger's Perception." PhD diss., School of Urban Planning, McGill University, 2015.

Digital Scholarship Lab. "Mapping Inequality: Redlining in New Deal America." https://dsl.richmond.edu/panorama/redlining/map/LA/Shreveport/areas#loc=13/32.4801/-93.7529.

Dimebag1980. "Shreveport City Profile." Urban Planet, 2009. https://www.urbanplanet. org/forums/topic/22745-shreveport-city-profile/.

Donors Choose. "Brown E. Moore Head Start." Accessed 2022. https://www. donorschoose.org/schools/louisiana/office-of-head-start/brown-e-moore-head-start/125841.

Downtown Shreveport. "Information on Incentives and Grants." Accessed 2020. https://downtownshreveport.com/ova_dep/grants/.

Driscoll, Kenny. "Black Maria America's First Police Transport Vehicle." Baltimore Police History, Dec. 30, 2023. https://baltimorepolicemuseum.com/en/black-maria-americas-first-police-transport-vehicle.

Drouaillet, Carlos. "Louisiana Strikes Down One of the Last Remaining Jim Crow Laws." *San Quentin News.* Feb. 6, 2019. https://sanquentinnews.com/louisiana-strikes-down-one-of-the-last-remaining-jim-crow-laws/.

Drug Policy Alliance. "Top Adviser to Richard Nixon Admitted That 'War on Drugs' Was Policy Tool to Go After Anti-War Protesters and 'Black People.'" 2016. https:// www.drugpolicy.org/press-release/2016/03/top-adviser-richard-nixon-admitted-war-drugs-was-policy-tool-go-after-anti.

Edwards, Roxanna, and Sean M. Smith. "Job Market Remains Tight in 2019, as the Unemployment Rate Falls to Its Lowest Level Since 1969." *Monthly Labor Review,* US Bureau of Labor Statistics, Apr. 2020. https://doi.org/10.21916/mlr.2020.8

Elkin, Maria. "What Everyone Gets Wrong About Affordable Housing." New America, Aug. 24, 2017. https://www.newamerica.org/weekly/what-everyone-gets-wrong-about-affordable-housing/.

Ellis, Paul. "How Nelson Mandela Created the Conditions for Success." Cambridge International Education, Mar. 28, 2019. https://blog.cambridgeinternational.org/nelson-mandela/.

Equal Justice Initiative. "Illegal Racial Discrimination in Jury Selection Documented in Caddo Parish, Louisiana." Aug. 24, 2015. https://eji.org/news/study-documents-racially-biased-jury-selection-caddo-parish-louisiana/.

———. "Nixon Adviser Admits War on Drugs Was Designed to Criminalize Black People." Mar. 25, 2016. https://eji.org/news/nixon-war-on-drugs-designed-to-criminalize-black-people/.

E-Reference Desk. "Caddo Parish, Louisiana." Accessed 2019. https://www. ereferencedesk.com/resources/counties/louisiana/caddo.html.

ESRI. "What Is GIS?" Accessed 2020. https://www.esri.com/en-us/what-is-gis/overview.

Fahy, Jennifer. "How Heirs' Property Fueled the 90 Percent Decline in Black-Owned Farmland." Farm Aid, Feb. 28, 2022. https://www.farmaid.org/blog/heirs-property-90-percent-decline-black-owned-farmland/.

FamilySearch. "Caddo Parish, Louisiana Genealogy." Intellect Reserve, accessed 2020. https://www.familysearch.org/wiki/en/Caddo_Parish,_Louisiana_Genealogy.

Federal Reserve Economic Data. "Unemployment Rate in Bossier Parish, LA." Accessed 2021. https://fred.stlouisfed.org/series/LABOSS5URN.

———. "Unemployment Rate in Caddo Parish, LA." Accessed 2021. https://fred.stlouisfed.org/series/LACADD7URN.

Feeding America. "Dedicated Response from Charitable Food Sector and Support from Public/Private Partnerships Help Reduce Food Insecurity in 2021." Sept. 8, 2022. https://www.feedingamerica.org/about-us/press-room/USDA-Report-for-2021.

———. "Hunger and Food Insecurity." Accessed 2021. https://hungerandhealth. feedingamerica.org/understand-food-insecurity/.

FEMA Maps. "Bossier Parish and Caddo Parish Hospitals and Urgent Care Facilities." ArcGIS Web Application, accessed 2022. https://fema.maps.arcgis.com/apps/ webappviewer/index.html?id=90c0c996a5e242a79345cdbc5f758fc6.

Ferrell, Jeff. "Migrating Shreveport Population." KSLA News, last updated June 15, 2006. https://www.ksla.com. https://www.ksla.com/story/5007203/migrating-shreveport-population/.

Ferrell, Scott. "25 Years of Casino Gambling in Shreveport–Bossier City." *Shreveport Times*, last updated Dec. 21, 2019. https://www.shreveporttimes.com/story/news/ local/2019/12/21/shreveport-bossier-city-has-seen-ups-and-downs-25-years-casinos/4408934002/.

Finch, Charles S., III. "The Black Roots of Egypt's Glory." *Washington Post*, Oct. 10, 1987. https://www.washingtonpost.com/archive/opinions/1987/10/11/the-black-roots-of-egypts-glory/1c3faf74-331c-4cc1-a6a0-3535fa3e098a/.

Finley, Keith. "Lynching." 64 Parishes, Dec. 21, 2012. https://www.64parishes.org/ entry/lynching.

Foley, Dennis. "Shreveport Sprawl, Lack of Density Don't Help Property Taxes." 710 KEEL, July 10, 2013. https://710keel.com/shreveport-sprawl-lack-of-density-dont-help-property-taxes/.

Foner, Eric, and Olivia Mahoney. "Americas Reconstruction: People and Politics After the Civil War." Digital History, 2003. http://www.digitalhistory.uh.edu/exhibits/ reconstruction/introduction.html.

Foundational Black Americans. "FBA History." https://officialfba.com/.

Freilich, Robert H., and Niel M. Popowitz. "The Umbrella of Sustainability: Smart Growth, New Urbanism, Renewable Energy and Green Development in the 21st Century." *The Urban Lawyer* 42 (2010) 1–39.

Friedman, Lisa. "What Is the Green New Deal? A Climate Proposal, Explained." *New York Times*, Feb. 21, 2019. https://nyti.ms/2GCkHjg.

Fuller, Neely, Jr. *The United Independent Compensatory Code/System/Concept: A Compensatory Counter-Racist Codified Word Guide.* Self-published, 2010.

Fulwood, Sam, III. "The Costs of Segregation and the Benefits of the Fair Housing Act." In *The Fight for Fair Housing*, edited by Gregory D. Squires, 40–56. New York: Routledge, 2017.

Gaille, Louise. "23 Advantages and Disadvantages of Qualitative Research." Vittana, May 17, 2017. https://vittana.org/23-advantages-and-disadvantages-of-qualitative -research.

Gamil, Marina. "Coptic: Ancient Language Still Spoken Today." Egypt Today, Aug. 8, 2017. https://www.egypttoday.com/Article/4/16207/Coptic-Ancient-language-still-spoken-today.

Gardiner, Alan H. "The Egyptian Origin of the Semitic Alphabet." *Journal of Egyptian Archeology* 3 (1916) 1–16.

Gary, Sheza. "Know the Benefits of Green Banking Sustainability on Our Environment." Finextra, June 1, 2022. https://www.finextra.com/blogposting/22365/know-the-benefits-of-green-banking-sustainability-on-our-environment.

Gershon, Livia. "How Stereotypes of the Irish Evolved from 'Criminals' to Cops." History, Dec. 18, 2017. https://www.history.com/news/how-stereotypes-of-the-irish-evolved-from-criminals-to-cops.

Gibbons, Ann. "How Europeans Evolved White Skin." Science, Apr. 2, 2015. https://www.sciencemag.org/news/2015/04/how-europeans-evolved-white-skin.

Gotham, Kevin F. "Racialization and the State: The Housing Act of 1934 and the Creation of Federal Housing Administration." Sociological Perspectives 43 (2000) 292–311. https://www.jstor.org/stable/1389798?seq=1.

Griffin, Chanté. "How Natural Black Hair at Work Became a Civil Rights Issue." JSTOR, July 3, 2019. https://daily.jstor.org/how-natural-black-hair-at-work-became-a-civil-rights-issue/.

Groeger, Lena, et al. "Miseducation: Is There Racial Inequality at Your School?" ProPublica, Oct. 16, 2018. https://projects.propublica.org/miseducation/district/2200300.

Gross, Terry. "A Forgotten History of How the U.S. Government Segregated America." NPR, May 3, 2017. https://www.npr.org/2017/05/03/526655831/a-forgotten-history-of-how-the-u-s-government-segregated-america.

Habitat for Humanity. "Energy Poverty." Accessed 2021. https://www.habitat.org/emea/about/what-we-do/residential-energy-efficiency-households/energy-poverty.

———. "7 Things You Should Know About Poverty and Housing." Accessed 2021. https://www.habitat.org/stories/7-things-you-should-know-about-poverty-and-housing.

Hanauer, Nick. "Better Schools Won't Fix America." Atlantic, 2019. https://www.theatlantic.com/magazine/archive/2019/07/education-isnt-enough/590611/.

Harriot, Michael. "When the Irish Weren't White." The Root, Mar. 17, 2018. https://www.theroot.com/when-the-irish-weren-t-white-1793358754.

Hayes, Adams. "Economics Defined with Types, Indicators, and Systems." Investopedia, 2021. https://www.investopedia.com/terms/e/economics.asp.

Hendley, Alexa, and Natasha Bilimoria. "Minorities and Social Security: An Analysis of Racial and Ethnic Differences in the Current Program." Social Security Bulletin 62 (1999) 59–64. https://www.ncbi.nlm.nih.gov/pubmed/10553615.

History.com Editors. "Jim Crow Laws." Feb. 28, 2018. https://www.history.com/topics/early-20th-century-us/jim-crow-laws.

Hochschild, Jennifer. "American Racial and Ethnic Politics in the 21st Century: A Cautious Look Ahead." Brookings, Mar. 1, 1998. https://www.brookings.edu/articles/american-racial-and-ethnic-politics-in-the-21st-century-a-cautious-look-ahead/.

Hofisi, Costa, et al. "Critiquing Interviewing as a Data Collection Method." Mediterranean Journal of Social Sciences 5.16 (2014) 61–64.

Holcombe, Randall. "Urban Sprawl: Pro and Con." PERC, Feb. 10, 1999. https://www.perc.org/1999/02/10/urban-sprawl-pro-and-con.

Holt, James. "The Topography of Poverty in the United States: A Spatial Analysis Using County-Level Data from the Community Health Status Indicators Project." Preventing Chronic Disease 4.4 (2007) 1–9. https://www.ncbi.nlm.nih.gov/pmc/articles/PMC2099276/.

Howard, Perry H. "Political Tendencies in Louisiana, 1812–1952: An Ecological Analysis of Voting Behavior." PhD diss., Louisiana State University, 1954. https://digitalcommons.lsu.edu/gradschool_disstheses/8115/.

Howard, Tenisha. "'The Secret African City': Ancient Egyptian Influences on Washington, D.C.'s Planning and Architecture in the 18th And 19th Centuries." Master's thesis, Cornell University, 2009.

Hughes, Allyson S. "Mixed Methods Research." Association for Psychological Science, Apr. 29, 2016. https://www.psychologicalscience.org/observer/mixed-methods-research.

Iberdrola Corporativa. *Innovación y tecnología.* Iberdrola, 2022. https://www.iberdrola.com/shareholders-investors/operational-financial-information/annual-reports.

Imhotep, David. *The First Americans Were Africans: Documented Evidence Expanded and Revised.* Self-published, Author House, 2021.

Institute for Transportation and Development Policy. "The High Cost of Transportation in the United States." May, 23, 2019. https://www.itdp.org/2019/05/23/high-cost-transportation-united-states/.

Institute on Taxation and Economic Policy (ITEP). *Who Pays? A Distributional Analysis of the Tax Systems in All 50 States.* 6th ed. 2018. https://itep.org/whopays/.

Insureon Staff. "Employment Discrimination Lawsuits: Case Studies." Insureon, 2014. https://www.insureon.com/blog/employment-discrimination-lawsuits.

iProperty Management. "Louisiana Landlord Tenant Laws: Renter's Rights and FAQs." Accessed   2020.   https://ipropertymanagement.com/laws/louisiana-landlord-tenant-rights.

Jan, Tracy. "Report: No Progress for African Americans on Homeownership, Unemployment, and Incarceration in 50 Years." *Washington Post,* Feb. 26, 2018.   https://www.washingtonpost.com/news/wonk/wp/2018/02/26/report-no-progress-for-african-americans-on-homeownership-unemployment-and-incarceration-in-50-years/.

Janofski, Craig. "What Is Poverty?" Extollo International, Aug. 8, 2019. https://www.extollo.org/post/2019/08/08/what-is-poverty?gclid=EAIaIQobChMIp-nMoMes6 AIVhJ6fCh2Z9g8PEAAYASAAEgIMf_D_BwE.

Jerrett, Michael, et al. "A GIS Environmental Justice Analysis of Particulate Air Pollution in Hamilton, Canada." *Environment and Planning* 33 (2001) 955–73. https://journals.sagepub.com/doi/pdf/10.1068/a33137.

Johns, David. "Disrupting Implicit Racial Bias and Other Forms of Discrimination to Improve Access, Achievement, and Wellness for Students of Color." White House Initiative on Educational Excellence for African Americans, 2016. https://sites.ed.gov/whieeaa/files/2016/10/Disrupting-Implicit-Bias-FINAL.pdf   (site discontinued).

Johnson, Glenn S. "Grassroots Activism in Louisiana." *Humanity and Society* 29 (2005) 285–304. https://doi.org/10.1177/016059760502900308.

Johnson, R. Burke, and Anthony Onwuegbuzie. "Mixed Methods Research: A Research Paradigm Whose Time Has Come." *Educational Researcher* 33.7 (2004) 14–26. http://www.jstor.org/stable/3700093.

Joiner, Gary, and Jaclyn Tripp. "Shreveport Was a Major Confederate Capital; Here's Why It Still Matters." KTAL News, last updated June 24, 2024. https://www.ktalnews.com/louisianas-lost-history/shreveport-was-a-major-confederate-capital-heres-why-it-still-matters/.

Jones, Janelle, et al. "50 Years After the Kerner Commission: African Americans Are Better Off in Many Ways but Are Still Disadvantaged by Racial Inequality." Economic Policy Institute, Feb. 26, 2018. https://www.epi.org/publication/50-years-after-the-kerner-commission/.

Jones, Martha S. "How the 14th Amendment's Promise of Birthright Citizenship Redefined America." Time, July 9, 2018. https://time.com/5324440/14th-amendment-meaning-150-anniversary/.

Jones, Syd. "Polish Americans." Every Culture, 2008. https://www.everyculture.com/multi/Pa-Sp/Polish-Americans.html.

The Joseph Smith Papers. "Grammar and Alphabet of the Egyptian Language, circa July–circa November 1835." https://www.josephsmithpapers.org/paper-summary/grammar-and-alphabet-of-the-egyptian-language-circa-july-circa-november-1835/1.

Kanbur, Ravi. "Q-Squared? A Commentary on Qualitative and Quantitative Poverty Appraisal." Q-Squared Working Paper 1, University of Toronto, 2005. 1–15. https://www.trentu.ca/ids/sites/trentu.ca.ids/files/documents/Q2_WP1_Kanbur.pdf.

Kaul, Greta. "White Flight Didn't Disappear–It Just Moved to the Suburbs." Minn Post, Mar. 21, 2018. https://www.minnpost.com/politics-policy/2018/03/white-flight-didn-t-disappear-it-just-moved-suburbs/.

Keilholtz, Jeffrey. "The Average Profit Margins for Autobody Shops." Career Trend, last updated Dec. 27, 2018. https://careertrend.com/list-7203350-average-profit-margins-autobody-shops.html.

Kimberlin, Sara. "Metrics Matter: Examining Chronic and Transient Poverty in the United States Using the Supplemental Poverty Measure." PhD diss., University of California, Berkeley, 2013. https://escholarship.org/uc/item/4j74x06w.

King, John B. "Giving Every Child in America a Fair Shot at a Great Education." US Department of Education, 2017. https://www.ed.gov/sites/ed/files/documents/press-releases/cabinet-exit-memo.pdf.

King, Sophia Y. "Environmental Jobs Don't Require Degree." US Green Technology, 2012. https://usgreentechnology.com/environmental-jobs-dont-require-degree/ (site discontinued).

Kotch, Alex. "Amid Deepening Child Poverty in the South, Glimmers of Hope." Facing South, July 24, 2015. https://www.facingsouth.org/2015/07/amid-deepening-child-poverty-in-the-south-glimmers.html.

KSLA News 12. "KSLA News 12 Investigates the School-to-Prison Pipeline in NWLA." Last updated Feb. 14, 2017. https://www.ksla.com/story/34500796/ksla-news-12-investigates-the-school-to-prison-pipeline-in-nwla/.

Kuddus, Abdul, et al. "Urbanization: A Problem for the Rich and the Poor?" Public Health Reviews 41 (2020) 1–4. https://doi.org/10.1186/s40985-019-0116-0.

Kwon, Sung Moon. "The Effects of Urban Containment Policies on Commuting Patterns." PhD diss., Portland State University, 2015. https://pdxscholar.library.pdx.edu/cgi/viewcontent.cgi?article=3305&context=open_access_etds.

Larino, Jennifer. "The Top 10 States People Move to When They Leave Louisiana." NOLA, Jan. 13, 2017. https://www.nola.com/news/business/article_9b8e2f84-4990-5c0d-b245-29d42f90ae4a.html.

Latitude. "Caddo Parish, Louisiana." Accessed 2020. https://latitude.to/articles-by-country/us/united-states/24826/caddo-parish-louisiana.

Leonard, Kimberlee. "Advantages and Disadvantages of Owning Your Own Company." Chron, Jan. 28, 2019. https://smallbusiness.chron.com/advantages-disadvantages-owning-own-company-21125.html.

Library of Congress. "Beginnings: African Immigration and Relocation in U.S. History." Library of Congress Classroom Materials. https://www.loc.gov/classroom-materials/immigration/african/beginnings/.

———. "The Civil Rights Act of 1964: A Long Struggle for Freedom." *Journal of American History* 102 (2015) 185–88. https://doi.org/10.1093/jahist/jav285.

Listing Bidder. "LA Avg Real Estate Commission Rate in Shreveport, Bossier City, LA." Accessed 2021. https://www.listingbidder.com/real-estate-commission-rates/real-estate-commission-rate-shreveport-bossier-city-louisiana/.

Liu, Jodi L., et al. "Beyond Neighborhood Food Environments: Distance Traveled to Food Establishments in 5 US Cities, 2009–2011." *Preventing Chronic Disease* 12 (2015) 1–9. https://pmc.ncbi.nlm.nih.gov/articles/PMC4552139/pdf/PCD-12-E126.pdf.

Local Housing Solutions. "What Is Affordable Housing and Who Needs It?" NYU Furman Center. https://www.localhousingsolutions.org/learn/what-is-affordable-housing-and-who-needs-it/.

———. "Zoning Changes to Allow for Higher Residential Density." NYU Furman Center, May 17, 2021. https://www.localhousingsolutions.org/act/housing-policy-library/zoning-changes-to-allow-for-higher-residential-density-overview/zoning-changes-to-allow-for-higher-residential-density/.

Lofton, Carmen. "Shreveport-Bossier Gaming Market Not Rolling Over in Defeat Despite Oklahoma Casino Competition." KTBS, Oct. 2, 2022. https://www.ktbs.com/news/arklatex-indepth/shreveport-bossier-gaming-market-not-rolling-over-in-defeat-despite-oklahoma-casino-competition/article_a03178aa-4027-11ed-ad74-3b7b1ac414b1.html.

Lomax, Michael L. "Six Reasons HBCUs Are More Important than Ever." UNCF. https://uncf.org/the-latest/6-reasons-hbcus-are-more-important-than-ever.

London.gov. "Policy 3.10 Definition of Affordable Housing." https://www.london.gov.uk/programmes-strategies/planning/london-plan/past-versions-and-alterations-london-plan/london-plan-2016/london-plan-chapter-3/policy-310-definition.

Long, Joseph. "What Is War? A New Point of View." *Small Wars Journal*, Dec. 5, 2012. https://archive.smallwarsjournal.com/jrnl/art/what-is-war-a-new-point-of-view.

Longley, R. "An Introduction to Psychological Warfare: From Genghis Khan to ISIS." ThoughtCo, Oct. 22, 2019. https://www.thoughtco.com/psychological-warfare-definition-4151867.

Louisiana Budget Project. "Payday Lending in Louisiana." Invest in Louisiana, 2016. https://www.labudget.org/paydaylending/.

Louisiana Casino Association. "Louisiana Economic Impact." Casino of Louisiana. https://www.casinosofla.com/how-louisiana-wins.asp.

Louisiana Civil Rights Trail. "A Story of Pride. A Story of Courage. Louisiana Civil Rights." https://www.louisianacivilrightstrail.com/?gclid=CjwKCAiAuaKfBhBtEiwAht6H70250jwjnmBxJxpph9Wti6ydRR5uBlEKQIyel_jsElOukeXSY1_1SBoCzKkQAvD_BwE.

Louisiana Department of Health. "Bossier Parish, Louisiana 2014–2016: Maternal and Child Health Profile." Last updated Aug. 2019. https://ldh.la.gov/assets/oph/Center-PHCH/Center-PH/maternal/IndicatorProfiles/Region7Parishes_14-16/Bossier_2014-2016.pdf.

———. "Caddo Parish, Louisiana 2015–2017: Maternal and Child Health Profile." Last updated Aug. 2019. https://Ldh.la.gov/Assets/Oph/Center-PHCH/Center-PH/Maternal/IndicatorProfiles/Region7Parishes_15-17/Caddo_2015-2017.Pdf.

———. "Health Data Explorer." https://healthdata.ldh.la.gov/.

———. "State Health Rankings Published: United Health Foundation Ranks Louisiana 50." Nov. 8, 2004. https://ldh.la.gov/news/1082.

Louisiana Housing Corporation. "Mortgage Credit Certificate Program." Accessed 2020. https://www.lhc.la.gov/mcc-homebuyers.

Louisiana Office of Public Health. *2005 Parish Health Profiles: A Tool for Community Health Planning; Caddo Parish.* Baton Rouge: Department of Health and Hospitals, 2005. https://ldh.la.gov/assets/docs/SurveillanceReports/php/PHP2005/PDF/Caddo/PHPCaddo.pdf.

Louisiana Public Defender Board. "School to Prison Pipeline Coalition." http://lpdb.la.gov/Serving%20The%20Public/Juvenile%20Justice/School%20to%20Prison%20Pipeline%20Coalition.php.

Louisiana State Civil Service. *State Civil Service Annual Report: Fiscal Year 2020–2021.* 2022. https://civilservice.louisiana.gov/files/publications/annual_reports/AnnualReport20-21.pdf.

Louisiana Workforce Commission. *Louisiana Labor Force Diversity Data Research and Statistics Division.* Department of Labor, 2018. https://www2.laworks.net/Downloads/Employment/AffirmativeActionPublication_2018.

Louisiana Workforce Information Review. *The Department of Labor, LA.* Louisiana Workforce Commission, 2021. https://www2.laworks.net/Downloads/LMI/WorkforceInfoReview_2021.pdf.

Mack, Natasha, et al. *Qualitative Research Methods: A Data Collector's Field Guide.* Research Triangle Park, NC: Family Health International, 2005.

MacNeil, Sara. "Cedar Grove a Banking Desert, Vulnerable to Predatory Lending." *Shreveport Times*, last updated June 24, 2019. https://www.shreveporttimes.com/story/news/2019/06/22/cedar-grove-a-banking-desert/1528496001/.

Manolas, Kasia. "What Is Rental Housing Discrimination?" Realtor Network, Feb. 7, 2022. https://www.avail.co/education/articles/what-is-rental-housing-discrimination.

March of Dimes. "Louisiana Infant Mortality Rate by Race." Accessed 2020. https://www.marchofdimes.org/peristats/ViewSubtopic.aspx?reg=46&top=2&stop=1&slev=4&obj=1.

Maxwell, Angie. "What We Get Wrong About the Southern Strategy." *Washington Post*, July 26, 2019. https://www.washingtonpost.com/outlook/2019/07/26/what-we-get-wrong-about-southern-strategy/.

May, Gerry. "Experts Weigh in on Perkins Future as Mayor After US Senate Defeat." KBTS, Nov. 4, 2020. https://www.ktbs.com/news/experts-weigh-in-on-perkins-future-as-mayor-after-us-senate-defeat/article_a551611e-1eec-11eb-8974-a798628289c8.html.

Mcarty, Erin. "Poverty Numbers Climbing in Shreveport/Bossier." 710 KEEL, Jan. 9, 2019. https://710keel.com/poverty-numbers-climbing-in-shreveport-bossier/.

McCargo, Alanna, et al. *Building Black Homeownership Bridges: A Five-Point Framework for Reducing the Racial Homeownership Gap.* Washington, DC: Urban Institute, 2019. https://www.urban.org/research/publication/building-black-homeownership-bridges.

McElfresh, Amanda. "Study: Louisiana's Education System Ranks Lowest in Nation." The Advertiser, July 31, 2017. https://www.theadvertiser.com/story/news/local/education/2017/07/31/study-louisianas-education-system-ranks-lowest-nation/525075001/.

McGaughy, Lauren. "Shreveport Becomes Second City in Louisiana After New Orleans to Pass Non-Discrimination Ordinance." NOLA, Dec. 11, 2013. https://www.nola.com/news/politics/article_fda3d765-1bee-5366-9ab6-e8d8d9ce52df.html.

McGrew, Chapman J., and Charles B. Monroe. An Introduction to Statistical Problem Solving in Geography. New York: Mcgraw Hill, 1999. https://www.book-info.com/isbn/0-697-22971-8.htm.

Mclean-Donaldson, Karen. "Racism in United States Schools: Assessing the Impact of an Anti-Racist/Multicultural Arts Curriculum on High School Students in a Peer Education Program." PhD diss., University of Massachusetts Amherst, 1994. https://hdl.handle.net/20.500.14394/15524.

Meckler, Lauren, and Kate Rabinowitz. "America's Schools Are More Diverse than Ever. But the Teachers Are Still Mostly White." Washington Post, Dec. 27, 2019. https://www.washingtonpost.com/graphics/2019/local/education/teacher-diversity/.

Melancon, Melissa V. "The Impact of the Louisiana Lottery on Salaries in Education." PhD diss., Louisiana Tech University, 1997. https://digitalcommons.latech.edu/dissertations/769/.

Mitchell, Brian Keith. "Oscar James Dunn: A Case Study in Race and Politics in Reconstruction Louisiana." PhD. diss., University of New Orleans, 2011. https://scholarworks.uno.edu/cgi/viewcontent.cgi?article=2413&context=td.

Morian, Dan. "Slave Owners and Their Insurers Are Named." Los Angeles Times, May 2, 2002. https://www.latimes.com/archives/la-xpm-2002-may-02-me-slavery2-story.html.

National Association for Latino Community Asset Builders. The State of Housing Affordability and Vulnerability in Houston: Preliminary Report. City of Houston and Community Development Department, Nov. 2018. https://houstontx.gov/housing/plans-reports/NALCAB-Report-090519.pdf.

National Center for Education Statistics. "Characteristics of Public-School Teachers." U. S. Department of Education, Institute of Education Sciences, 2021. https://nces.ed.gov/programs/coe/indicator/clr.

National Committee to Preserve Social Security and Medicare (NCPSSM). "Black Americans and Social Security." https://www.ncpssm.org/our-issues/social-security/african-americans-and-social-security/.

NeighborWho. "Janet LN, Glen Cove, LA." Accessed 2022. https://www.neighborwho.com/lp/244743/3/building-report.

News and Politics. "Payday Lending in Louisiana." Slideshare, Feb. 15, 2014. https://www.slideshare.net/bagertjr/civic-academy-payday-21514?from_action=save.

New York Life. "Common Questions." Accessed 2022. https://www.newyorklife.com/newsroom/common-questions.

Norris, Dave, and Amanda Norris. Community Foundation of North Louisiana. 2020. https://cfnla.org/wp-content/uploads/sites/28/2020/10/Community-Counts-2020.pdf.

North Louisiana Economic Partnership (NLEP). "Caddo Parish Competitive Advantages Help Businesses Succeed." Accessed 2019. https://www.nlep.org/Regional-Data/Regional-Profiles/Caddo-Parish-Profile.aspx#Communities.

———. "Locations, Expansions and Closings in North Louisiana." 2022. https://www. nlep.org/Relocation-Expansion/Expansions-Locations-Closings.aspx.

Northwest Louisiana Council of Governments. "Public Transportation Planning Study of the Shreveport–Bossier City Urbanized Area." New Orleans: AECOM Technical Services, 2015.

NPR. "How Jacob Loud's Land Was Lost." Interview by Keith Romer and Jacob Goldstein. NPR, *Planet Money*, transcript, Apr. 7, 2021. https://www.npr.org/ transcripts/983897990.

Obenga, Théophile. *A Lost Tradition: African Philosophy in World History*. Paris: Source Editions, 1995.

Odhiambo, Walter, et al., eds. *Quantitative and Qualitative Methods for Poverty Analysis*. Kenya Institute for Public Policy Research and Analysis, 2005. https://www.saga. cornell.edu/saga/q-qconf/proceed.pdf.

O'Lear, Cassidy. "How Do Racial Disparities Affect Housing?" FamilyPromise, Feb. 28, 2022. https://familypromise.org/latest/racial-disparities-housing/.

Ostlund, Kidd U., et al. "Combining Qualitative and Quantitative Research Within Mixed Method Research Designs: Methodological Review." *International Journal of Nursing Studies* 48 (2011) 369–83.

Pager, Devah, et al. "Sequencing Disadvantage: Barriers to Employment Facing Young Black and White Men with Criminal Records." *Annals of the American Academy of Political and Social Science* 623 (2009) 195–213. https://doi. org/10.1177/0002716208330793.

Parker, Simon. *Urban Theory and the Urban Experience: Encountering the City*. 2nd ed. New York: Routledge, 2015.

Partelow, Lisette, et al. "7 Great Education Policy Ideas for Progressives in 2018." Center for American Progress, Mar. 28, 2018. https://www.americanprogress.org/ article/7-great-education-policy-ideas-progressives-2018/.

PayScale. "Cost of Living in Baton Rouge, Louisiana." Accessed 2021. https://www. payscale.com/cost-of-living-calculator/Louisiana-Baton-Rouge.

———. "Cost of Living in Bossier City, Louisiana." Accessed 2021. https://www. payscale.com/cost-of-living-calculator/Louisiana-Bossier-City.

———. "Cost of Living in Shreveport, Louisiana." Accessed 2021. https://www. payscale.com/cost-of-living-calculator/Louisiana-Shreveport.

Perlstein, Rick. "Exclusive: Lee Atwater's Infamous 1981 Interview on the Southern Strategy." *Nation*, Nov. 13, 2012. https://www.thenation.com/article/archive/ exclusive-lee-atwaters-infamous-1981-interview-southern-strategy/.

Perry, Andre M., et al. "The Devaluation of Assets in Black Neighborhoods." Brookings, Nov. 27, 2018. https://www.brookings.edu/research/devaluation-of-assets-in-black-neighborhoods/.

Pharr, Jennifer R., et al. "The Impact of Unemployment on Mental and Physical Health, Access to Health Care and Health Risk Behaviors." International Scholarly Research Notices (2012) 1–7. https://doi.org/10.5402/2012/483432.

Pointer, Eric. "Premiere of Documentary About Civil Rights Movement in Shreveport Draws Large Crowds." KSLA, last updated June 28, 2018. https://www.ksla.com/ story/38536880/premiere-of-documentary-about-civil-rights-movement-in-shreveport-draws-large-crowd/.

Pravitasari, Andrea E. "Study on Impact of Urbanization and Rapid in Urban Expansion in Java and Jabodetabek Megacity Indonesia." PhD diss., Kyoto University,

2015. https://repository.kulib.kyotou.ac.jp/dspace/bitstream/2433/202752/2/dtikk00140.

Prison Policy Initiative. "Louisiana Profile." 2018. https://www.prisonpolicy.org/profiles/LA.html.

Public Broadcasting Service. "Africans in America: Europeans Come to Western Africa Part 1." PBS. https://www.pbs.org/wgbh/aia/part1/1narr1.html.

Quillian, Lincoln, et al. "Hiring Discrimination Against Black Americans Hasn't Declined in 25 Years." *Harvard Business Review*, Oct. 11, 2017. https://hbr.org/2017/10/hiring-discrimination-against-black-americans-hasnt-declined-in-25-years.

Ragusett, Jared. "Essays on Urban Sprawl, Race, and Ethnicity." PhD diss., University of Massachusetts Amherst, 2009. https://scholarworks.umass.edu/cgi/viewcontent.cgi?article=1659&context=open_access_dissertations.

Rajkumar, Tajpertab. "Poverty: A Descriptive Study of Attitudes and Aspirations Among Selected Respondents in North Baton Rouge (Louisiana)." PhD diss., Louisiana State University, 1985.

Ravallion, Martin, et al. "New Evidence on the Urbanization of Global Poverty." *World Bank Policy Research Working Paper* 4199 (2007) 1–48. https://ssrn.com/abstract=980817.

Reames, Tony. "Combating Energy Poverty in the U.S." Kleinman Center for Energy Policy, Apr. 20, 2021. https://kleinmanenergy.upenn.edu/podcast/combating-energy-poverty-in-the-u-s/.

Richardson, Jason, et al. "Redlining and Neighborhood Health." NCRC, accessed 2021. https://ncrc.org/holc-health/.

Rizvi, Syed. "Biggest Sources of Immigrants to Shreveport." Stacker, Apr. 21, 2022. https://stacker.com/stories/7992/biggest-sources-immigrants-shreveport.

Robinson, Jill R. "Land Use Behavior of Private Landowners at the Urban/Rural Fringe." PhD diss., Ohio State University, 2004.

Rodrigue, John. "Slavery in French Colonial Louisiana." 64 Parishes, Mar. 11, 2014. https://64parishes.org/entry/slavery-in-french-colonial-louisiana.

Rong, Dong. "Impact of Urban Sprawl on U.S. Residential Energy." PhD diss., University of Maryland, 2006.

Rutherford, Ian. "Ancient Greek and Egyptian Interactions." OUP Blog, Apr. 14, 2016. https://blog.oup.com/2016/04/greek-egyptian-interactions-literature/.

SAS. "Statistical Analysis—What Is It?" Accessed 2020. https://www.sas.com/en_us/insights/analytics/statistical-analysis.html.

Schmidt, Roger. "Commercial vs. Industrial Applications: Focus on Cold Applications." *Insulation Outlook*, June 1, 2007. https://insulation.org/io/articles/commercial-vs-industrial-applications-focus-on-cold-applications/.

Schmitt, Angie, et al. "Shreveport Mayor Votes to Bulldoze a Black Neighborhood to Build a Highway." StreetsBlog USA, Aug. 22, 2017. https://usa.streetsblog.org/2017/08/22/shreveport-mayor-votes-to-bulldoze-a-black-neighborhood-to-build-a-highway/.

Schottman, Jill. "The History of Reparations Payment." Accessed 2021. https://study.com/academy/lesson/reparations-definition-overview.html.

Scott, Loren. "Northwest Louisiana." BIZ, 2020. https://bizmagsb.com/article/a-history-of-the-shreveport-bossier-economy/.

Sertima, Ivan. *They Came Before Columbus: The African Presence in Ancient America.* New York: Random House, 2003.

Sewell, Summer. "There Were Nearly a Million Black Farmers in 1920. Why Have They Disappeared?" *Guardian*, Apr. 29, 2019. https://www.theguardian.com/environment/2019/apr/29/why-have-americas-black-farmers-disappeared.

Shaw Environmental and Infrastructure. *Caddo Parish Regional Water/Utility District Master Plan Final Report—Caddo Parish-Shreveport.* 2012. http://la-caddoparish. civicplus.com/DocumentCenter/View/638/FINAL-Report-for-Caddo-Parish-Phase-4_11-8-12?bidId= (site discontinued).

Sherris, Jacinta. "Online Payday Loans Louisiana: Options for Payday Loans in Louisiana." MoneyLion, Mar. 26, 2020. https://www.moneylion.com/learn/online-payday-loans-louisiana/.

Shreveport Area. "Banking." Deposit Accounts, accessed 2021. https://www.depositaccounts.com/local/shreveport/.

Shreveport/Caddo Metropolitan Planning Commission. *Shreveport-Bossier Metro Area.* 2016. http://shreveportcaddompc.com/wp-content/uploads/2016/01/Appendix200420–20WZHA20Market20Evaluation 20Memoranda_201308131551203231.pdf.

Shreveport Louisiana. "City Council." Accessed 2021. https://www.shreveportla. gov/201/City-Council.

Shreveport Metropolitan Planning Commission. "Getting Around: Transportation and Mobility." Chapter 8 in *Great Expectations, City of Shreveport.* https://www.shreveportcaddompc.com/home/showpublisheddocument/1501/637520162569530000.

———. *Great Expectations: Shreveport-Caddo 2030 Master Plan.* City of Shreveport, 2010. https://www.shreveportcaddompc.com/boards-commissions/reports-policies-presentations/reports/shreveport-caddo-2030-master-plan.

———. "Population and Land Use Trends." Chapter 3 in *Great Expectations, City of Shreveport.* https://www.shreveportcaddompc.com/home/showpublisheddocument/1491/637520162550130000.

Shreveport Times. "Unemployment Rate Caddo Parish." Accessed 2020. https://data. shreveporttimes.com/unemployment/caddo-parish-la/CN2201700000000/.

Shy, Yulbritton. "'This Is Our America, Too': Marcus B. Christian and the History of Black Louisiana." Master's thesis, University of New Orleans, 2010.

Simerman, John. "More than 1,500 Louisiana Inmates Were Convicted by Divided Juries, New Report Says." NOLA, Nov. 17, 2020. https://www.nola.com/news/courts/article_ddba16a8-2929-11eb-9072-ff7a00598e9f.html.

Simon Fraser University. "What Is Sustainable Community Development? Centre for Sustainable Development." Accessed 2022. https://www.sfu.ca/sustainabledevelopment/Archives/what-is-sustainable-community-development. html.

Slevin, Peter. "In Aetna's Past: Slave Owner Policies." *Washington Post*, Mar. 9, 2000. https://www.washingtonpost.com/archive/politics/2000/03/09/in-aetnas-past-slave-owner-policies/faa58ed3–51ba-44e6-b59f-c36ae181e093/.

Smart Growth America. "What Is Smart Growth?" Accessed 2022. https://smartgrowthamerica.org/what-is-smart-growth/.

Smith, Chuck. "Caddo Commission Votes to Discourage 'Bank Deserts.'" Red River Radio, June 27, 2019. https://www.redriverradio.org/post/caddo-commission-votes-discourage-bank-deserts.

SNDi Trends. "Street-Network Sprawl in Shreveport, Louisiana, United States." Sprawl Map, 2015. https://sprawlmap.org/places/unitedstates/louisiana/shreveport.html.

Solomon, Danyelle, et al. "Systematic Inequality and Economic Opportunity." Center for American Progress, Aug. 7, 2019. https://www.americanprogress.org/article/systematic-inequality-economic-opportunity/.

Southern Poverty Law Center. "Discrimination Complaint Filed Against Louisiana's Jefferson Parish Public Schools." May 17, 2012. https://www.splcenter.org/news/2012/05/17/discrimination-complaint-filed-against-louisiana%E2%80%99s-jefferson-parish-public-schools.

Spokeo. "Who Lives on N Greenbrook Loop, Shreveport, LA 71106." Accessed 2022. https://www.spokeo.com/N+Greenbrook+Loop+Shreveport+LA+addresses.

SporTran. "Shreveport LA. Public Transportation." Accessed 2021. https://www.sportran.org/.

Stacker. "The Black Homeownership Gap in Shreveport." Mar. 22, 2022. https://stacker.com/louisiana/shreveport/black-homeownership-gap-shreveport.

———. "Incarceration Rates Demographics in Louisiana." Mar. 10, 2022. https://stacker.com/louisiana/incarceration-rates-demographics-louisiana.

Starkey, Brando S. "White Immigrants Weren't Always Considered White and Acceptable." Andscape, Feb. 10, 2017. https://andscape.com/features/white-immigrants-werent-always-considered-white-and-acceptable/.

Stebbins, Samuel. "Shreveport, LA Is Among the Most Dangerous US Metro Areas." 24/7 Wall St., last updated Nov. 9, 2021. https://247wallst.com/city/shreveport-la-is-among-the-most-dangerous-us-metro-areas/.

———. "This Is the Parish with the Lowest Child Poverty Rate in Louisiana." The Center Square, July 18, 2022. https://www.thecentersquare.com/louisiana/this-is-the-parish-with-the-lowest-child-poverty-rate-in-louisiana/article_33ae7805-85f8-5715-b3af-6cf9bdb72b16.html.

Stebbins, Samuel, and Evan Comen. "These Are the Worst Cities to Live in Based on Quality of Life." USA Today, June 13, 2018. https://www.usatoday.com/story/money/economy/2018/06/13/50-worst-cities-to-live-in/35909271/.

Stirling Properties. Retail Market Survey: Shreveport–Bossier City. 2015. https://www.stirlingprop.com/wp-content/uploads/market-research/Shreveport-Bossier-City-Retail-Survey-November-2015.pdf.

———. Retail Market Survey: Shreveport–Bossier City, LA. 2018. https://www.stirlingprop.com/2018/10/31/retail-market-survey-shreveport-bossier-city-la/.

Stoll, Michael A. "Job Sprawl and the Spatial Mismatch Between Blacks and Jobs." Brookings Institution Metropolitan Policy Program Survey Series (2005) 1–13. https://www.brookings.edu/research/job-sprawl-and-the-spatial-mismatch-between-blacks-and-jobs/.

———. "Job Sprawl, Spatial Mismatch, and Black Employment Disadvantage." Journal of Policy Analysis and Management 25 (2006) 827–54. https://www.jstor.org/stable/30162764.

Stony Brook University. "Humans Living in East Africa 200,000 Years Ago Were as Complex in their Behavior as Humans Living Today." Newswise, Feb. 16, 2011.

https://www.newswise.com/articles/humans-living-in-east-africa-200–000-years-ago-were-as-complex-in-their-behavior-as-humans-living-today.

Strand, Palma J., and Nicholas A. Mirkay. "Racialized Tax Inequity: Wealth, Racism, and the U.S System of Taxation." *Northwestern Journal of Law and Social Policy* 15.3 (2020) 265–304. https://scholarlycommons.law.northwestern.edu/cgi/viewcontent.cgi?article=1200&context=njlsp.

Streetscape. "Downtown Shreveport." Accessed 2020. https://downtownshreveport.com/streetscape/.

SuburbanStats. "Current Caddo Parish Louisiana Population Demographics and Stats 2019 and 2020." 2020. https://suburbanstats.org/population/louisiana/how-many-people-live-in-caddo-parish.

Tadele, Rediet. "Tignon Law: Policing Black Women's Hair in the 18th Century." Amplify Africa, 2020. https://www.amplifyafrica.org/post/tignon-law-policing-black-women-s-hair-in-the-18th-century.

Talamo, Lex. "Struggling to Survive." *Shreveport Times*, Jan. 27, 2016. https://www.shreveporttimes.com/story/news/2016/01/27/struggling-survive/78846170/.

Tashakkori, Abbas, and John W. Creswell. "The New Era of Mixed Methods." *Journal of Mixed Methods Research* 1 (2007) 3–7. https://doi.org/10.1177/1558689806293042.

Tech and Solutions. "5 Ways Geographic Information Systems (GIS) Can Reduce Poverty." *Borgen*, Mar. 18, 2016. https://www.borgenmagazine.com/geographic-information-systems-to-reduce-poverty/.

Themba-Nixon, Makina, et al. *Persistence of White Privilege and Institutional Racism in US Policy: A Report on US Government Compliance with the International Convention on the Elimination of All Forms of Racial Discrimination.* Transnational Racial Justice Initiative, 2001. https://racism.org/index.php?option=com_content&view=article&id=1386%3Aprivilege01&catid=69&Itemid=165&showall=1&limitstart=.

Thomas, William B. "Black Intellectuals' Critique of Early Mental Testing: A Little-Known Saga of the 1920's." *American Journal of Education* 90 (1982) 258–92. https://www.jstor.org/stable/pdf/1085111.pdf.

Thonddara, Romanee. "Using GIS and Spatial Statistics to Target Poverty and Improve Poverty Alleviation Programs: A Case Study in Northeast Thailand." *Applied Spacial Analysis* 5 (2011) 157–82. http://link.springer.com/article/10.1007/s12061-011-9066-8.

TMG Consulting. "Retail and Commercial Market Assessment." Part 3 in *Shreveport Common Market Assessment.* 2014. https://www.shreveportcommon.com/tmg-real-estate-market-study.

Town Charts. "Caddo Parish Louisiana Education Data." Town Charts Education. https://www.towncharts.com/Louisiana/Education/Caddo-Parish-LA-Education-data.html.

Turner, Margery A., and Felicity Skidmore, eds. *Mortgage Lending Discrimination.* Washington, DC: Urban Institute, 1999. https://www.urban.org/sites/default/files/publication/66151/309090-Mortgage-Lending-Discrimination.PDF.

United for ALICE. "Research Center: Methodology." 2020. https://www.unitedforalice.org/methodology.

United States Senate. "The Senate Passes the Thirteenth Amendment." Accessed 2019. https://www.senate.gov/artandhistory/history/minute/Senate_Passes_the_Thirteenth_Amendment.htm.

United Way ALICE Project. *ALICE: A Study of Financial Hardship Louisiana.* United Way, 2019. https://issuu.com/louisianaassociationofunitedway/docs/18uw_alice_report_la_-_used_for_iss/1.

United Way of Northwest Louisiana. "Day 7: Housing and Redlining." Accessed 2021. https://unitedwaynwla.org/equity-challenge-day-7/.

University of Washington Population Health Institute. *2022 State Report: Louisiana.* County Health Rankings and Roadmaps, 2022. https://www.countyhealthrankings.org/reports/state-reports/2022-louisiana-state-report.

UPI. "AT&T to Lay Off Nearly 900 in Shreveport." UPI Archives, July 5, 1985. https://www.upi.com/Archives/1985/07/05/ATT-to-lay-off-nearly-900-in-Shreveport/4517489384000/.

US Bureau of Labor Statistics. "Occupational Employment and Wages in Baton Rouge—May 2020." Southwest Information Office, July 14, 2021. https://www.bls.gov/regions/southwest/news-release/2021/occupationalemploymentandwages_batonrouge_20210714.htm.

———. "Occupational Employment and Wages in Shreveport–Bossier City—May 2020." 2021. https://www.bls.gov/regions/southwest/news-release/occupationalemploymentandwages_shreveport.htm.

———. "Occupational Employment and Wages in Shreveport–Bossier City—May 2021." 2022. https://www.bls.gov/eag/eag.la_shreveport_msa.htm.

———. "Occupational Employment and Wages in Shreveport–Bossier City—May 2022." 2023. https://www.bls.gov/regions/southwest/news-release/occupationalemploymentandwages_shreveport.htm.

US Census Bureau 2017. "American Community 1-Year Estimates." Census Reporter Profile, Bossier Parish, LA, 2018. https://data.census.gov/all?t=Employment+and+Labor+Force+Status:Industry:Occupation&g=050XX00US22015&y=2017.

———. "American Community 1-Year Estimates." Census Reporter Profile, Caddo Parish, LA, 2018. https://data.census.gov/all?t=Employment+and+Labor+Force+Status:Industry:Occupation&g=050XX00US22017&y=2017.

US Census Bureau 2018. "American Community Survey 1-Year Estimates." Census Reporter Profile, Bossier Parish, LA, 2019. https://censusreporter.org/profiles/05000US22015-bossier-parish-la/.

———. "How the Census Bureau Measures Poverty." 2018. https://www.census.gov/topics/income-poverty/poverty/guidance/poverty-measures.html.

US Census Bureau 2019. "ACS 5-Year Estimates Education Attainment Caddo Parish." Accessed 2020. https://data.census.gov/cedsci/table?t=Educational+Attainment.

———. "Bossier Parish Louisiana Summary." Accessed 2021. https://www.census.gov/quickfacts/bossierparishlouisiana.

———. "Caddo Parish Louisiana Summary." Accessed 2021. https://www.census.gov/quickfacts/caddoparishlouisiana.

———. "East Baton Rouge Parish Louisiana." Accessed 2019. https://data.census.gov/cedsci/table?t=Populations+and+People&g=0500000US22033&y=2019&tid=ACSDP1Y2019.DP05.

US Census Bureau 2020. "Bossier Parish: Explore Census Data." Accessed 2021. https://data.census.gov/table?t=Owner/Renter+(Householder)+Characteristics:Owner/Renter+(Tenure)&g=050XX00US22015&y=2020.

————. "Caddo Parrish: Explore Census Data." Accessed 2021. https://data.census. gov/table?t=Owner/Renter+(Householder)+Characteristics:Owner/Renter+(Ten ure)&g=050XX00US22017&y=2020.

US Census Bureau 2021. "Caddo Parish: Explore Census Data." Accessed 2021. https:// data.census.gov/table?t=Commuting%3AEmployment%3AEmployment%2Band %2BLabor%2BForce%2BStatus%3AIndustry%3AOccupation&g=0500000US220 17&y=2021&tid=ACSDP1Y2021.DP03.

US Census Bureau 2023. "Bossier City Monthly Housing Cost 5-Year Estimate 2023." Accessed 2025. https://data.census.gov/table/ACSST5Y2023. S2507?q=Bossier+city.

US Census Bureau 2024. "Shreveport Monthly Housing Cost, Year 2024." Acessed 2025. https://data.census.gov/table/ACSST1Y2024.S2506?q=Shreveport+city.

US Census of Housing 1990. "Louisiana: Summary Population and Housing." US Department of Commerce, 1992. https://www.census.gov/prod/www/decennial. html.

US Census of Population and Housing 2000. "Louisiana: Profiles of General Demographic Characteristics." US Department of Commerce, 2001. https:// www2.census.gov/census_2000/datasets/demographic_profile/Louisiana/2kh22. pdf.

————. "Louisiana: Summary Population and Housing." US Department of Commerce, 2002. https://www2.census.gov/library/publications/2003/dec/phc-2-20.pdf.

US Census of Population and Housing 2010. "Louisiana: Population and Housing Unit Counts." US Department of Commerce, 2012. https://www2.census.gov/library/ publications/decennial/2010/cph-2/cph-2-20.pdf.

US Census of Population 1990. "Louisiana: General Population and Characteristics." US Department of Commerce, 1992. https://www2.census.gov/library/publications/ decennial/1990/cp-1/cp-1-20.pdf.

US Department of Housing and Urban Development. *Analysis of the Shreveport–Bossier City, Louisiana Housing Market.* Comprehensive Market Analysis Report, 2006. https://www.huduser.gov/portal/publications/pdf/CMAR_ShreveBossLA.pdf.

————. *Comprehensive Housing Market Analysis: Shreveport–Bossier City, Louisiana.* Comprehensive Housing Market Analysis Report, 2008. https://www.huduser. gov/publications/pdf/cmar_shreveportla.pdf.

————. *Comprehensive Housing Market Analysis: Shreveport–Bossier City, Louisiana.* Comprehensive Market Analysis Report, 2012. https://www.huduser.gov/portal/ publications/pdf/ShreveportLA_comp_12.pdf.

————. *Comprehensive Housing Market Analysis: Shreveport–Bossier City, Louisiana.* Comprehensive Housing Market Analysis Report, 2021. https://www.huduser. gov/portal/publications/pdf/ShreveportBossierCityLA-CHMA-21.pdf.

US Government. "Housing-Related Complaints." USA.gov, accessed 2021 https://www. usa.gov/housing-complaints.

US News and World Report. "Bossier Parish Public Schools." Accessed 2021. https:// www.usnews.com/education/k12/louisiana/districts/bossier-parish-102011.

————. "Caddo Parish Public Schools." Accessed 2021. https://www.usnews.com/ education/k12/louisiana/districts/caddo-parish-112818.

————. "Linwood Public Charter School in Louisiana." Accessed 2022. https://www. usnews.com/education/k12/louisiana/linwood-public-charter-school-203230.

Vandal, Gilles. "Bloody Caddo: White Violence Against Blacks in Louisiana Parish, 1965–1876." *Journal of Social History* 25 (1991) 373–88.

Vaughan, Tim. "10 Advantages and Disadvantages of Qualitative Research." Poppulo, 2021.   https://www.poppulo.com/blog/10-advantages-and-disadvantages-of-qualitative-research.

Vines, Matt. "Affordable Rental Housing in Severe Shortage for Louisiana's Lowest Earners." LSUS Shreveport, June 9, 2025. https://www.lsus.edu/affordable-rental-housing-in-severe-shortage-for-louisianas-lowest-earners.

Wake, John. "The Shocking Truth 50 Years After the 1968 Fair Housing Act: The Black Homeownership Paradox." *Forbes*, May 16, 2021. https://www.forbes.com/sites/johnwake/2019/05/16/the-shocking-truth-about-the-u-s-black-homeownership-rate-50-years-after-the-1968-fair-housing-act/?sh=6c197bfb63ba.

Walker, Richard. "The New Deal Didn't Create Segregation." *Jacobin*, 2019. https://jacobinmag.com/2019/06/the-color-of-law-richard-rothstein-review.

———. "What Was the New Deal?" Living New Deal, 2019. https://livingnewdeal.org/what-was-the-new-deal/.

Walker, Robert. "100 Things That You Did Not Know About Africa." African American Male Resource Center, Chicago State University, 2006. https://www.csu.edu/dosa/AAMRC/news1.htm (page discontinued).

Weatherspoon, Floyd. *African American Males and the U.S. Justice System of Marginalization*. New York: Palgrave, 2014. https://doi.org/10.1057/9781137408433.

Welsing, Frances Cress. "The Cress Theory of Color-Confrontation." *Black Scholar* 5.8 (1974) 32–40. http://www.jstor.org/stable/41065722.

Wendling, Mike. "US Election 2016: The Factory That Symbolizes Donald Trump's Appeal." BBC News, Nov. 4, 2016. https://www.bbc.com/news/election-us-2016-37856565.

White, Douglas, and Mary Lois White. *Rental Housing Affordability in Louisiana 2023*. LSUS Center for Business and Economic Research Report. https://www.lsus.edu/Documents/CBER/CBER%20Reports%20page/Rental%20Housing%20Affordability%20in%20Louisiana%202023.pdf.

White House. *Giving Every Child a Fair Shot: Progress Under the Obama Administration's Education Agenda*. Department of Education, Jan. 30, 2016. https://obamawhitehouse.archives.gov/sites/default/files/docs/giving_every_child_fair_shot_050316.pdf.

———. "Inflation Reduction Act Advances Environmental Justice." Aug. 17, 2022. https://www.whitehouse.gov/briefing-room/statements-releases/2022/08/17/fact-sheet-inflation-reduction-act-advances-environmental-justice/.

———. "Justice 40 Initiative." 2022. https://www.whitehouse.gov/environmentaljustice/justice40/.

Wittkower, Dylan. "Discrimination." In *Spaces for the Future: A Companion to Philosophy and Technology*, edited by Joseph C. Pitt and Ashley Shew, 37–64. New York: Routledge, 2018.

Williams, Chancellor. *The Destruction of Black Civilization: Great Issues of Race from 4500 B.C. to 2000 A.D.* Chicago: Third World, 1987. https://www.scribd.com/doc/156636864/Chancellor-Williams-Destruction-of-`Black-Civilization.

World Population Review 2021. "Baton Rouge, Louisiana." Accessed 2022. https://worldpopulationreview.com/us-cities/baton-rouge-la-population.

———. "Bossier City, Louisiana Population." Accessed 2022. https://worldpopulationreview.com/us-cities/bossier-city-la-population.

———. "Bossier Parish Louisiana." Accessed 2022 https://worldpopulationreview.com/us-counties/la/bossier-parish-population/.

———. "Caddo Parish Louisiana." Accessed 2022. https://worldpopulationreview.com/us-counties/la/caddo-parish-population/.

———. "East Baton Rouge Parish." Accessed 2022. https://worldpopulationreview.com/us-counties/la/east-baton-rouge-parish-population.

———. "Shreveport, Louisiana Population." Accessed 2022. https://worldpopulationreview.com/us-cities/shreveport-la-population.

Wyatt, Ashonta. "The Lived Experiences of Black Males in Special Education: A Phenomenological Study of Parents and Students." PhD diss., Xavier University of Louisiana, 2019.

Wyse, Susan E. "What Is the Difference Between Qualitative Research and Quantitative Research?" Snap Surveys, 2011. https://www.snapsurveys.com/blog/what-is-the-difference-between-qualitative-research-and-quantitative-research/.

Yin, Robert K. *Case Study Research: Design and Methods.* 3rd ed. Thousand Oaks, CA: Sage, 2003. https://iwansuharyanto.wordpress.com/wp-content/uploads/2013/04/robert_k-_yin_case_study_research_design_and_mebookfi-org.pdf.

Yong, Ed. "The New Story of Humanity's Origins in Africa." *Atlantic*, July 11, 2018. https://www.theatlantic.com/science/archive/2018/07/the-new-story-of-humanitys-origins/564779/.

Zapotosky, Matt. "Charleston Church Shooter: I Would Like to Make It Crystal Clear, I Do Not Regret What I Did." *Washington Post*, Jan. 4, 2017. https://www.washingtonpost.com/world/national-security/charleston-church-shooter-i-would-like-to-make-it-crystal-clear-i-do-not-regret-what-i-did/2017/01/04/05b0061e-d1da-11e6-a783-cd3fa950f2fd_story.html.

Zhongxi, Ren, et al. "Are Chinese Descendants of an African Eve?" China.org.cn, Nov. 24, 2009. http://www.china.org.cn/china/2009-11/24/content_18944317.htm.

Index

www.ingramcontent.com/pod-product-compliance
Lightning Source LLC
Chambersburg PA
CBHW071849270326
41929CB00013B/2158